The Next India-China War
Near or Never

Volume 1

N. Haridas

Published by

7/22, Ansari Road, Darya Ganj, New Delhi-110002
Phones : +91-11-40775252, 23273880, 23275880, 23280451
Fax : +91-11-23285873
Web : www.atlanticbooks.com
E-mail : orders@atlanticbooks.com

Branch Office
5, Nallathambi Street, Wallajah Road, Chennai-600002
Phones : +91-44-64611085, 32413319
E-mail : chennai@atlanticbooks.com

Printed in India at Nice Printing Press, A-33/3A, Site-IV,
Industrial Area, Sahibabad, Ghaziabad, U.P.

Preface

As an Indian who lived through and saw the convulsions of the 1962 India-China war days, and its inglorious conclusion humiliating India, my thoughts are violently agitated how India pointedly and permanently targeted by an imperial China, can keep her freedom and independence in the long-run. Political policies continuously change and along with that every country's strategic policies. But regarding India-China relations, there is no change and scaling down in the hostile policy of China, and this hostility only continues to grow more intense. In the meanwhile, it is argued by the left intelligentsia that in recent years considerable progress has been achieved in India-China relations, especially in the economic sector and that is a positive sign. But by making a review of the policy of China regarding the border dispute, there is no sign that she is prepared to make any concession and return the land she has conquered, especially the Aksai Chin. India's loss of Tibet as the buffer stands out worse than America losing the Chinese mainland to the communists in 1949. This momentous loss is more grievous as it came only because of New Delhi's naïve and impotent leadership who unashamedly capitulated before the Chinese conquest of the land of the Lamas. That is a loss which can never be remedied and repaired, and Tibet remains the permanent haunt of strategic India. Aksai Chin and the McMahon Line are only the by-products of the Chinese conquest of Tibet.

The wrong state of India's policy and strategy is that even after the 1962 defeat, India continues to be an unallied loner in the international politics. While looking forward, the real fact is that economically and militarily, India is smaller than

China and possibly, that second place is to continue. The border dispute between the two countries is the boiling concern and the frequent border skirmishes can escalate into a full war any time. Wars and world wars have been fought not by one country with another country. Powers group and regroup into blocs and allies, and they fight under strategic unity. To face the stronger China, why the strong India is not making any scheme to make a military alliance with any powerful country, and that question remains mysteriously unanswered by New Delhi, which refuses to come out of the shell of Non-Alignment. Even the Filipinos, who protested against the presence of American forces and sent them away, are now calling the American forces back, because of the rising threat of China and her imperial forays into the South China Sea. Japan, living under a peace constitution, is now struggling to get out of the peace clause, and getting ready to defend her territory against China, rattling swords. It is true that China is no more communist but an imperial country, more chauvinistic than the Mongol Ming and Qing dynasties, and towards this reality, all Asian nations are now waking up, and India too is up but with no purposive plan. China's befriending Pakistan, the committed American ally and nuclear arming the latter are looked as a diplomatic and strategic puzzle, but it is turned out to be thoroughly realistic. The hangovers of Non-Alignment are still constraining the thoughts of New Delhi and the country's top political tribe. If India wants to defend her honour and freedom against the rising China, she should find her military allies immediately.

There are new political and strategic developments in East Asia, South Asia, and South-East Asia ignited by the new power-pretenions of China. The latest development is the Japanese Prime Minister Shinzo Abe opening a new chapter in Japanese defence strategy, perhaps recalling the militant ways of Japan during the first half of the twentieth century. Japan is governed by a Peace Constitution which rather prohibits the use of force for dissolving international disputes. But, still the emerging necessities have caused a big change in the national politics and now the Japanese people have begun to think whether they can shoulder the responsibility of defending their own country instead of mortgaging that impossibility to the United States. They also doubt whether the Japan-America Security Treaty will promptly alert Washington in times of need as many Presidents are hesitant to intervene in big crises. Different lessons have to be learnt by Japanese people regarding the changing and softening role of the United States in bitter areas of struggle, like Iran, Israel, and the Middle-East. In these threats, America is playing a 'climb-down' theory which sends different messages on different occasions.

The Unites States is no more the hegemonic power that it had been during the whole of the twentieth century. That era began to decline during the end of the twentieth century and especially through the climb-down theory of many United States Presidents, like Ford and Carter who simply surrendered. China now hopes that she can replace the United States in Asia in the new power struggle coming through the decades. China now plays the game which is aggressive and imperial though it is more covered up and subtle than during the hegemonic Mao days. One cannot rule out the possibility of China's reasserting her imperial claims on the borders of India and her new policy regarding the expansive South China Sea. On another occasion, when a future United States President is as weak as Carter or Obama, China will attempt to make inroads into other parts of Asia and the Pacific, and the Indian Ocean. Already a charter has been laid out to establish her sea lane control of the Indian Ocean and the Pacific.

But this new assertion by China is also facing new challenges from her one-time allies, proxies, and satellites. Vietnam, Cambodia, Laos, and North Korea are no more her servants at command. While Japan, the third largest economy in the world, wants to take over her national defence in a more aggressive way. The rise of India as an economic power is throwing new challenges to the hegemonic ambitions of China. India too is well on road to become a superpower. Though constrained by her coalition politics and popular democracy, Indian economy is viewed as sound enough for long-run development and growth. It is often argued that the rise of India is of great advantage to the United States and the joining hands among Japan, India, and the United States will be an effective formation to check the rabid ambitions of Red China. Now Asia is thinking more effectively of forming a power triangle between Washington, New Delhi, and Tokyo, and this will be an effective check on Chinese adventurism and aggressiveness.

In this book, the author wants to argue on the point how India, having inherited a very violent Chinese policy on the border, can stand against China in future and he does make certain suggestions on how India, by reorienting her defence strategy and by disowning Non-Alignment in toto, can stand against China. In the natural course of events, the rise of new economic and military powers in the world cannot be stopped at any point of time. And so is the rise of China and India as the new economic giants. India has been following a weak defence policy and capitulative China policy since independence and that is largely due to the ideological predilections and illusions of Pandit Jawaharlal Nehru. India has suffered a lot and at least now she must recognize what is the proper course of her future policy. Since 1949, China has mounted many wars, invasions, and aggressions, but India did not go to war even in safer places like Korea, Afghanistan, Iraq and cut a sorry figure as a military power. That means India is militarily harmless, and if a country is militarily harmless, what will be its fate is the harsh lesson of long history. The new developments in Asia and Africa offer splendid opportunities for India to follow an aggressive but fraternal foreign policy.

War comes when the people do not want it and so the war imposes itself on enemy nations when they are least prepared for it. But one cannot say that the war has not been intended by any of the combatants. The history of the world is the history of thousands of wars and their peaceful aftermaths. The title of the book suggests that the author is not a votary of the war and does not adore war as a means of dispute resolution. As an Indian citizen who is a living witness of the India-China war of 1962 and its inglorious conclusion leaving a permanent wound in Sino-India relations, the author has been thinking about the next war between the two Asian giants and its devastating aftermath. For any Indian citizen, a new war between the two countries is haunting and they are therefore obsessed with that nightmare. The writer never argues for war and revenge; he argues for peace, and the arguments and pleadings maintained throughout the book focus on how to avert the next India-China war. A war in the nuclear age is not a war to be won but to be lost by both adversaries.

When both sides are prepared and equipped for war and both sides are well aware of the capacity and readiness of the opposite side, an adventurous jump by one party into the battlefield is not to be expected smoothly. The author emphasizes that both the Asian giants should avoid war at any cost. And he hopes that the emerging leadership of both countries, including Xi Jinping and Narendra Modi will think that way only, even at the cost of material sacrifice. He wants to make it clear once more that this book is not a plea for a new war. The border dispute always burns and it is burning in the hearts of the people on both sides of the Himalayas, but author's plea is to avoid war.

N. Haridas

Contents

VOLUME II

Part III

Part IV

Part I

Chapter 1

Introduction

The New Imperialist in the East

1) China's rise as the new economic giant of the east and the next super-power dramatically alters the political and military equations of Asia. This change is outstanding since 1978, when Deng Ziao Ping emerged the new man of China's destiny. Chinese militarism and imperialism revives its fury only after the communist seizure of power in Beijing (1949), when the world saw the sudden appearance of the Chinese conqueror throwing head long into the Korean War. In 1950, Communist China plunged into Korea to challenge the power of the United States, who ineptly stood down in the Chinese Civil War, a stand down which the democratic world would deeply regret later. But what rattled Free India was the invasion of Tibet by the Peoples Liberation Army (PLA) in 1950 under the false bogey of 'liberation' and under the cover of the Korean War then raging, and that too much before the communists has consolidated their hold over the mainland. The invasion of Tibet cannot but cast China's imperial shadow all over East Asia and South Asia, but the Indian Prime Minister Nehru, out of his idealistic and one-sided camaraderie with the Chinese dragon was determined to invent friendship with the communist foe outrageously and demonstrably on imperial rampage and its sad result is free India facing the multi-pronged, multi-level threats from the dragon. These threats are ideological, military and economic. True the economic threat need not always be bad. In 1950, an alarmed Asia and the world warned Nehru about

the new enemy in the making in Peking. Even before 1944, the British in India had warned the Indian leadership of the plans of the Chinese Communist Party (CCP) to seize Tibet, but Nehru never cared to hear these cautions, who acted the left leaning socialist and apologist of world communism and consequently Chinese imperialism, wanted to camaflouge and euphemise this mortal danger from the north, and its legacy is the border dispute. Even six decades after independence, India is facing a hostile Pakistan supported by an aggressive China in committed conspiracy against her. After 1991, India too is a fast growing economic and military power. Too obvious to comment that the India-China rivalry is well on its way causing a new arm race in Asia and in this frenetic race China certainly is the 'Big Brother' and India the 'Small Brother'.

2) The media world is abuzz with big stories like China building hundreds of miles of underground tunnels to hide her nuclear bombs from surprise attacks, as surprise attack is the projected strategy of any nuclear power. China wants to keep her nuke power most secure, and finds the tunnel system giving the high guarantee and well known that nuclear powers keep a large part their warheads and missiles in deep underground silos. China's mammoth war infrastructure and structure, feverishly laid across the country, unless visible through the satellite eye and spy cameras, are known to the world only through whisper, hearsay, the Internet and its off springs. Before 1989, communist countries, and more particularly the Soviet Union and satellites, were making high claims about their military buildup, which looked as fantastic as unreal, but at last these hollow claims exploded through the sudden Soviet collapse. About their military power, communist countries publish bloated statistics to bully the enemy and energise the sagging morale of their depleting international cadres. In the sixties and seventies of the last century, such Soviet claims looked terrible, but when the Marxian edifice came down like a castle of cards in 1989, not only the world but the Marxian's also stood dumb-founded in disbelief. What happened to the sprawling Marxian empire built so impenetrable and invincible? Having shed the core theory of communism for the sake of capitalist wealth creation, Red-

China, since 1978, went anti-Marxian and market friendly, in spite of she displaying the images of Marx, Engels, Lenin, Stalin and Mao, as backdrop for the grandstanding party meets and congresses. China cares to reinform the believers that Marx and Lenin still reign as the communist messiahs. It is a different question that even in capitalist China, the state continues to guide its economics and finances through party priorities and the finances supporting the country's fast expanding infrastructure is almost wholly under state control, but at the same time the economy is recording a speed not realised by any country, Japan included. Experts differ whether this high speed spells out hard economic pragmatism or the miracle of speed?

3) Nehru's pacifism and camaraderie towards China led to the 1962—Sino-Indian War, and this war and humiliation alone would convince Nehru that China was out to undo Non-violent India. Still he was feeling hesitant to equip India against the aggressive China. More than half century passed since the war, and in her increasing aggressiveness China eludes the border talks by beating about the bush. India is entitled to get back the conquered territory, but China not only refuses to return Aksai Chin, but now lays claim over the Indian state Arunachal Pradesh, an area of about 90000 sq. kms. After the imperial era of Mao Tse Tung and Chau En Lai, many new rulers came and went in Beijing, but the Indian demand for restoration lies in China's cold storage of defiance and India continues her pleas at the doorstep of Beijing. Recently, after the November 2012 power-transfer in Beijing, the Sino-Indian border dispute and territorial dispute are again put in the back seat by the new rulers. The new President of China Xi-Jinping has returned to Beijing after a farmhouse rendezvous with the American President—Barak Obama. In May 2013, Li Kiquang the smiling, soft spoken Chinese premier made a pleasant landing on New Delhi and he reported that China is ready to settle the border dispute on new proposals. After 1988, there were several negotiation rituals, but China is in no mood to accept the fact that she is the aggressor (of Tibet and Aksai Chin) and India the victim, and the stalemate continues. In spite of occasional silver linings in the diplomatic sky, the India-China border impasse continues,

and this is the most feared flash point for another war in Asia which may breakout without notice or declaration as in 1962. See how China, after 1959, hijacked the Hindu-Chini-Bhai-Bhai Days into the violence of the 1962 war. How did Hitler hijack the peace-loving Europe into the cauldron of the Second World War, drawing all Europe, Asia and the Americas into the inferno of 1939-45.

4) Indian democracy still doubts if Communist China is the committed enemy of India? Anyone examining the Sino-Indian history after 1949 need have no doubts. Surprising that even after 1962, there are differing voices in the country mainly based on the propaganda of the Indian left and the left-media. In hard experience the dragon enmity is deep-rooted, malicious and ideologically inveterate. Why Red-China abruptly turned the enemy, overturning the long history of the two great Asian civilisations, must be enjoined with the violent theory and practice of world communism, declaring war on freedom and civilisation. There existed no Chinese imperial design against India before 1949, but the history and precedents of the past need not guide the rulers and regimes of the future, and red-China abruptly overturns her past to implement her new naked imperialism. Things turned upside down in 1949, when India, to her surprise, found the new enemy, multi-dimensional, ferocious, and blood thirsty appearing in different forms on different occasions. Red-China raised her imperial hood, first against Tibet, and when she could go home from Tibet unpunished of that horrendous crime, it was inevitable she will pounce upon India lying prostrate and undefended before her. Red-China was confident that she had nothing to fear from that philosopher ruler of India—Jawaharlal Nehru.

5) There existed no common border between India and China any time during known history. The imperial British, as their basic policy, wanted to avoid a common border with the Middle Kingdom, and on that reason the former even refused to annex Tibet during the 19th and 20th centuries, only to keep Tibet as the buffer between British India and the Chinese empire. The British wanted the monastic territory of Tibet, long and wide, wild and mountainous, as buffer not only between India

and China, but between India and Russia also. Standing between India and Tibet is the snow-clad Himalayan massif, which the monks and rishis alone ever tread and domiciled, but never traversed by any foot solder of conquest. Budhism, a cardinal faith and religion of China, travelled to that country from India through the mountain passes and seas. Genghis Khan—the Mongolian tyrant conquered Asia up to Peking and Europe up to Kiev. Ivan the Terrible was the Khan's tax-collector. Mongols subjugated China for a while and reached Tibet, but over whelmed by the Tibetan faith and culture allowed the Tibetans to govern themselves under the supervision of the Khans. From Tibet the Mongols did not cross into India. The Chinese dynasties, from the Ming to the Manchus, were never a threat to India and this historic brotherhood stood long and exceptional. When the Chinese revolters overthrew monarchy during 1911-12, and the republic was inaugurated, India was a British colony and all talk in republican China then was how to liberate India from the British yoke, and how better it would be to co-exist with a free India. Republican China acted unimperial. Chinese leaders Sun Yat-sen and Chiang Kai Shek were prominent advocates of pleading for India's freedom and they wished to see the emergence of two Asian giants side by side, and Sun was hoping these two future titans to become democracy's bulwarks in the east. That fraternity existing through thousands of years, will collapse abruptly in 1949, when the communists seized power in Peking. Indian leaders Mahatma Gandhi and Jawaharlal Nehru got all support from the rulers of Nationalist China in their war for freedom. Though the people of India, after 1949, were deeply concerned about the motives of an adversary China, the Indian ruler Jawaharlal was jubilant and euphoric about the communist seizure of the mainland, but this Sino-Indian bonhomie was short lived until the dragon landed the first back-stab on India, through the rape of Tibet in 1950. In the beginning, it seemed a mystery why Red-China turned the enemy when free India stood collaborationist and compliant to the high crimes of the CCP. Then the Indian patriot cannot miss the argument that the main reason for China's high handed hostility was India lying a very soft target before the predatory dragon.

6) The arguments made here points to the existential necessity of India keeping her powder dry to avoid again the Nehruvian folly of preaching gospel to the wild dragon. The caution is true that India is smaller to China economically and militarily and this second place (of India) is not going to change in the near future. After 1949, the Chinese threat has only increased and it seems there is no escape from that danger. India succumbing before the military power of China, will produce too many dominos among the Asian democracies and this write up dares to make some unconsidered suggestions to be considered by free world and free India. The history of Communist China says that when the going is tough, Mao and company had the wisdom to turn aside or turn back. When India is ready for war, there will be no war, but how the big India will fight the bigger China is the big challenge facing the former's strategic calculus.

7) As the most populous and one of the most liberal democracies of the world, India faces several popular and populist problems to make the country's public opinions converge to the cause of national defence through the instrument war. At the same time China, being a single party dictatorship, faces little political obstacles in coordinating and building her war machine and making her war policies efficient and effective. Even after the 1962 war and India's pathetic defeat, there is a section of political opinion in the country doubting whether China is the political and military adversary of India. Such different, rather diffident domestic response against the Chinese enemy is part of the left party's political strategy, and the Indian left lead this China friendly campaign as an ideological crusade, trivializing and covering up the Chinese threat. Is Communist China the foe of democratic India is the question often asked by the Sinophiles? Do they dare ask this question even after China refuses to engage in any kind of meaningful talk on Aksai Chin and Arunachal? The so-called Indian intelligentsia are unwittingly playing into the hands of the Chinese imperialist and pawns. A class of traitorous doubters pretending as peaceniks sabotaged France's war efforts during the run up to the Second World War. During the First World War President

Poincare, deeply worried about the fate of France under some peace-champions appointed Clemenceau as prime minister, who acting swiftly arrested several pacificists as war criminals and tried them in military courts and jailed them. No surprise, thereafter the tide of war was turning surprisingly in favour of France and soon Marshall Foch would drive away the Germans from the Marne battle fields.

8) The world in awful about the emerging China, and the stunning statistics of her whopping economic growth is terrifying. Communist China's invasion of Korea, Sinjiang, Tibet, and India even at the threshold of the revolution left the permanent scare and suspicion on her neighbours. The world talks louder about the China rising, and the more they talk about, the more puzzled they become. Twentieth century started with wars and revolutions that changed the course of the history and geography of empires, especially of the European empires. While the First World War changed the political landscape of Europe into radically different geographical shapes, the October Revolution in Russia launched a new threat to human civilization long accepted and surviving through of tens of thousands of years. French Revolution is called the biggest political divide in living memory, but that uprising posed no threat to civilization and man's pursuit of happiness. French Revolution was truly bloody regarding France and the Parisians but it promised man a new dawn of liberty. What it wanted was to change the autocratic ruling class and it exhorted to replace the emperors, kings and tyrants with peoples' leaders and elected rulers. The call of the French Revolution dismayed and later destroyed monarchies and empires, but never saddened the great majority of humans including workers, peasants and the commons. The world rejoiced and is still rejoicing at the message of the French Revolution, and the great majority of humans have no hesitation in embracing the call of the Revolution for equality, fraternity and liberty. All subsequent revolutions, let it be the many popular revolts in Europe, the February and the October Revolutions in Russia, the Communist Revolution in China and the too may and too frequent revolutions taking place in Latin America claim they are the inheritors of the message of the

Bastille. The world continues to ride on the call of the French revolters. True, the Parisians drew their inspiration from the American War of Independence.

9) What happened in the Communist Revolution in China! Was the 1949 Communist capture of power a popular revolution? Chiang Kai Shek was elected President of China in 1948 under the new Constitution, with a massive majority, but the Communist refused to attend the National Assembly in Nanking, and instead they went for the Civil War. The election of Chiang was on popular vote, but the communists would only laugh at popular verdicts, and they repudiating the popular verdict, fought the Civil War which was fought across China between the Communists and the Kuomintang. At last Mao Tse Tung defeated the Kuomintang and overthrew the Chiang regime and seized the throne of Peking. It was a war which the communists have won. How can it be popular revolution when the majority of the people refuse to accept it? Had Mao Tse Tung gone for a free and fair election—(he will never do it) he would have got a resounding popular no? The same the case of Russia, China or Cuba. Mao won power through guerilla war and war, and he ascended the throne as the communist Genghis Khan of China whose most urgent priority and plan was not economic reform, but the destruction of the civil society. He believed a bankrupt population will not get the physical stamina to overthrow the communist tyranny. As the Red Genghis Khan, he invaded the monastic territory of Tibet and annexed it. He was a strategic genius and he made it sure that in the heat and the tumult of the Korean War (started by his proxy North Korea) he could camaflouge his outrage on Tibet. In 1950, the Indian ambassador K.M. Panikkar in Peking and B.N. Rau in the UN played their cards well to camaflouge Chinese imperialism and conquest of Tibet. Or, if Panikkar and Rau refused to defend India's murderous enemy—Mao Tse Tung, they would have got the sack from that Indian patriot and apologist of China—Pandit Jawaharlal Nehru. Strange diplomatic puzzle how Nehru allowed Panikkar to continue in Beijing once the latter acted against his instruction. Neglecting Nehru's directive, Panikkar told China that India accepts China's 'sovereignty' ever Tibet,

(instead of 'suzerainty') and this acknowledgement was patently an act of treason. But Nehru's biased favour towards Panikkar prevailed over his patriotism and allowed Panikkar to continue his anti-Indian game in Beijing. The Chinese invasion and seizure of the defenceless Tibet remains the biggest strategic setback for free India, and it is very different from Kashmir or Ladakh. Let us look back to the British certainty and firmness on this issue before 1947. British India wanted to keep Tibet the independent buffer and the permanent security wall between India and China. To keep that buffer secure and stable, the British were ready to arm-twist their military power over which then the Sun did not set. Only because of Nehru's unstrategic love affair with China, Tibet changed into India's permanent haunt. Nehru was never sorry that he betrayed the Tibetans who are now hopelessly battling for independence.

10) Here I attempt to make a look into India's immediate past, and suggest certain measures to defend Indian territory in future years. May be in some places my suggestions will look dangerous and chauvinistic to the peaceniks, but remember these suggestions and pleadings are to avoid a war and not to precipitate war. As Oliver Cromwell declared four centuries ago, keep the gun powder always dry. When the two economies are galloping fast, its result will inevitably be the biggest arm race in Asia and that race can stumble into a shooting war. Under strategic scenario, it is arms and unfortunately nuclear arms that keep the peace of the world. Had Nehru been a fighter, he could have saved Tibet from China in 1950 by a small amount of muscle flexing as he could have saved Kashmir for India in 1948 but his illusions about the power of moral arguments came in the way. Panikkar, Krishna Menon and B.N. Rau gave the advice which Nehru very much wanted to get as the zealous China—apologist, and they sold their opinions and kept their jobs. Nehru during his long rule never initiated a war and never ventured into a battle field and that was free India's weak and dangerous strategy. General Thimmayya—a celebrated C-I-C, in his farewell address to the Indian armymen, wailed if he was leaving them as cannon fodder for the Chinese guns—and that prophecy would soon come true in October 1962.

11) Even half century after 1962, it appears much strategic waters did not flow down the Jamuna. Successive rulers in New Delhi would prefer to harp on the danger from Pakistan—a smaller power, and the Sino-Indian border dispute lay in the freezer from 1962 to 1988 when India herself (Rajiv Gandhi) took the initiative for talks. But the border talks with Beijing, like the materiologist's weather report, continues uncertain, vague and unidirectional. Indian leaders go to Beijing and Chinese leaders come to New Delhi, but Beijing never coming ready to talk the real border, and they go on beating about the bush. India remembers that the 1962 Chinese attack on India was a surprise move when it was still the harmony of the Hindi Chini Bhai Bhai Days. It was true that the relations had already gone cool and China gave enough signs that she has plans only to victimize, insult and punish India, but Nehru and his courtiers in New Delhi took it all as mere bluff or vain talk. Communist China always acted in fraud, and deceit and she made it often demonstrably. All along her strategic behaviour had been that where the going is tough she will pull back even unceremoniously and dishonourably. Sinologists warn that the next Chinese attack on India also can happen anytime and in surprise. At the same time do China apprehend an unpredictable Indian foray into Tibet or Singiang? Free India is too innocent to cause such apprehensions though China falsely calls the bogey of Indian imperialism which does not exist. The transfer of power in Beijing in 2012 though with tumult and fan fare also does not give any room for new hope. As generally assumed, under communist rule the change of the person of the ruler does not cause radical changes in state policy. The new Chinese premier Li Kiquang announced that his first foreign touchdown will be New Delhi, and he kept the promise. India, the victim of aggression is waiting and China the aggressor is dodging, and the stalemate continues. Li Kiquang's call to the people of India to solve the boundary issue and his further call for a joint Sino-Indian alliance in all fields to make the power of Asia competent to challenge the world, makes impressive reading and this diplomatic offensive the Indians appreciate only. But will China move away from her hostile stance? Again no signs.

12) While China's economic miracle dazzles the world, India follows the process at a slower pace. The economic rise of China is truly startling, but for a country like India, threatened and beaten by China by arms, this giantly growth of the enemy is not simply economic miracle, but the war chest to fund the huge Chinese war machine in the making. As a rising economic and military power, India certainly adds to the hegemonic worries of China. But the threat from China is the fulcrum of the world debate of the 21st century. While the west see this Chinese threat a very dangerous international issue, regarding India, it is of existential concern. Most of the Asian nations too view this threat with anxiety and alarm. While the Chinese economy is galloping at the fastest pace in known history, the Indian economy is growing at a lesser pace, probably due to her democratic, populist and coalition constraints inhering a popular democracy. India looks back that Monarchic China, and Kuomintang China did not turn adversaries. It is only after the communist seizure of power in 1949 that Red-China suddenly jumped on board, as Asia's new conqueror. Sardar Patel's warning to Prime Minister Nehru that Chinese communism is a more chauvinistic form of nationalism was taken by the latter in careless abandon, but after the 1962 war, the latter must have been nostalgically recalling the prophetic words of his late colleague and political opponent.

13) Unlike the Japanese imperialists during the first half of the 20th century, communist imperialism, since 1950, has been dangerously coloured by the romances of a political ideology, claiming to transcend national barriers and boundaries. More important that China, like Soviet Union after 1946, has been riding on the wave of post-war red imperialism, having a permanent corps of ideological soldiers in every country, and more powerfully in Asia. The Communist parties in each country play the role of China's spokesman and often as her political fifth column and many Asian democracies are in political compromise with these political agents of China. This Marxian corps, more active and adamant in post-war years, are shackling and demoralizing the nationalist forces in every state, they providing red imperialism the enduring advantage

of a political ideology masking her crude conquests of Tibet, Singiang and Aksai Chin. These Chinese forays are professed as revolutionary missions. But how long can naked aggression be covered up under the ideological mask? In the 21st century almost all Asia takes China as a real threat, and this fear is not imaginary but real. China is building a huge war machine targeting the neighbours, and more pointedly India and Japan.

14) Daring Chinese imperialism is causing scare all through Asia and South Asia and this muscle flexing has become more prominent after the demise of the Soviet state. Till 1972, Chine was blatantly aggressive and conducted herself insensitive to popular opinion in the neighbourhood and world opinion at large when she ruthlessly marched into Tibet, Korea and Singiang and Aksai Chin. Her detente with the United States in 1972 was the turning point when she could end her isolation and begin behaving diplomatically and according to international rules. After the 1962 war with India, China's only military adventure was the Vietnam invasion of 1979, and thereafter her imperialism has been confined to the suppression of revolts in Tibet and Singiang and her taunts against India in the border. But her economic change over into China Incorporated in 1978 suddenly caused a paradigm shift is her economic and military relations with South Asia, East Asia and South East Asia as her economy will rise world class thoroughly integrated with the global economy. As its natural consequence the economic rise has brought in more friends and less foes. South Korea, Japan, Thailand, Indonesia, India, Malaysia and Singapore and Australia are fast growing economies. South Korea, Japan and Taiwan who had gone into the American camp exclusively after the 1953 Korean armistice are now the big business partners of China. China is South Korea's biggest export destination and the Asian economic giant Japan is China's biggest trading partner. Indonesia, though a rising democracy at logger heads with communist insurgency, is another trade and business partner. Singapore—the business hub and the junction of international trade, transshipping and manufacturing, is a state ruled by the majority ethnic Chinese, but keeping away from political affinity with Beijing. Though politically controlled by the Chinese majority, Singapore's limited democracy is more affiliated with the democracies of Asia and the west. Philippines keeps political distance with Beijing, but business relations with Beijing are picking up. Thailand is another miracle economy in the Far East doing big business with China. A good part of China's whopping requirement of raw material, especially ironore has been supplied by Australia and the Australian economic boom is heavily related to this insatiable Chinese quest. China is America's prominent trade partner and the US investment is the rich source of China's Foreign Direct Investment. Growing China is making large investments in Africa for recovery of raw materials and the Chinese foray into Latin America are wide and aggressive. Chinese communism is being reformed in this way and the country is no more the isolated rouge elephant of the east as she was between 1949 and 1972.

15) China is slated to become the biggest economic power on earth within three or four decades and India is expected to reach the third place when the United States will slip into the second place. With large area, the largest population and a stable and authoritarian political order, the limit for China's economic and military rise is perhaps the sky itself. True there are skeptics and critics who contend that the Chinese economy is dangerously unstable and it is a bubble that will burst anytime. Largely state controlled and regulated, the country stood the slowdown of 2007-08, though allegations of economic and currency manipulations are rife. The point to be stressed is that the domestic capacity of China to consume is huge, and even in the event of world recession, with her billion plus consumers at home, she could stand many economic storms. The economic world calls the 21st century as the century of 'Chindia'. The rise of China is spectacular, and her new economic muscle allows her military muscle to grow terrific, and the history of Chinese imperialism in Korea, Tibet, Singiang and India drives most Asian countries scary. At this juncture the economic take off of the Far East, East Asia and South Asia too opens a new chapter in the economic dynamism of region. The economic growth of Asia generally shall benefits every country in the region compelling each to develop a vested interest in the growth of

Chindia. But the way the Japanese industrialization during the first half of the 20th century unsettled the peace of Asia and the Pacific and radically upset the balance of power of peace loving Asia, is the new concern against the military rise of China. The risk point is that while China leads the race, India and rather recently Japan under her new dynamic leadership are opting only to follow the Chinese lead, which strategy is slated to fail in the final tier. Given the prevailing political mood there is only distant possibility that the Asian giants—India and Japan will go for the strategy to walk in front of China instead of chasing the Chinese trail.

16) From 1950 on, India has been saddled with a territorial dispute with the China and this is because of the Chinese invasion of Tibet and Aksai Chin. The Chinese invasion of Tibet really rattled India and Nehru, but Nehru simply lay low only to capitulate at last. The border question exploded and the impasse continues long 1962. Now very strong arguments are heard in India and abroad for a consensus with China on the question whereas the conservatives contend that there is not yet any sign relenting on the part of China ever since 1949. The compromisers argue that between 1959 and 1962 Chau En Lai came with several proposals for a settlement of the border, but Nehru rejected all these proposals outright, and this Nehru stand though principled, was unpragmatic under the existing ground realities. The Chinese premier's proposal was only to make India accept the existing Chinese claims, encroachments and annexations and China withdrawing from no place. Compromise is more easily said than done. The argument regarding the ground realities by the pragmatists forget the fact of the invasions and annexations made by China since 1949. In 1950, she invaded Tibet, and though India was shattered by this outrageous breach of faith, but Nehru simply surrendered, and the responsibility for this invasion has to be squarely laid on the defeatism and pacifism of Nehru. True, long after there is no meaning in blaming Nehru's naïve past, his gullibility and ungallantry who rendered so much of unwanted, unsolicited and unacknowledged services for the callous and blood thirsty China. That China finally pushing him to the brink infuriated him though this Nehru realization came too late. After a series of bitter betrayals, Nehru's position against China began to harden and so in 1959 he refused to bite the next hook thrown at him by Chau En Lai and the result was the 1962 war. The war and the defeat of India left the permanent wound of humiliation on the Indian psyche. China conquered Tibet which stood the buffer between India and China through history and this invasion was illegal, illegitimate and outrageous. It was the inept and innocent Nehru who himself invited the PLA standing at the Sino-Tibetan border to jump across the Tibetan plateau and come to the Tibet-India border. Euphoric about his success in Tibet, Mao felt that China can commit any outrage on India and he conquered and annexed Aksai Chin—an area of 38000 sq. kilometers of Indian territory in Kashmir. Arunachal Pradesh, which China calls 'Southern Tibet' was not a disputed territory in 1962, and after occupying it in the war China beat and hasty retreat from Arunachal. But now China says she has legitimate claim over the area and some Chinese generals recently declared that if the PLA wants, they can recapture Arunachal within hours. This is the ground reality behind Chau's compromise move. But the compromisers argue that overlooking the fact of the invasions of Tibet and Aksai Chin, India shall go for a compromise with China, allowing the latter enjoy all the fruits of naked aggression. Historic that a peace obtained through surrender can never be real peace and that will be peace uneasy. The contenders for peace ask India to swallow all bitter pills of naked aggression only for the sake of consensus. Let the border impasse continue, better than peace through capitulation.

17) China's provocations continue over her peace offers. Now she says that the boundary between Kashmir and Tibet has never been clearly marked and so Aksai Chin is not a disputed area but part of Tibet. State boundaries are often not clearly marked, but a border dispute affects both ways. If China contends that their claim comes up to Aksai Chin, Indian can claim that the Kashmir state includes in addition to Aksai Chin, 50,000 square miles from Tibet, and can present the same kind of arguments advanced by Chau against Aksai Chin. The general practice and understanding is that though the boundary

is not defined by walls or watersheds or rivers, both sides are well aware through which place approximately the boundary runs. The Chinese contention that the McMahon Line is a British imperial legacy is a rude challenge to history. How Tibet remained independent till 1950 is a British legacy, free India is a British legacy, the handing over of Hong Kong to China in 1997 is a British legacy, and the present day Singapore, Burma and Malaysia too are British legacies. Until Britain left these colonies the Chinese were only mute witnesses to British imperial power under whom China also reeled until 1945. The argument of the compromisers is that it is very difficult to undo the conquest and annexation of Tibet and Aksai Chin by China, and therefore India, with a better sense of pragmatism shall go for accepting the Chinese outrage on Tibet and India. No country with an iota self respect can accept such a command to stand down. China never says that over these annexed lands she is willing for any compromise. It is a different question whether India can retake and redeem these lands by force when negotiations fail. Negotiations in the present way going on is slated only to fail.

18) Another argument in favour of this losing compromise is the multiple benefits India and Tibet are to secure through striking a peace deal with China. The point is that keeping the border dispute in the back-burner, if India and China can join hands economically, it will inaugurate an era not only of Asian economic resurgence but the Asian economic dominance of the world. Twenty-first century envisages that the new economic power houses of Asia are China and India, and Chindia can challenge the world economic order. This plea is not an illusion, but truth, if only China had acted unimpirical. Ever since the founding of the PRC, India had been pleading for peace and cooperation at the doorstep of Beijing, but the latter spurning these offers with contempt and rubbishing it through false accusations and finally through aggression. After the 1962 war, China never showed an inclination to return the territory she occupied. Marginal adjustments are negotiable but not wholesale, substituting surrender for reconciliation. It is history that all Indian efforts at cooperation and unity resulted in the invasion of India in 1962.

19) Because of globalization mutual trade between India and China is growing fast after 2000, and it is set to hit the target of 100 billion dollars in the near future. But trade expansion is a two way traffic benefitting both parties and through expanding trade, China may not be doing India any strategic favour. It is good there is economic cooperation. Even after 1962, India refuses to seek any military ally, much less a powerful ally like the United States. Only in the George W. Bush era, India chose to join hands with the USA on certain strategic programmes like the Indo-US Nuclear Deal, arms purchases, joint military exercises and so on, but India is not yet a military ally of the super power. Vietnam, after 1975, is a friendly country to India, but made to suffer the Chinese invasion of 1979, when India did not move a little finger in favour of Vietnam. Important to see the stand of China after the 1962 war. She is fomenting trouble for India, by aiding the rebels in the North East and the Maoists insurgents inside by supplying them with arms, money and sanctuary. China went to Sri Lanka which lies at the doorstep of India. China is an important strategic partner of Sri Lanka in the latter's fight against the Tamil separatists—the LTTE. China is involved in building ports and vital infrastructure in the Simhalese island. Already plans are afoot by China to rebuild the port of Gwardar near Karachi and she wants to open a road-cum-rail link to the Indian Ocean through Kashgar (Singiang), Tibet, Aksai Chin and Pakistan Occupied Kashmir (POK). It is China who nuclear armed Pakistan, and the strategic and economic alliance between Pakistan and China remains deep and committed. Pakistan has no other enemy today than India and this Sino-Pak partnership is exclusively aimed at containing India. China's role in the recent coup in Maldives is clear and manifest, and the Waheed coup and his blatant anti-India acts cannot but be with the blessings of powerful foreign forces, and in this respect the main suspect is China. The Myanmar junta came smoothly under the Chinese spell when the unpopular junta sought friends and recognition abroad—and the free world promptly denouncing and deserting the junta Myanmar was moving fast into Chinese embrace and the Chinese ride into Burma became smooth and clear. There many arterial transport

projects are initiated by China to get a direct opening to the Bay of Bengal from the Yunnan province through the Irrawaddy plains and other rail and road connections are on fast track. India's hostile attitude towards the junta gave the Chinese the easy climate to control the politics of the junta for a long time, and only after 2001 India will change her policy and begin to befriend the junta even against American advisory. Gradually international pressure would force the junta also to change course and the democracy leader Aung San Sui Kui has been released a change very much against the wishes of Communist China who is going across the world is search of autocracies and tyrannies to buy their support and friendship. Certainly the Middle East Spring and the ouster of the dictators of Egypt, Tunisia, Lybia are blows to totalitarian China. But like the South East and the South Asian nations, the suspicion and fear of a rising China have come to affect the people of Myanmar also, and of late Rangoon takes the words of China only with caution. This change in Myanmar is favourable to India, but the efforts of New Delhi to exploit the new opportunity still appears unenthusiastic and unmotivated.

20) In the international domain of diplomacy and strategy China's efforts are consistently to exclude India from actively engaging the ASEAN nations. Considering the size of the respective economies, India cannot compete with China in Asia or Africa or Latin America in economic invasion. China makes big use of her powerful economy to influence not only non-democracies, but many democracies also. Presently China's influence in the ASEAN is large. Her massive assistance to Cambodia forces that country to obstruct India's active role in the body. Not to say about the non-aggressive stand of India in these forums. In the Shanghai Co-operation Organization (SCO), China consistently moved to prevent the participation of India, and in the SAARC, China tries her most to stop India from becoming even an observer. Fundamentalist Iran is the best friend of China and China's support to the genocidal Syrian regime of Bashar Assad is unashamably anti-people and partisan. The diplomatic as well as military moves of China right from 1949 never showed any sign of she moving away from her path of confrontation with India. But India's efforts to break out of these Chinese webs spun around her, continues belated, half hearted and vague. When China grows big, it is a fact that Asia and India also grow big, but China goes ahead with a scheme in political and strategic advance planning, which combines ideological as well as military imperialism whereas the Asian powers including Japan and India wake up occasionally only to find the Chinese threat growing ominous and fearful.

21) China actively cultivates the Asian countries to find allies, wards and friends among them, but the imperial behaviour of China in Tibet, Korea, Vietnam and India has cast a negative shadow upon almost all Asian countries except perhaps North Korea and Pakistan and of late Iran. Countries like South Korea, Japan, Australia, Philippines, Indonesia, Singapore, Malaysia, Thailand and so on view China with suspicion and fear, and to abate this fear the recent conduct of China in world affairs, offers little hope. It is a recent development that the peace loving Japan has been aroused to fight back, and the immediate provocation is the Senkaku island in the South China Sea near the Okinawa prefecture. Three million square miles of South China Sea has been claimed by China as her exclusive backwaters. To the South China Sea, there are several littoral states like Vietnam, Japan, Philippines, Indonesia, etc. who lay claim to the mineral rich bed of the sea. Senkaku was occupied by US forces in the Second World War, and handed over to Japan to administer, and Japan is in possession since 1945. China claims the island citing the historical reason that once upon a time Okinawa had paid tribute to the Chinese emperor. The Senkaku issue now hots up and the new Japanese premier Shinzo Abe (the grandson of the former premier Nobusuke Kishi) is alerting the people promising to defend Japan against Chinese imperialism. He asserts that in spite of the peace clause in the Japanese Constitution, he can make Japan a nation state capable of defending herself. Against China weaving a web around India, particularly in the Indian Ocean area, the South China Sea offers a counter weight to meet China in the east, provided India rises proactive. It must be said that wherever there is effective resistance, China had only backed down. Unforunate to say that for the thorough success of Chinese imperialism in Asia, the main guilt lies on the docility and defeatism of the post-war leadership of the United States and free India. India even dissuaded the United States from checking the Chinese rape of Tibet in 1950, a policy that allowed the dragon to ride through the Tibetan plateau like knife cutting butter. No strategic default of free India is worse than the fall of Tibet to Communist China.

CHAPTER 2

Big Splendour Called China

22) While the world confers superlatives on post-1978 China, they forget the history that the Chinese economy was the biggest economy in the world for centuries, and the Middle Kingdom sat in the high seat until the beginning of the 19th century when industrial revolution in the west pushed her into the background. Covering a land mass of about 3.5 million square miles and a population of 1350 million, China is a giant in political economy, and no surprise that when she rustled her feathers again and rose up to act, she holds the breath of the world. About the Chinese empire in long slumber, that super-statesman and military genius—Napoleon Bonaparte warned 'let the sleeping giant sleep'. Moralized as the most ancient civilization deeply religious, cultural and scholarly, China pioneered epoch-making scientific inventions and discoveries. She invented writing paper, invented printing and the movable type, invented gunpowder and fireworks China's fireworks and gunpowder travelled across the world enabling the west to develop the fire arms and killer machines of mass murder during the 15th, 16th, 17th and the 19th centuries. Chinese emperors sent naval expeditions to Africa and the Far East, many centuries before Vasco De Gama sailed to Kozhikode, Goa and Macao. More than a millennia ago China introduced competitive examination to find out high talent for civil service and that practice was copied by Britain and the west only in the middle of the 19th century. For naval war, she invented the deadly flame-throwers. Confucianism the national moral

philosophy governs Chinese life for the last 2500 years. The Middle Kingdom continues the biggest Buddhist country in the world, in spite of she being the dedicated adherent of Confucius and Lao Tse. It is religious history's high point that Buddhism went to China the Far East and South East Asia from India.

23) China is history's greatest builder and her national symbol is the Great Wall, built through centuries to save the country from the northern barbarians. The Great Wall continues the most spectacular human construction even in the 21st century. If the gigantic Roman Colliseum stands to represent the heyday of the Roman empire, the Great Wall, famously sighted by the moon walkers, declares the splendour and power of bygone Chinese majesty. Her great emperor Shihuangdi (259-210 BC) built his own huge tomb underground, about 30 km away from the ancient capital of Xian. It is a massive mausoleum, rather a palace complex constructed by five lakh workers during the course of 36 years. This mausoleum complex includes the world famous life-size Terracotta Warriors—6000 in number—now the most sought after tourist destination in China. In 1974, some workers digging a well struck an underground cellar which turned out part of the tomb complex. The excavation goes on endless, and archeologists say it may take many decades to complete the job. The Forbidden City in Beijing, the residence of Chinese emperors attracts more than 80000 visitors a day. This palace complex is known as the biggest and the most articulate royal residence in the world. Emperor Quilong constructed the sprawling and beautiful Summer Palace, its gardens and hunting grounds in Chengdu—150 km away from Beijing. The Grand Canal speaks high of ancient China's irrigation technology and water locks. Perhaps these locks provide the principle for the multi-level construction of the Panama Canal. The Grand Canal, constructed by the emperors, is a wonderful irrigation as well as travel, transport and flood control system which is a navigable duct of about 1200 miles. China—the maker of chinaclay earthenware exported it to the world through the Silk Road, the mountain passes and ships. Specially made Chinese pottery was used by the Ottoman emperors to detect poison in food. A Chinese princess accidentally discovered tea and China

is the inventor as well as the largest producer of silk. Napoleon, looking at these wonderful and gigantic feats cautioned the world 'Let the sleeping giant sleep' and for many centuries China slept and soundly too. That slumber has to end and it ended during the middle of the 19th century, when the empire suddenly opened its gates to the world. Again for the real dragon triumph to happen, the world had to wait till 1978—when Deng Ziao Ping the wizard of a statesman inaugurated China's economic liberalization, and the achievements of liberalization look explosive and awful.

24) China is a subcontinent with the world's largest population, and in the usual course her rise as a super power is no cause for surprise. The surprise is that rise has been delayed so long. She has the wherewithal for economic giantism. The Chinese emperors enjoyed the grand vision that they are the biggest and the longest surviving monarchy in the world. At present Russia and Canada are bigger in land area. In between came and went so many empires—the most outstanding being the Roman empire which lasted about two millennia, ending in 1454. The Mongolian empire of the 13th century and Russian, Ottoman, Astro-Hungarian, Hohenzhollern, Portuguese, Spanish, British, Dutch and the French empires also receded into history. Twentieth century came as the age of dissolution of monarchies and the age of freedom. In 1911-12, the more than two and a half millennia old Chinese empire came crashing down and the republic was born but her ride to democracy remains rough and tumble. Civil wars, foreign wars and warlords hampered the development of freedom in China. The Kuomintang who succeeded the empire had a very struggling existence till 1945, when the Japanese invader was humbled. After the world war, the civil war between the Kuomintang and the Communists was set to explode, and it exploded sooner. In the fight, the corrupt, indisciplined and unloyal forces of the Kuomintang were kneeled, and Mao Tse Tung winning power on 1st October, 1949, reached Beijing as the new Helmsman of the Communist empire in the east. Like Lenin, he unleashed a reign of terror and presided over a disastrous economic experiment. Though collapsing on the economic front, he was a conqueror

and empire builder par excellence, and without wait he annexed the soft under belly of Asia—the lands of Tibet, Singiang, Inner Mongolia and India's Aksai Chin. But his reckless policy on collectives, communes and mass purges, took the country to economic agony, doom and disaster but still not causing his political collapse. Mao followed the Lenin strategy that any kind of economic discontent can be overcome by ruthless terror and kill, and thus he survived the most dangerous economic malaise called the Great Leap Forward. The pragmatists in the CCP who wanted to relanuch China into the road to economic takeoff had to wait till 1976—when Mao died. Winning the power struggle of 1976-78, the reformists introduced the new policy of market economy. Napoleon cannot go wrong—the giant has been awakened.

25) Liberalised China, who underwent thorough economic liberation and liberalization, is now the world's second largest economy and military power and the biggest military power in Asia, dwarfing the Japanese militarists of the thirties and forties of the last century. As said earlier, China had constructed many among the biggest in the world, and again doing the same. In 1950, India inherited the second biggest railway system in the world with 55000 kms of tracks, and free India added only 10000 kms to the British stock. In 1949, China possessed only 12000 kms of rail roads, but in 2012. China has 80000 kms of rail roads—an addition of 68000 kms during the last 60 years, and she plans to increase it to 120000 kms—a spectacular feat demanding huge resources, planning and technology. In 2013, India does not run a superfast train—and does not have one on the drawing board. China has 10000 kms of superfast rail tracks, though this reputation suffered a setback in the 2011—crash. Poor quality construction and corruption are alleged as reasons. China built the largest sea bridge in the world above the Shandong Bay, built the longest and the highest rail road connecting eastern China with Lhasa—a distance of 10000 kms. She is the largest producer of steel and the second largest producer of automobiles in the world. Toy exports from China accounts for 65 per cent of the world total. Her ship building industry is expanding and she is building aircraft carriers. She has

the world's largest standing army of 2.3 million, and the second largest air force. Her maritime power is not yet big threat, but growing with bases on the periphery of the Indian and Pacific Oceans. Since 1964, she is a nuclear power and from 1983, a thermonuclear power. The economic rise of China, though supporting her imperialism shall complement the economy of the world, and in economic calculus, this is a universal plus factor. Her military rise is alarming and her accelerating aggressiveness more alarming. In the midst of the giantly economic strides she is making certain clandestine economic moves being questioned by the economic world. China's foreign exchange reserves are a whopping $3.2 trillion, nearly a double of India's GDP. Sixty-five million Chinese tourists travel abroad every year and the majority airborne. The biggest contingents of foreign students in Europe and the United States are Chinese. Due to the frenetic pace of industrialization, nearly one half of the Chinese people are now urban dwellers and so goes on the stupendous statistics of liberalized China. The urban slums are proliferating and that is inevitable. The latest Beijing contention is that India is not her competitor and a Chinese general put it recently that China does not consider India a challenge to her power politics. True, the economic and military records of Nehru's India had been hopelessly unimpressive and sickly for China to ignore India. Given the size, resources, and the population of China, the above data is no cause for surprise, but the rise pushing the Asian concerns high.

26) In the statistics of this whopping hugeness of China's rise, critics find big negatives, voids and holes. They say the main threat to rising China is the country's political system which continues authoritarian, repressive one party rule, and the harassing political issue before Beijing is how long can China, the hotbed of liberalism, revolts and rebellions for political and democratic rights, can get on with the totalitarian system sitting heavy on people's rights. While this political nightmare stares at the Chinese state, her dazzling economic rise certainly gives new confidence to the people. Another issue is the threatening rate of industrial pollution. Rapid industrialization and economic take off is making China the biggest polluter in the world.

In her frantic race to become the economic-super-power, she produces dangerous quantities of toxic gas and ash, and the capital city of Beijing suffers a pollution which is ten times of the highly industrialized Japan in the neighbourhood. It is true that during the fifties and sixties of the 20th century, Japan also was alarmed by the rising rate of pollution, but the people and the state rushed up with remedial measures, and these measures caused immediate reduction and ease, and at present the Japanese pollution rate is only one-tenth of certain parts of China. In the mad race to produce more, China showed criminal neglect of its environment and now she fears pollution related diseases are rising, threatening the health of the nation on fast move. Before parting, the former president Hu Jintao, cautioned against the country's frenetic growth rate, and he declared that the fast growing Chinese economy is dangerously unstable. When growth is heavily dependent on exports, a slowdown in the major economies of Japan, the United States and Europe cannot but hit China's growth. Still it is merited record that the economic downturn of 2008-09 has been successfully negotiated by Beijing, though presently the growth rate has come down from 12 per cent to 7.5 per cent and that not bad performance at the time of world recession.

27) The economic world accuses that the market oriented Chinese economy is still regulated by state funds and bank funds which are generously allocated according to political priorities which fails to make economic sense. She builds infrastructure on a huge scale without caring for the economic returns it makes. Critics argue that China's heavy investment in bridges, sea-bridges, superfast trains, and multi-lane highways are not based on careful economic evaluation. Huge amount of public funds are ploughed to finance these projects, whose future returns are not certain and many major highways and bridges are yet to pick up the expected traffic. One example is the 24 kms long sea-bridge over Shangdong Bay. There is feverish activity in building more hotel rooms, but hotel occupancy is less than 60 per cent. Energy and water are subsidized by state causing large waste of public funds. Local governments are the owners of land, and they want to improve the finances of local bodies by selling more land to industries and thereby create more funds for local bodies. But such sales deprive the farmer of agricultural farms they want to cultivate. Acquisition of agricultural and residential land for industries creates resentment among the people, and resistance and riots in these places are a common sight. In the era of economic freedom, the mass political murders as in the Mao era are never more the usual and uniform state response against riots and revolts, though a repeat of the 1989. Tiananmen crackdown cannot be ruled out. This change is manifest, and after 1989, instead of retreating, the people have become more alert and assertive of political rights. Trade unions and labour, though unorganized, are increasingly on the warpath. China's cheap labour, which had once been the magnet of the foreign entrepreneur is no more cheap and foreign companies and corporate houses complain about the rising labour cost in China—which inevitably is the other cost a fast-pace industrialization shall bear. Investors say that to get permission and license for new enterprises needs time and bribery, as nepotism, favour and other forms of corruption have come to affect the decision-making process more thoroughly. All kinds of political and bureaucratic corruption abound China, and many believe that scourge has come to stay. The former Politbureau member and the superstar of Chunking's economic and social miracle has recently been sentenced to life imprisonment (September 2013) sending shock waves across China, but the billionaires among Chinese leaders and princelings are on the increase only. Commentators say that the former President Hu Jintao's son is a big business magnate and the Prime Minister Wen Jiabao's family business runs into billions and corruption without accountability is a burning question in China. The richer the country becomes, the more corrupt her face turns.

28) After the Communist Party settled down in power, there emerged a privileged political class which is the inevitable consequence of any political system popularly unremovable. The CCP claims to have a membership of more than 60 million, and there is scramble for enrolling in the CCP, because of the special privileges conferred on members, and the status they

command in society. As Lord Acton said, power tends to corrupt, and absolute power corrupts absolutely. China is under communist absolutism and that absolute power corrupts. World watchers say that in corruption, Russia and China sit on the top rung of the ladder and what bedevils the Chinese society is the absolute pollution of politics and environment through absolute corruption and toxic gas. Massive industrialization starting in 1978, China produces enough toxic ash to fill a 100 × 60 meter pond every 2½ minutes. While pollution rises alarmingly, only lately Peking starts to think how seriously it threatens life in the country. Beijing is one of the most polluted cities in the world, though it is the capital and home to the greatest and the biggest palaces in the world. Environmentalists say with pollution escalating in leaps and bounds, it is possible that China, and especially her urban conglomerations may turn into unlivable dens. The same China goes abroad in voracious search of mountainous quantities of raw materials like iron ore, coal and oil from new sources like Australia, Africa and South America and while processing these materials, the amount of carbondioxite it will throw up in future looks frightening. Industrialization corrodes the nation's agricultural life. How Japan lowered the high rate of pollution in the 1960s and 1970s can be emulated by the speeding China. While buying more and more oil and coal the Chinese rulers, fail to see the ghost of pollution threatening man's blood, breath, and food. Alarmists say it is time China apply brake on the blind rush.

29) The Chinese rulers, including the new rulers Xi Jinping and Li Kequiang are worried how corruption will endanger the country's future, and the future of the CCP. The governor of one province gifted a luxury yatch to his mistress. Another lover, more voluptuous, daring and jealous, hijacked him, and for a time she ran the administration of the province selling favours for a price. She became a multi-millionaire. The scandal reached its nemesis by the dismissal of the governor, and the royal mistress migrating to Hong Kong to start new business. In 2011, more than eight lakh party cadres were investigated and 140000 charge sheeted for corruption, but how many will be finally punished remains the big if. All agree that what threatens the state the most are corruption, the rise of princelings and a highly privileged ruling class. The posh area of Beijing is reserved for the residence of the ruling class with palatial edifices. The members of the Peoples' Congress, the 200 strong Central Committee, and the twenty-five member Polit-bureau have a new Forbidden City built for them. Fearing chemical contamination of fruits and vegetables, about 15000 acres of garden land near Beijing is specially cultivated with fruit trees and vegetables using organic manure, and this is to feed the ruling class, making the communist aristocracy more real than apparent. The rise of princelings angers the people more than anything. The heirs of the revolutionaries of the past, including the daredevils and titans of the Long March of 1934-35 are some of the princelings. Chau En Lai who lost his parents early, was adopted and brought up by an uncle. In turn Chau En Lai adopted Li Peng and a number of girls. It was Li Peng who later as prime minister became instrumental in suppressing the Tiananmen revolt of 1989 with the blessings of Deng Ziao Ping. Chau's adopted daughter became head of the state theatre. As premier, Chau led a very ordinary like befitting a socialist, but Chairman Mao was different. Mao kept a number of palaces around the country reserved for him. He travelled in special trains accompanied by hundreds of women friends and mistresses. He institutionalized the "Thoughts of Mao" and unleashed violence against the opponents. His aristocratic and monarchic lifestyle was the talk of all China, but who will open his mouth against him? His designated (dynastic) successors were the Gang of Four, but they fell flat in the post Mao power struggle, and the Mao dynasty was gone forever. Bo Xi Lai—the most efficient mayor of the sprawling city of Chunking, was the architect of many brilliant economic projects and programmes creating tens of thousands of jobs in the city. His record as commerce minister under Hu Jintao was outstanding. Now his wife stands accused and convicted as party to the conspiracy and murder of a British businessman who was partner in her business empire. Bo Xi Lai, now expelled from the CCP and sentenced for life for corruption and nepotism was once tipped to the top post of the country. He was sent to Chunking from Dalian and under him Chunking witnessed exponential industrial development. The leadership admits that his competence as an administrator has been unsurpassed by any, but because of indiscriminate corruption, he fell by the wayside. Reports say the CCP, through the Bo Xi Lai trial, wants to send a strong message down the power hierarchy against corruption and this malaise reaching endemic proportions, it has started to eat into administrative vitals. Warnings are fired that corruption that killed the Kuomintang administration is fast returning to haunt the Communist Party of China. Wen Jiabao has accumulated wealth like anything and that charge has seriously dented his liberal image. As the media and people are gagged, there appear no public criticism, but the people know the goings on in every detail and they are furious. Lord Acton cannot go wrong and power, whether it is monarchic, Marxist or dictatorial corrupts. Soviet Russia showed it and China shows it. Now what Beijing fears the most is the ghost of corruption, but unlike in a free society there is no whistle blowers to expose the criminals. Many new generation leaders like Li Ping, Bo Xi Lai, the present president Xi Jinping, and the new Prime Minister Le Kequiang are called the princelings of past leaders, having godfathers and guardians in critical places of the power structure.

30) There is no rule of law in operation but China engages enough number of judges to decide the large number of civil and criminal cases speedily. The number of judges in the country are about two lakhs, whereas India, maintaining one of the most justice oriented and free and fair judicial systems in the world, has only around 20000 judges and magistrates to adjudicate the millions of disputes and crimes which a free society throws up in the usual course. It is the CCP who directs every state institution including the judges. The party maintains that any decision shall give first priority to safeguard the interests and good name of the CCP, and most likely that decisions will be in compliance of this party dictat. Important to note that unlike the Mao era, liberal China is no more a closed-door, cloistered society. What angers people the most are corruption, party aristocracy, princelings, income disparity between millionaires and ordinary men, the difference in the living standards of urban dwellers and village peasants and so on. Deeply disturbing that the families of the members of the Polit-bureau, the Military Standing committee, the Central committee, the province chiefs, etc. become millionaires and billionaires through state run business and private business. Incidentally, I refer to the story of pre-revolution Chau En Lai running many industries and businesses and even money shops across China and Hong Kong to raise funds for the party. For this purpose he was exploiting his official position in the Kuomintang government very deftly. He ran an opium plantation also to raise money for the party, though officially the CCP opposed opium trade. The totalitarian system bans political dissent, and the absence of whistle blowers enables the party to stride along or run amuck. What will Karl Marx do with these brokers and movers of personal fortune? To crown these maladies is the denial of political rights and human rights. Is the Tiananmen revolt the grand finale of public protests?

31) About economic practices, traders and economists accuse China of violating treaties and breaching commercial morals done often covertly. China is a member of the World Trade Organisation (WTO), but she is accused as mass producing cheap goods and dumping it in world markets. Also they accuse that massive export quantities are achieved through unseen state subsides not visible on the surface. No country in the world faces so many accusations of commercial fraud in so many international meets. The big worry of the outside world is the economic sabotague China plays through the almost perpetual devaluation of the Yuan. Economists warn that the Chinese economy is as fragile as a bubble, that being a complex combination of too many bubbles that can burst any time. Against this harsh judgement of the outside world, the Chinese rulers are not perturbed. They feel such charges are levelled against any rising economy, and in the long run, defying the dooms day apologists, these economies stand up. China contends that the New York stock market crash of the 1920's did not destroy the economy of the United States, though it bankrupted the credit system and caused long-term recession and it needed the violent shocks of the Second World War to neutralise the waves of the crash. China is big, and the Chinese economy also is big and it is growing fast but certainly with its attendant spins off, both positive and negative and that is the Chinese logic. The German economist Edward Chancellor calls the Chinese economy a series of bubbles. But the economy's strength as well as its weakness is that it continues state regulated. Again the question is whether the warnings of the Soviet economy will go irrelevant in the case of China.

32) Modernists believe that economic growth lays the high road for man's pursuit of happiness; but social scientists argue that the welfare of the people cannot be built on the laws of arms, much less on capital and profits and this is the weak point in the socialist argument. A capitalist economy is the latest ideological challenge to world Marxism and to the Chinese Communist Party (CCP). Economic pundits warn that an overacting, overheating economy is in urgent need of negotiating the plateau and they say economic growth is not a sprint but a marathon. But rights activists are vehement in questioning the relevance of high economic growth, when it keeps the people under political bondage, and they protest that it is the inhuman side of China's Marxian humanism.

33) The plea made in this book is how a democratic, non-violent India will meet the challenge of an over-armed, anti-democratic, paranoid China. The main obstacle in the way of free India's strategic thinking is her monastic vow not to make any military alliance with any power in the world, big or small. This Nehru fad rose to the level of a political creed, immobilising Indians into the stupor of pessimism. For this pacifist Indian policy to succeed, all countries in the world shall swear that they will not attack India, so long as the latter continues non-aligned and non-violent. Indeed a fantastic proposition in the world of power politics. Nehru—the author of non-alignment, and a historian himself, never enquired whether his policy was not a challenge to the natural tendencies of man. The world fought thousands of wars, and in many of these wars, a small power was facing a big power with the help of allies, protectors and guardians. Look back to 1955 and immediately after to see what has been the relevance of Non-Alignment, except inviting total discredit and insecurity

for India. In 1962, when India lost the border war with China, the diplomatic and strategic world could only laugh at Non-Alignment, and that humiliation continues the running sore on India's international image. Keeping the border dispute in the back burner, now India and China are entering a new trade regime, which admirably is accelerating to meet a 100 billion dollar mark. But by examining the Chinese conduct all through from 1949, it appears wishful thinking that she will relent on her imperialism. She encroaches into POK—the Indian territory under Pak occupation and (April 2013) she advances 19 kms into the India's Dapsang in Ladakh and set up a camp. Good news China withdrew from there after a month. Aggressive Beijing objects to the visit of India's president and prime minister to Arunachal Pradesh which was followed by the next Chinese salvo objecting to the visit of India's defence minister to the state. Against these diplomatic snubs, the Indian response continues evasive and diffident. Political strategists warn that China may attack India in Kashmir or Arunachal in the near future, and in that contingency, they ask, how will India defend herself. In military strategy, the best form of defence is offence, but Non-Aligned India will not even dream of an offensive war. More humiliating to Indian patriotism that this suicidal Nehru policy continues to rule the Indian mind even after 1962 also while the military muscle of China has grown manifold since. Non-adventure, writ large on her non-violent face, India dithers to act dangerous, the two exceptions in the history of free India being Indira Gandhi taking the big decision in 1971 to liberate Bangladesh, and Narasimha Rao in 1991 taking the plunge into the non-populist, non-socialist waters of market economy. In the Bangladesh War, Indira emerged the heroine of Asia. In 1991 Narasimha Rao, inaugurated India's new name as the world-class economic dynamo. Rao redirected India's foreign policy westward, asserting that the country cannot any more be a camp follower of world communism. In 1996, Rao bid adieu to power, and thereafter India's foreign policy stagnates where he left it. Having no military ally to call in, in a future conflict with China, Indian security and defensibility once again remain in the high-risk category, in spite of she joining the nuclear club in 1973.

34) There is an opposite school who will dismiss India's fear of China, which they call a vested fear, and the end product of Non-Alignment. They ask whether this high, rather mortal fear of China is justified in the 21st century, and again they ask why the Chinese threat cannot be overcome by India radically changing her military calculus and strategy in the coming years? Certain that even before 1949, the Chinese communists laid down the scheme and programme to target India and invade and subjugate Tibet and Singiang. Lenin declared that the path of communism in Asia runs through Calcutta (then capital of British India). It is the regret of India that her China policy, crafted and codified by the credulous leadership then reigning in New Delhi, offering apologies to world communism, still reigns supreme in the South Block. Ever since the revolution of 1949, the policy of Red-China had been to escalate confrontation, and India will only be lucky if there is no repeat of the 1962, or its worse in a future war. When national security makes it essential to enter into military alliances and compacts with other powers to make national defence certain and guaranteed, why India, many times invaded even by the smaller Pakistan, and once thrashed by Red-China, refuses to go for a military alliance with a democratic power like the United States, and make her security as much guaranteed as that of Japan, Taiwan and South Korea? Since its festive and bombastic founding in 1955 at the Afro-Asian Conference in Bandung, what is the balance sheet of Non-Alignment, except pushing India into uncalled for humiliations and surrenders? When the Chinese threat rises apparently and really, what is the military option for India to defend herself? In the 1971 Bangladesh War, India was wearing the life-jacket of the Treaty of Friendship with Soviet Union—then the Big power. But in the 21st century, the Soviet successor—the Russian Federation is no more Big, and no more committed to India. India remembers that in 1962, it was the Anglo-American arms supply, so prompt and unconditional, that forced China to call a unilateral ceasefire and withdrawal from the North-East. Perhaps China then was capable of a limited

war only or she wanted to teach India a lesson, as she used the same strategy of attack and withdrawal in her Vietnam invasion 1979. In 2013, it is harsher truth that India does not match the military might of China in any manner, and therefore too dangerous to think of self-defence. If Joseph Stalin—the captain of murder and genocide and the inveterate foe of human rights and human freedom, could ally with the democratic bourgeois and arch reactionary—the United States of America in 1941 to fight Hitler, why not India ally with the same United States who continues the world's strongest democracy while India is the largest? Between these estranged democracies, human rights and human liberty shall build the enduring bond. A military alliance of the powerful Asian democracies comprising India, Japan, South Korea, Vietnam, Indonesia, Philippines and Australia can be an effective check on Red China, but that scheme presently and immediately looking somewhat hazy, complex and remote, an alliance with the United States is the immediate option before India to deter the hissing dragon. Full scale Japanese rearmament is the other Asian alternative to counter China, but this change is to come through a basic policy shift in Washington and Tokyo, and the consequent policy changes to happen in Seoul, Hanoi, Jakarta, Manila, Bangkok, Kuala Lumpur, and Canberra. But a joint Asian defence scheme against China may take time to materialise, and while thinking of war, stress will be on the immediate rather than on the mediate.

35) Another more optimistic school argues that the internal politics of China are under pressure to move towards a fully liberalised political order, and her economic interests going truly global, China will not go as reckless and blood thirsty as she had been under her Helmsman—Mao Tse Tung. In this respect the question facing India once again is whether her national security can be mortgaged to the good will and good conduct of an unpredictable, treacherous foe. If China is a rapidly growing economic giant, many Asian countries too are growing fast, but in military strategy the latter still going, ununited, uncoordinated and haphazard. The latest tensions in the South China Sea do not give room to think that China is mellowing. In real practice Chinese imperialism has no political colours. Assume China

goes democratic! Will she relent on Tibet and Aksai Chin? A democratic China may not be unduly reckless but she too will not go for a manifestly losing compromise and democratic China also will want to keep Tibet and Aksai Chin. No country wants to play evidently unpatriotic. Australia and Japan are even now significant military powers, but producing no united voice for a common Asian defence strategy. These powers are concerned and seriously concerned of China's military rise and imperial pretensions, and interesting that historically these concerns are comparable to China's mounting fears about the rise of a militarist Japan during the first half the twentieth century.

36) Biographers say that even as a boy, Mao was fond of hearing stories of the military exploits of great conquerors like Genghis Khan, Timur, Kublai Khan, and Napoleon. His role models were Lenin and Napoleon and not Marx, Engels and Rosa Luxumburg. When power came to his hands in 1949, what he did first was to conquer the territories lying invitingly undefended in the neighbourhood. From this dangerous game of striking at the soft underbelly of Asia like Tibet, Singiang, and Aksai Chin, Mao came out with flying colours. In the imperial onslaught, China avoiding Japan, Taiwan and Philippines from the hit list, was primarily because the Pacific waters provide no safe cages and hideouts for red-guerillas; and secondly because she cannot immediately lock horns with the powerful United States, supposedly guarding these territories. When America fought hesitant and dithery wars against Red-China in Korea, Vietnam, Cambodia and Laos, all other Asian countries chose to run away from these battle zones, terrified of the dragon's aggressive sound and revolutionary fury. Communist China's misinformation campaign that she was fighting liberation wars for freeing Asia from Western imperialism and colonialism was eminently successful, that plea having too many Asian takers including Nehru. With Nixon and Kissinger placing the seal of approval on imperial China in 1972, the latter was suddenly appearing on the world stage the decent guy, purged of all sins including the past crimes and high crimes against humanity, but certainly with the huge spoils of naked conquest safely in her kitty. In whitewashing China's bloodstains of genocidal aggression, the historic advantage she enjoyed was the suicidal acquiescence of India into the abrupt disappearance of the huge territory of Tibet—a buffer protecting India all through history. Nothing endangered the territorial safety and security of India than the dragon rape of Tibet, but Nehru—the ruler of India sat there blind to this danger and this was precursor to the rout and defeat an isolated and estranged India will suffer in the 1962-war. This defeat was rather a foregone conclusion. This victory, was giving China the new image of an Asian bulldozer rolling forward. Immediately after the 1962-war, Pakistan, though the committed American ally in Asia, somersaulted into the Chinese camp, but surprisingly her umbilical cord with the United States unsnapped. Pakistan reinforced the bond by ceding a portion of POK in Kashmir to China and this was the Ayub masterstroke in running with the hare and hunting with the hound. This Pak-breach of faith against the United States was evidently unloyal, but after some years, this mistrust and misconduct will be largely repaired by the former brokering the 1972—thaw in Sino-American relations. After 1972, Asia acquiescing in the imperial demands of China became more usual.

37) When the Chinese economy was liberated by Deng in 1978, India lay there the sick economic person of Asia, parrotting socialist slogans. Chinese economy started to surge ahead voracious and ferocious but no Indian politician dared to come out to advocate market economy, much less plead for urgent economic reform and regeneration, and for too long, the Indian politicians lay there intimidated and immobilized under Nehru's 'Socialist Pattern'. For the Socialist diehards, market economy was political anathema and ideological sacrilege. If Marxian China chooses to grow into an economic giant through the capitalist route, that was only China's business was the reaction of the Indian socialists. And sheer political accident that in 1991 Narasimha Rao, the unkown human dynamo and political dark-horse, was elected Prime Minister of India. Who did know then that this silent, soft-spoken, scholastic polyglot and loyalist of the Nehru family, was holding so harsh an un-Nehruvian, un-Indira economic philosophy defiantly harboured in his heart? When Nehru died in May 1964, Lal

Bahadur Shastri, another dark-horse, was picked up to succeed, and within days, this tiny man was asserting himself as the new leader, tough, pragmatic and if necessary ruthless enough to make Indira herself to complain that the new prime minister was departing from her father's path. Shastri, the tiny-giant, gave new confidence to the nation, but as he died after a brief stint in office, the great promise he held out could never be assessed, but certainly his start was momentous. From the fifties to the nineties, the socialist blackmail of Indian economy remained so thorough that no political leader, except Rajaji, Ranga, Masani and the so-called 'bourgeois renegades', came out in the open to oppose Nehruvian statism. Narasimha Rao adopted a new and different strategy, determined to take India to the new era of economic giantism, and thereby end the economic invalidity of the world's largest democracy. It was a time when even political titans, fearing political ostracism, could not make a whisper against socialism, when the socialist demagogues stalked the land. So Rao had to bury socialism through a ticklish operation that may look unprincipled, but he was confident that the end would justify his means. The wizard he discovered to drive the economic steamroller forward was Dr. Manmohan Singh—till that day an academic and an economic technocrat. Rao and Manmohan, as builder and designer, reorganized and reconstructed the economy in speed, and very quickly both earned the confidence and adulation of the world and the people of India, who for so long were groping in economic darkness. Like the Deng magic in China, the Indian economy too would enter the era of miracle. There is no doubt that this all powerful resurgence of India will anger and surprise China, till then looking down on India as the economic and military pariah. China should change her policy as India, the other rising giant of Asia, would start casting her rising economic shadow on the dragon. The world assumes that in the 21st century, China and India are in economic race, and some economists believe that in due course the Indian economy may outgrow China's, as the inherent strength of the former may prove more potent in the long run. Some experts are of the view that the Chinese miracle contains a large body of economic manipulations. Mitt Romney

—the Republican candidate for the 2012 US presidential race calls China the dishonest devaluer. Many high ranking Chinese leaders (privately) admit that the published statistics of China are simply to feed the Chinese masses and to surprise the world. Still the truth is that China is big, and her economy too ought to be big, and her military power comes through economic power.

38) Apart from the total denial of political rights to the people, the revolts in places like Tibet and Singiang for secession, autonomy and independence are lately making new internal and international inroads. For a communist state, the real and permanent threat is from her own people, who want to be free and free themselves from the jaws of collectivist terror. The teachings and writings of European revolutionists and thinkers like Moore, Hobbes, Rousseau, Kant, Hegel, Marx, Bakunin and others stormed into China, when during the second half of the 19th century, the Chinese monarchy decided to open the Middle Kingdom to the outside world. The Chinese empire, closed to the open world for centuries, when suddenly opening, the knowledge inflow from the west came like an avalanche, catalyzing peoples' power to challenge the dynastic power of the monarchy itself. It is history this challenge led to the overthrow of the Qings in 1911-12. The Chinese republic was inaugurated by Sun Yat-sen, but his ride to democracy was not smooth. The republic came so suddenly that that it was unorganized and uncoordinated. Part of this confusion was caused by Sun himself, who as the leader of the revolution, led the Kuomintang party to power. Though the leader of the revolution, Sun was prepared to give only limited rights to the people in the beginning. After Sun's death in 1925 Chiang Kai Shek, through a series of coups, succeeded him, and the latter as the new patriarch, ruled China from 1925 to 1949. Though a military dictator, Chiang was paying obeisance to the ideals and teachings of his mentor and co-brother Sun Yat-sen, but the former could only preach but could not practise democracy. While the Kuomintang paid lip service to human rights, the communists blacked out all the rights of man, including his biological rights. Who can deny the fact that presently the world is democratizing at an accelerating pace? In the midst of

this surge of democratic territory, how can totalitarian China keep her people—one fifth of all humanity—under communist bondage is the formidable challenge facing Red-China and the world communist movement.

39) China is the only powerful communist state with a fool proof terror machine at it command to make her turbulent people obey. But Beijing will remember that in 1989, the more perfect Soviet terror machine broke up in an explosion of public anger, with dangerous repercussions thrown across China itself. The real threat to the communist state is her own people asking for political rights. When the winter of economic rights has already come, can the spring of political rights be far behind? To fan this domestic fire, the new uprising for democracy in the Middle East, the rise and release of the democratic forces particularly in Myanmar (Burma) are the latest events, battering the Chinese state left in undemocratic isolation.

40) Some facts about the titanic rise of Red-China and her economy are as above. The theme of the book is to invite the thoughts of the reader to the question how a democratic India will face an authoritarian, aggressive China in future. In many places in the write up, the author is aware that he speaks not as an impartial observer or historian (which I am not) but as an Indian nationalist concerned about how non-violent India will meet the imperial China. The author's patriotism often may conflict with the visions of impartial comment. While telling the course of the recent history of these two Asian giants, the author's fright about China as the opponent out to destroy democratic India may appear too barbed and abrasive, but I hope and wish there will be no future war between India and China.

41) To understand the (deceptive) communist policy and practice in internal and international affairs, and the wholesale breach of promise they commit against people, I relate cursorily the events in Tsarist Russia, particularly about the weak ruler called Nicholas II, the Russian Socialist Revolutionary Party, its liberal leaders like Luvov and Kerensky and their inept handling of the February Revolution (see appendix). The refusal of Luvov and Kerensky to withdraw Russia from the Great War, the revolt of the generals that almost killed the Kerensky Government, the German conspiracy to allow Lenin safe passage to Russia, Lenin's audacity, adventure and decisional precision in calling the insurrection of October 25, Trotsky's leadership of the Red Army and the Brest Lito Vsk Peace Pact surrendering the major part of European Russia to Germany are some of the natural as well as manmade events that helped Lenin to consolidate his power which in the beginning looked loose, unsettled and uncertain. Here the case of China is different. The historic watershed was she opening to the world during the second half of the 19th century. The policies of Sun Yat-sen and Chiang, and the Japanese invasion were factors that destabilised the Kuomintang rule that finally paved way for the communist takeover in 1949. The Stalinist terror state, the decline and fall of the Soviet Union, Mao's pre-revolution ideological moderation including his soft policy towards the middle class before 1949, his game of hide and seek in guerilla campaigns, the pervading American defeatism in post-war years, and the blind admiration of Chinese militarism and imperialism by Asian democracies are visited in the discussion. The conclusion is that whether it is political rights or military confrontation, democracies come pitifully at the receiving end. The Achilles' Heel of post-war democracy is that she has become dangerously defensive. Still the strong point guarding the morale of the freeman is that the communists, in their scramble to make new history fail to read history, much less read their own political history since the Manifesto. The stories of communist terror regimes born through outrageous breach of promise, breach of faith and political gangsterism, as practised from the days of the October Revolution, the communists deliberately ignore. The weakness of democracy is that she has gone down apologetic and unadventurous. Again the basic issue is how the unadventurous democrat will make his future strong.

Chapter 3

Communism's Hour of Triumph in the East

42) Why the rise of a democracy as economic and military power house like the United States, post-war Japan or post-war Germany does not threaten and frighten the world, as the rise of authoritarian and totalitarian regimes like Hitler's Germany, Stalin's Russia or Mao's China? Historians recall that till the beginning of the 19th century, the Chinese empire was the biggest economic power on earth. It dropped out of the race to the top slot during the coming centuries. After Kublai Khan the Mongolian emperor of China, the monarch of China were not conquerors, in spite of many dynasties coming and going. The majority Hans did not recognise the Manchus as the legitimate ruler though the former conquered and consolidated the Middle Kingdom under them. From the sixteenth century onwards, even travel and inter-course with foreign countries were banned by the state, and China lived a closed society, cut off from the turbulent world of scientific inventions technological and industrial revolution, political revolts and Western colonization, and this isolation continued till the middle of the 19th century. Being a consolidated, large empire comprising more than three million square miles of land area, the Western conquistadors in the beginning did not find China an easy target for colonization, like India or the unpopulated Americas. During the 19th century came the wakeup call that the inward looking China turned outward. Large number of Chinese students went abroad seeking Western education, and therewith started the inflow of Western revolutionary political ideas into China. The Revolution of

1911-12 overthrew the monarchy, and the Kuomintang under Sun Yat-sen took over. In 1912, Sun Yat-sen became president of the new republic for ten weeks, and he was forced to hand over power to the co-conspirator and militarist warlord Yuan Shikai. Yuan ruled like a dictator till 1916 when he died. In 1913, the first democratic election was held in China. Sun Yat-sen, though the most popular leader thought China was not mature enough to jump into democracy in one leap and wanted to found an authoritarian state in the beginning, and showed little interest in popular mandate. But his deputy in the Kuomintang party Sogren opted for election and in the 1913 general election he won the majority mandate. While waiting in Shanghai to board the train to Peking to be sworn in as the new prime minister, he was assassinated probably by the agents of Yuan Shikai. What would have been fate of republican China had Sogren been allowed to assume power remain always the big puzzle in Chinese history. After the death of Yuan Shikai in 1916, Sun established his government in Nanjing but he could extend his rule only over a limited area over South East China. Later he changed his capital to Canton. He was aided and advised by the Soviet Government, and made an alliance with the communists and started receiving aid and advice from Moscow. During this time, taking advantage of the disappearance of the monarchy, many provinces and regions came under warlords and under these pressures real anarchy was prevailing over China. Under Soviet guidance the Kuomintang party was re-organized on Soviet lines, and that was the real reason how the party apparatus stood in tact up to the October Revolution of 1949. Sun was an internationalist aiming a world revolution and to add to his woes he was a bad administrator. Betrayed by his own illusions, Sun died a disappointed man in 1925. After Sun's death virtual anarchy and war-lordism prevailed. He was succeeded by the young general—Chiang Kai Shek—who was a capable, adventurist and adept politician, but often a bad military commander. It was his military policy that failed him in his dream of making this cradle of civilization the mighty Kuomintang empire. During 1926-27, Chiang's Northern Expedition could make violent strides and many warlords in the

North were suppressed. He was then in alliance with Moscow and the Communists. He felt could not go forward with his communist comrades. He believed Communism and Bolshevism were the diseases of the heart whereas Japanese imperialism the disease of the skin. Chiang's strong moves through the Northern Expedition made strides in the reunification of China. Tragedy would come from the Japanese islands. The Japanese invasion of Manchuria in 1931 and the general invasion of China in 1937 would upset all Chiang plans and calculations. The Kuomintang consolidation of power could not be completed as the Japanese raids, conquest and colonization continued till 1945. It was the allied victory against Japan and the Axis powers in 1945 that brought big relief and honour to China and Chiang, and all territorial losses suffered by China from 1895 to 1945 were suddenly repaired and these territories returned to Chiang on a platter by the Allies. Having gained the confidence and esteem of Joseph Stalin, Chiang could solve the major part of his territorial disputes with Russia, though some remained. While Chiang was triumphantly riding the victory parade of 1945, as one of the Big Five, the impending civil war was casting its black shadow on Kuomintang power. The Civil War was fought between 1946 and 1949, but being repudiated and abandoned by America in the hour of crisis the Kuomintang had to surrender the mainland to communists and flee to the island of Taiwan. The government also crossed the Formosa straits and migrated into the Island nation as the New Nationalist China. Chiang himself flew down to Taipai. Mainland became the Peoples' Republic of China. Once the PLA under Mao Tse Tung won mainland China for the communists, the bad days for India started, and the crisis in Sino-Indian relations was inaugurated. If Chiang had been a companion in India's freedom struggle one of the midwives attending on the birth of free India, Mao suddenly leaped atop the Himalayas as India's new and inveterate enemy. Then starts the tumultuous and bloody adversary era in Sino-Indian relations. Even before the consolidation of the communist revolution and power over the mainland the communist war council in Beijing decided that the empire building programme will go on, hand in hand with the demolition of the existing political order, and no sooner the PLA was subjugating Tibet and Xinjiang and then jumping into the Korean War. Sad commentary on Washington and New Delhi that the Chinese invasion of Tibet was accomplished under the cover of the den and tumult of the Korean War. The Korean War (1950-53) was inspired and instigated by Communist China as part of her clandestine programme of revolution through naked conquest, which international communism was ruthlessly advocating and preparing for, since October 1917. America entered the war to defend South Korea under UN auspices, and fought to rescue the Syngman Rhee regime. When the war raged and prolonged for years, the world, scared and weary of the agonies of the Second World War, feared that it may escalate into the Third World War, perhaps resulting in nuclear confrontation between the big two. America deployed about 1.8 million troops in the Korean theatre, and 34000 died in the battlefield. MacArthur—the hero of the Second World War in the Pacific, recommended a massive invasion or even a nuclear strike of China, if need be. Frayed by the Second World War, but still holding the mantle of world policeman, America rather the Democratic Party so promptly entering the Korean fray, has already decayed into a very reluctant faction. Then see how dangerously and abruptly the American fortunes in Asia tumbled since 1949, especially after the Korean debacle. Till 1949, Chiang's Nationalist China was America's staunchest ally and protégé in the east. When the communist revolution was turning mainland China into the red-army bastion, the massive sacrifices made by America in men and material in the Pacific theatre in the world war, were all washed down the Pacific waters. Never America thought that so suddenly she will be faced with the wholesale ill luck of the huge continental mass, and the most populous nation turning against her own saviour in the Second World War. May be the people of America now wish how easier and better it would have been to defend Chiang by arms, than throwing her to the communist wolf. The truth is that Truman has become an unwilling fighter in post-war years, though her presence in the war-theatres of the world continues ubiquitous. Unfortunate that about the Chinese Civil War America was deeply divided into pro-Nationalists and pro-Communists. Human Rights is facing the crude reality that not only the United States, but the democratic countries as a class, have demoralised into reluctant and hesitant defenders, afraid of the terrors and tribulations of the battlefield. They are obsessed with the suicidal urge to end any ongoing war at the earliest, and if need be through dishonorable, withdrawals and capitulations. The modern demagogues, are mortally afraid that a running war is the most nasty business to lose vote in the next election. This democratic wobbling caused by the pangs, fatigues, and privations of war, is the chief agent urging the anti-democrat to challenge the really superior economic and military power of world democracy.

43) Chiang Kai Shek, succeeding Sun Yat-sen as China's ruler, had to fight parallel wars with his political enemies at home the communists and war-lords, and the foreign enemy—Japan. He had to fight parallel enemies not only before the Second World War, but during the war itself. The war in the Pacific ended in the destruction of Japanese militarism, and Chiang's China will turn out the biggest and immediate beneficiary of the huge American sacrifices made in the Pacific battlefields. America won the war against Japan and won it thunderously, and 1945 saw Chiang at the head of the victory parade of the Allies, as the equal among the Big Five. But this euphoria will last less than four years, and Chiang's huge war gains were soon to be robbed by Mao Tse Tung thoroughly. And who thought in 1945 that the great victory wrested by America, was going to be hijacked so soon by the cold-warring communists? But this alone happened and America is yet to recover from that shock. For what good did America spill the blood of hundreds of thousands of her sons in the Pacific waves jungles and islands? Were it all to enthrone the arch enemy of democracy in the Forbidden City? Was not the billions of dollars poured down by the American tax payer into the Pacific, enough to buy a continent, as she bought Louisiana from Napoleon and Alaska from the Russian Tsar? Where have gone these bounties and sacrifices? This was the tragic finale of the Chinese Civil War. America's post-war doubts and vacillations were throwing her strongest ally into the wilderness of the Taiwan Island, and this policy impotency

of the Truman administration is taken by strategists as the worst American blunder in the post-war years. Truman had his own reasons to keep away but do these reason justify the loss of China to Communism? He complained all American arms and money poured down on the lap of the Kuomintang were misappropriated and stolen by the thieves and rascals among the Kuomintang. But the question is whether it was possible for America to prevent the Kuomintang collapse by making a direct entry. Even the threat of direct intervention would have saved the Kuomintang. During the height of the Civil War, when the PLA forces were in ropes, America imposed an arms embargo which gave the interval for the PLA to regroup, redeploy and rearm. In fact in the home turf the defeatists in America had won their fight against the gallant and the adventurists. American democracy is rich and power packed, but it is weak diffident and cowardly, demoting the post-war New World into a tribe of capitulators. With the loss of China to Marxian despotism, the American superman fell flat in her first post-war wrestling match with the totalitarians. Defeatists in America argued that the Chiang regime was corrupt, indisciplined, incoherent and inefficient and therefore deserving the fall. If the Kuomintang were corrupt and inefficient, can they be made non-corrupt and efficient overnight by injecting a sudden doze of moral stimulus? The real question was whether America was capable of fighting the Chinese Communists and defeat them? An America, capable of defeating Japan and Nazi Germany could have defeated the Chinese Communists also. When the Allies defeated Japan in the world war also, the Kuomintang government and army were corrupt and inefficient, but on that excuse America did not fail to defend Kuomintang China against Japan. It is to be pointed out that America was never satisfied of the quality of Kuomintang fight against Japan. But in the Chinese Civil War, America was not even ready to take the side of Kuomintang openly. The Nationalists went haphazard and disintegrating because there was not forthcoming even an American promise of direct intervention. When America directly entered the Vietnam War in 1962, was the administration of Ngo Din Diem efficient, non-corrupt and competent? If Diem had been competent and capable, he would have sought American help only to conquer North Vietnam, and not to defend the South. Diem was autocratic, corrupt and unpopular, but under him the people had a hundred times more freedom than under communist tyranny. When North Korea invaded the South in 1950, what was the condition of the Rhee government? He was dictatorial and corrupt, but courageous, pro-American and nationalistic, and under him the human rights of the people were far better than under the totalitarian North Korea. With resolute American intervention, Rhee was rescued, and now after six decades South Korea is a prosperous economy, a semi-democracy moving towards democracy, and standing firm on the side. She built herself as one of the bulwarks of free Asia's and more important thing is that the people of South Korea are on their way to make a fully free society. In the Vietnam War, America intervened thunderously, but the pervading American defeatism was once again forcing her rulers to slow down, change horses midstream, and withdraw when with so much of blood, arms, money and infrastructure pumped down and deployed, the war could have been won. Very strange that American battle field is now commanded by the unelected media.

44) As the military commander taking charge of a disintegrating, and leaderless China in 1926, the achievements of Chiang Kaishek were high and historic. He played the key role in reuniting the country after the fall of the Manchus, and he re-established the central authority which the idealist Sun Yat-sen thoroughly failed to rebuild. The misfortune was he never got the peace to completely overcome the problems of destabilization plaguing China after the fall of the monarchy. During of Japanese invasion, he had to shift his capital three times, and at last had to go into the interior city of Chunking situated behind the Yangtse Gorges and sit there till the end of the Second World War. While fighting the Japanese, he had to collaborate with the communists as well as confront them on different occasions and theatres. But for the Japanese villain, he would have and could have completed the consolidation of the Kuomintang power, and established himself as the unchallenged ruler of China. True, he committed very serious

mistakes in military strategy in the Civil War, but he never got the peace to sit down and work out. Once the world war was over, the communists turned against, Chiang pointing their gun at him point-blank. He was the real ruler of China from 1925 to 1949 and emerged the unquestioned national icon. He rose as the popularly acknowledged commander of the country to fight Japan, and his leadership in this respect was accepted by the communists and Mao Tse Tung himself. But he, reigning as war commander and fighter for a quarter century, accumulated a lot of popular discontent against him especially he acting a military ruler but apparently working under the Sun ideals. Fighting war is always the wrong game in populist politics, and power incumbency is a liability for any popular leader and political party. During his administration, a section of the people supported the Communist Party for the latter's popular and humane political policies so cheatingly displayed before the Chinese common man. China, in the 19th and 20th centuries, was a country perpetually in revolt. As usual, the initial, moderate approach of the communists towards the landlords and industry was a pretense. After the capture of total power, the communists will disclaim, disown and denounce all past promises, and unleash ceaseless terror on the people. The CCP gagged the peoples' mouth. As Lenin declared "promises are only to be broken like crack-nuts". Today there is a thousand times more discontent and anger against the communist rulers, but totalitarian suppression is so massive and bloody that there is absolutely no vent or fissure in the iron curtain for a peoples' revolt to break out and so the overthrow the totalitarian state through armed revolt is an illusion. If a fraction of the American troops deployed in Korea had been sent to China during the Civil War, the outcome would have been the opposite. With a contingent of US troops stationed even as reserve, the massive indiscipline, demoralization and the avalanche of defections from the Kuomintang ranks at the last stage could have been arrested. Even after Chiang fled to Formosa, there was still left large contingents of Kuomintang soldiers in the capital and in many places in the mainland, who too, because of desertion by commanders, defected to the PLA finally. At last it was an avalanche of defections from the KMT.

45) During the Civil War, many American generals were sent to China to devise and recommend plans to re-organise and rescue the Kuomintang, but all were unanimous in finding that the Kuomintang body was unusually sick and incorrigibly corrupt. Direct intervention by the United States alone was the only remedy, but the Truman administration was not ready to undertake this big job, and this US policy did the final undoing of the Kuomintang. American moderates and defeatist like General Marshall were very particular to give the message to the communists that there will be no direct US intervention in any case and in any contingency. While this open US stand has encouraged the communists, it demoralised the Kuomintang further down. So far as the 1350 million Chinese and their human rights are concerned, it is to be noted that even the Japan occupied regions like Manchuria were enjoying a far better rights regime than under Mao. Japan was occupying many parts and pockets in the mainland and large Japanese army units stood in different locations in China especially the Kwantung Army in Manchuria after 1931. It was the American hesitancy and irresolution in the Civil War that would later impose on her the tragic burden to fight the many losing wars in Korea, Indo-China and Vietnam. These post-war battles were also lost only due to the diffidence and irresolution of the demagogic leadership in Washington. In spite of these uncertainties, political commentators contend that Kuomintang had a good chance to win the Civil War, had Tom Dewey won the American Presidency in the 1948 run. No doubt these are now only the ifs of history, but very unfortunate ifs for the world democracy and the human rights activists to contend with.

46) It was Chiang's permanent obsession and worry all through the reign how to meet the indomitable Japanese, but never there coming the defeat of Japan until the end of the Second World War. In the world war, he was lucky to be proxy to the American victory in the Pacific, and so entitled to share the bumper harvest of total Allied triumph. Chiang, who captured absolute power in a series of military coups after the death of Sun Yat-sen, was at first facing the rising power of the war lords, the communists and trade unions in the north. He took it

upon himself his fundamental task to fight the communists first, and consolidate his power-base all over the vast subcontinent, then facing the grim prospect of disintegration after the fall of the Qings. Trained in Japan as military cadet, he remained the favourite of Lenin and Stalin, and strangely the Stalinist favours continued up to the communist victory in 1949. The Chiang-Stalin love-affair was in good shape, even in the face of the Chinese communists and the twenty-eight Bolshevists complaining to Moscow that Chiang was treacherous, unreliable and anti-communist. But Stalin refused to snub Chiang even when the latter was hunting down communists in their thousands, while professing and pretending loyalty to Moscow. Even after the Northern Expedition and the mass slaughter of the communists in Shanghai in 1926, Chiang was able to play Moscow against the home communists, and playing this dual role, he was taking the fight to the north more ruthlessly. After gaining the consolidation of the north by defeating many warlords, he emerged the acknowledged ruler of China and remained so until 1949, when conceding victory to the communists, he fled the mainland, taking his government and followers to the island of Formosa (now Taiwan). When China was overrun by the communists under Mao, that was communism's finest hour in the 20th century. In the loss of China, the once triumphant Truman administration and America were facing their worst political disaster in foreign policy and military strategy. America's Pacific hero in the Second World War—General Douglas MacArthur, who then too was continuing in command of the Pacific forces, was the US Commander in the Korean operations also in the beginning. The North Korean invasion of South Korea was launched, five years after the American victory over Japan in 1945—through the atomic decimation of the Japanese cities of Hiroshima and Nagasaki. Truman contends that the Second World War would have dragged on for more years, had not America used the atom bomb, and so runs his logic and excuses for committing the ghastly crime. The murder of the two cities shocked the conscience of the world so badly that the world still refuses to condone Truman and America, of this genocidal monstrosity. But the Trumanities argue that had not the atom bomb been employed demonstrating its apocalyptic power of destruction, the Japanese were preparing to fight the defence of their homeland with all the bitterness and ferocity of a patriotic defence of the motherland, causing much heavier human loss on both sides, probably running into many millions. In that case, America estimates that at least a million more of her soldiers would have fallen before overrunning the Japanese islands. And the Japanese casualties would have been a many multiple of this. But to the comfort of Asia and especially of Red-China, post-war Japan was ordered to turn her face away from arms and war, and thereafter a democratic Japan was taking no part in the fight against communist imperialism anywhere in Asia, Europe, Africa and Latin America. This isolation has been imposed on her, in spite of she being the staunchest post-war ally of the United States in Asia. Post-war Japan not only went democratic, but also declared her absolute repudiation of the armed path. This (Japanese) conversion into peace is the main reason why communist imperialism could make a walkover in China, Tibet, Sinjiang, Inner Mangolia, the Indian borders, Vietnam, Laos and Cambodia. Strategists complain that America, in post-war years, has become a hesitant warrior, obsessed with the comfort of her 'limited-war' concept, and thereby taking the country and clients to the morass of unlimited defeats. Unfortunately, this new American policy of pacifism has encouraged and emboldened the Chinese dragon go imperial after an interregnum of eight centuries after the Mongol adventures into South East Asia. Economically liberalized modern China says that a wealthy China need not be ideologically isolationist and autarchic and today her main trading partners are Europe, Japan, the United States, South Korea, Australia and India. Very quickly Communist China's pragmatists have learned to repudiate and renounce the decaying economic debilitations of the Leninist-Stalinist construct, which demands all economic powers, including goods and services, in the hands of the totalitarian, insensitive bureaucrat. This process muzzles the noise and voice of the free people. The Lenin-Stalin programme feared that a well fed, and decently clothed citizen is a bourgeois, and potential danger to the totalitarian state.

47) Mao Tse Tung was the most successful empire-builder of his time. His political failure was that his political ideas were making no sense to make Communist China an economic power houses. It is basic theory that a big military power has to be a big economic power also, whereas for Mao, political power was most important, and economic power cames second. Mao's high priority was to eliminate all voices of dissent, and to achieve this target, he employed different types of elimination processes like mass-trials, the Great Leap forward, Let The Hundred Flowers Bloom, and the Cultural Revolution. These projects were aiming to suppress dissent and destroy the economic and cultural foundations existing almost permanently. In spite of causing so much of havoc through senseless, vandalistic demolition and destruction at home, Mao believed that China can conquer at least the whole of Asia by his army of guerillas, saboteurs and Fifth Columns. He trained them to be tricky enough to feed parasitically on enemy resources, and fight the enemy too. This guerilla power unleashed mindless violence and massacres in Indo-China. Mao's first testing ground to experiment with his imperial formula was Tibet, where he was lucky to have a sincere collaborator in the pious, dreamy Indian leader—Jawaharlal Nehru. Nehru, the secret admirer and ally of world communism, who will handover Tibet to the imperial dragon on the silver platter of voluntary capitulation. Again post-war Asia is to contend with the intriguing puzzle that Mao was again lucky to have a committed pacifist in post-war Japan, winking at Red-China's imperial crimes. There erupted protests and violent debates in Europe and America why Tibet, the historic buffer-state between India and China, has been so suicidally ceded by India to a voracious China, and that too to the total surprise of Mao himself. Dalai Lama—the ruler and religious supremo of Tibet, had to flee to India in 1959, because of the dragon threat to his life and power but in this case, Nehru showed the courtesy to give him asylum, but conditional on the latter living a non-political monk in India. The question continuously asked is why China repeats her threats against India after the latter allowed China to make a naked conquest and annexation of Tibet, which is the huge trophy India presented to her even

before the heat of the revolution has subsided. Through this act, Nehru was acting as the patron of Chinese imperialism. In 1950, Sardar Patel had to post a strong reminder on Nehru that all Indian exertions and endeavours in the world arena, supporting the Communist revolution in Peking, have been rubbished and negatively reciprocated by Mao and Chau En Lai, and then what is the purpose and use of India giving the most-favoured nation-clause diplomatic treatment to a declared adversary. Unfortunate for free India that Sardar Patel and Nehru were politically in opposite poles—Patel favouring a pro-democracy, pro-west foreign policy, and Nehru bent on taking up revolutionary causes, which in practice was to favour the genocidal causes practised by totalitarian Russia and genocidal China in spite of Nehru being no lover of violence and repression. After India became independent, Nehru took up the cause of liberation of the African and Asian colonies from Western colonial rule, as the fundamental plank of India's foreign policy. Fortunately for Russia and China, they then had no colonies in Africa and Asia, except the new Chinese colony of Tibet and Russia's East European satellites. Nehru will accept only one enemy for India, and that was the west, and more particularly America and Britain. When China committed the rape of Tibet in 1950, the people of China were a famished, poverty-stricken mass with millions dying of manmade and state-induced famines, and state-terror. But the Indian communists and Nehru were singing the songs of praise of the Chinese Revolution, and this was to camaflouge the high-crimes, that red-terror and red-imperialism were staging in and out of China. The Indian communists acted as the committed ideological surrogate of China, and they making no secret of their anti-national stand. But after the 1962, Chinese invasion of India, the Indian communists had made a strategic retreat temporarily from their pro-China polemics, but again, with the support of the leftist media, they resurfaced and threw themselves into the political mainstream of the country. Immediately after the Chinese attack in 1962, the Indian Communist Party (unsplit) passed a revolution with a large majority condemning the Chinese invasion and supporting the stand of India—but not making this resolution public. Leaders like EMS and A.K. Gopalan were upset and they recorded their powerful dissent which sowed the seeds of split and reports say this conflict of patriotism was the real reason for the 1964 split later. That year the Indian Communist Party split into two the nationalists and the internationalists. More than half century after the war the China-loyal Indian Marxists are there as the unostracised, radical class standing aright on India's political landscape. As in the Soviet Union and Red China, Indian communism's war against economic capitalism has lost much of its cutting edge in the politics of globalisation.

48) Communist China, till 1972 was a country living internationally outlawed, and therefore able to run amuck, as the rogue elephant of the east. In her forays she was interfering militarily and politically in the internal affairs of any country in Asia, Africa and Latin America. In the fifties and the sixties of the 20th century, the communists were on rampage in Malaya and Indonesia where they, under the command and patronage of international communism, were organising sporadic as well as massive armed revolts in many places and pockets. In Malaya they actually pushed the government to the brink when the practical-minded government, by commissioning British help, put down the insurrection, and established democracy with the king as the symbolic head. In fact Malaya (now Malayasia) was rescued from communists by British forces. This was followed by the country's short-lived union and honeymoon with Singapore, but this union soon broke up. Anyhow this failure to unite did not result in the much feared disintegration of the two countries, inviting communist coups. While Malaya could build her economy powerful to survive the communist threat, Singapore—that 200 square mile island discovered by Raffles and colonized by the British in the 19th century wrote its new history as the third economic miracle of Asia after Hong Kong and Japan. British colonisation of Singapore was followed by a massive influx of Chinese immigrants. After the grant of independence, the island nation under the hard-hitting pragmatism of her legendary leader Lee Kuan Yew, emerged the trading, manufacturing and shipping hub of the east, and a bright jewel in the Pacific seaboard. The island is another economic

superstar of Asia, following Hong Kong. Though populated and ruled by a Chinese majority, the ruling party is anti-communist and pro-west, refusing to ally with Red-China politically. Nor they pay homage to Chinese communism because of ethnic or ideological affinity. This island, though a guided democracy, is a vibrant economic power.

49) In the fifties and sixties of the last century, world communism went on the rise and this rise, was accomplished through a two-way invasion. The first was ideological, which in many places was backed up by guerilla war. The second stage was through direct military conquest. To start a guerilla war in a country, at first they prepare the ground through the native communist party whose loyalty is wholly and unquestionably to international communism, as it formerly was to the Comintern. Communists do not acknowledge a mother country. This unprecedented ideological internationalism has been enjoyed and exploited by Russia and China through the national communist parties across the world, whether it is in Eastern Europe, Western Europe, Vietnam, Cambodia, Laos, Malaya, Indonesia or India. After the Chinese attack on India in 1962, the Indian communists suffered the split (not by name) into nationalists and internationalists. After the 1962 India-China war, the Communist Party (Marxist), declared that the border between the two countries remains undefined, and therefore they cannot say whether the claim of China is wrong. Thousands of communists were in detention under security laws, but no detenu charged with the crime of treason. Nehru—the communist patron, euphemized this anti-national stand of the communists as political dissent. The national communist parties in Asian countries acted as the sabotage arm of International Communism, doing advance-firing for the actual communist invasion to follow immediately. Many countries could put down these Fifth Columns through armed suppression, but many could not or did not do so, due to their liberal human rights regime, or due to their military weakness or because of vague liberalism or weak leadership.

50) In Indonesia, the founding President Mohammad Sukarno went into the anti-Western camp from the beginning

of his country's liberation from Dutch-rule. During the world war, Japan occupied Philippines, Indonesia, Indo-China, Burma, Malaya and Singapore, but after 1943, when the Japanese fortunes in the battlefield began to tumble, they instigated the nationalist parties to strengthen their fight against the Dutch in Indonesia, the British in Burma, Malaya and Singapore and the French in Indo-China. At one stage Japan compelled the reluctant Sukarno to declare the independence of Indonesia from Dutch rule, and this declaration later clothing Sukarno with the aura as the leader of the war of independence. Japan was allied with the Indian National Army (INA) led by Subhash Chandra Bose, but in their fight against the British, the Japanese refused permission to the INA to seize Tripura during the battle of Kohima, in which thousands of Indians laid down their lives. The war was turning against Japan, and an Allied victory was in sight. One story goes that Subhash Chandra Bose wanted to escape the Japanese strangle hold, and so he was planning to escape to Russia and in the rash bid, his plane crashed in the Taipei airport and thereafter nothing was heard of him. Another story goes that he escaped into the wilderness and was roaming a Sadhu. But indisputable that the liberation movement in Indonesia, Indo-China, Singapore, Malaya, etc., were aided and abetted by the Japanese militarists in their desperate bid to weaken powers like the United States, France, Denmark and Britain. After the war, Indonesia was granted independence by the Dutch and Sukarno emerged its supreme leader. He refused to ally with the west, and was practically ruling the country as dictator, which policy the west was hesitating to admire and reluctant to endorse. This charismatic, pleasure-seeking ruler was getting immediate recognition from the communist block, and he, for political advantage, was veering towards a socialist dictatorship of his choice. The dictatorial and totalitarian policies not finding favour with the west, it was natural for him to turn to the communist-block for acceptance and recognition, which Russia and China readily accorded for the asking. To be reiterated that any attempting dictator, or even an elected dictator like N. Krumah of Ghana or Sukarno of Indonesia was finding it easy to rig and sabotage popular ballots, and cling on to power. By declaring himself a 'socialist' any dictator was becoming in the seat of power safe. A military dictator like Gamal Abdul Nasser of Egypt was proclaiming that he is the only socialist in the Middle East, and he renamed Egypt a 'Socialist Republic'. For Sukarno too, socialism became the strategic bandwagon for him to mount, only to cover up his tyrannical omissions and sins. But his socialist programmes were taking the resource-rich Indonesia rapidly into economic ruin. Among the independent nations newly freed from foreign rule, Indonesia was comparatively a prosperous economy even during the colonial days. The Indonesian communists, being a powerful armed unit, were hoping that with considerable infiltration into the state apparatus already accomplished, a communist takeover of the country was clearly on the cards, but to their dismay at the last moment the army will enter. The army chief Suharto, in a swift move, toppled Sukarno and took over. While the Suharto military rule continued for 25 years, he was accused of purging the state establishment of communists, through a merciless liquidation programme, in which thousands of communists, were led before firing squads. So far as the east and the Pacific seaboard are concerned, the Suharto coup was a big setback for communist imperialism Asia but still the communist bulldozer was ruthlessly steamrolling into Indo-China. The Chinese frustration was that a country of 250 million people was slipping away from the fast expanding communist empire in the east, and this setback will weaken and slacken the future red-offensives. As done by Chiang Kai Shek in his Northern Expedition, and more particularly in Shanghai, the Suharto cleaning operation, reduced the Communist Party of Indonesia into a mere shadow of its past self. The Suharto rule was dictatorial, but very successful in the economic front, and a growing economy and resulting prosperity gave a longer life for army-rule, especially when he did not stumble into the kind of adventures recklessly pursued by Sukarno through his muddled empire building adventures. As he enjoyed the reign of a quarter century, Suharto could ensure that the serious threat of communist guerilla-terror is eliminated. Had Sukarno continued in power, the loss of Indonesia to communism was clear possibility, and such loss would have been another big blow to world democracy, in spite of Suharto not being a democrat. Needs to emphasize that the Suharto coup indirectly enabled the country to return to democracy, once his rule was over-thrown by popular revolt. Suharto founded no political dynasty. On the other hand, had Indonesia gone communist, there would have been no return to democracy even in remoter days, as it happened in Russia, North Korea and China. A nuclear-armed communist Indonesia would have become another deadly threat to free Asia, as the country is another fast emerging economic power. Recent events would say that any totalitarian economic order is prone to disintegration sooner than later, as it happened in Eastern Europe and Russia. Sometimes it endure longer by adopting the Chinese model of market economy, as the half-way house between freedom and political terror, but now such thoughts are hypothetical regarding the most populous Islamic country.

51) Mao Tse Tung himself will confess later that but for the Japanese invasion of China, there would have been no communist revolution in China. The Japanese had battered and damaged the Kuomintang state-apparatus beyond repair, and this beating continued until the end of the Second World War. Japan invaded Manchuria in 1931 and established her semi-colony there called Manchukuo. More than a (quarter) million Japanese were brought in and settled there immediately, and more would follow. Manchuria, though an occupied territory, was at once turning into the industrial hub of China. But when the Second World War broke out, Japan, an ally of Germany and Italy, prepared her scheme named the "Greater East Asia Co-Prosperity Sphere" without any effective coordination with her ally Germany and this non-co-ordination now appears very strange to military strategists. In 1941, in breach of this alliance, Japan entered into a Non-Aggression Pact with Soviet Russia, which friendship continued till the last days of the Pacific War. In 1941, the Russo-Japanese Non-Aggression Pact may not have sounded so much controversial as Hitler and Russia were still allies. Russia and Germany jointly invaded Poland. In total breach of faith after some months, Hitler would turn his guns against

Bolshevik Russia violating the German Soviet comradeship in arms. But the surprise is that even after Soviet Russia somersaulted into the Allied camp, this Russo-Japanese Non-Aggression Pact continued, very much to the chagrin of Japan, but to the advantage of Russia Finally in July 1945, Stalin would unilaterally repudiate this pact and suddenly invade Manchuria. Supporting the American offensive against Japan. This Russian defection and deceit the Japanese never anticipated. Japan, was fighting the United States and Britain and wanted to renew this pact, but Stalin, after the Yalta Conference, remained elusive keeping Japan in the guessing game. The day the atom bomb was dropped on Hiroshima, Russia launched a massive invasion of Manchuria, and then alone Japan could know the Stalinist betrayal. It was too late for Japan to retaliate and turn back from her fatal commitment in Pearl Harbour. When Hitler turned his guns against Russia in 1941, the Japanese Foreign Minister Matsukuo Yosuke strongly pleaded in the cabinet to attack Russia from the east, but the militarists, ignoring him, opted for Pearl Harbour. If the Yosuke advice had been heeded in Tokyo, the outcome of the war would have been very different. Germany and Japan were following their own independent rather contradicting strategies, and this non-co-ordination finally proving fatal for both. For the Axis, the greatest opportunity in the war was forfeited by Japan, when Hitler attacked Russia in 1941. Following the Nazi thrust from the west, if a corresponding invasion of Russia had been mounted by Japan from the east, the Soviet defences would have crumbled in no time, and possibly the industrial and fertile plains of European Russia would have gone to Germany, and the large, expansive eastern Russia, occupied, colonized and probably industrialized also, by Japan. When the Pearl Harbour decision was being debated by the Japanese Cabinet, the Japanese Foreign Minister Matsuoke Yosuke had just returned from Moscow, after receiving a very affectionate send off by Stalin himself at the railway station. Still he alone emphatically pleaded in the cabinet to attack Russia through Vladivostok. He was overruled by the militarists, and the Konoye cabinet resigned, and the indomitable, but reckless Tojo took over. In October 1941,

Stalin was in grave fear of a Japanese attack from the east. The Russian spy in Tokyo Richard Sorge—(a German national) was regularly monitoring Tokyo's power corridors and reporting to Moscow on Japan's war plans. The master spy informed Stalin that Japan has no plan to attack Russia, and the Tokyo war-council is planning differently. Later this spy, caught by the Japanese counter intelligence, was executed. Hitler attacking Russia, and Japan attacking Pearl Harbour were the turning points in the Second World War, sealing the fate of the Axis. The Tojo cabinet was opting for the impossible, as Pearl Harbour was Japan's most desperate, rather blundering gamble. At the same time, the Japanese grievances against the United States cannot be called unreasonable or imaginary. Before the war, the United States was the main source of oil and raw materials like serape iron and oil, but America, in order to protect Kuomintang China, was clamping export bans against Japan. Japan felt she was being forced into economic suffocation, and she has to seek alternative sources, or face economic ruin. America wanted Japan to withdraw from China, but Japan was already the colonist of Manchuria having more elaborate schemes to conquer more China. The alternative was to seek iron-ore from Manchuria and to capture the oil fields of Dutch-Indies (Indonesia), which she accomplished swiftly. But a war with the resource-rich, technology leader like the United States was suicidal for Japan on any reason but the latter planned that way only. After a devastating attack on Pearl Harbour, her leaders, particularly the navy had laid down the strategy for a separate peace with the United States, but FDR would not agree, forcing Japan to choose the ruinous route. In the process, Tokyo decided to exempt Russia, because in 1941 she had no serious grievance against Russia, though fighting Russia in Manchuria and Inner Mongolia. Prime Minister Konoye's last minute plea with the American Secretary of State Cordell Hull, for a direct meeting with President Franklin D. Roosevelt was repeatedly rebuffed, and a distraught Konoye, caught between the militarists at home and the rude American state department, resigned, paving way for the militants to takeover the reins in Tokyo. Historians contend that a paranoid American state department and State

Secretary Cordell Hull were fearing that in a direct meeting with FDR, the president—the generous man he was, was likely to give away too much to Konoye. The president agreed to meet Konoye, but Hull and advisors sabotaged the scheme at the last moment. In retrospect, it can said that Cordell Hull too shall take the blame for the Pearl Harbour strike. Surprising that the recent researchers will discover that the Pearl Harbour attack was welcomed by America, as FDR was very much in need of a pretext to enter the war on the side of the Allies, and the military top brass in Washington never relayed the intelligence about the impending Japanese strike to the local commanders in Pearl Harbour. Washington was warned by several countries about the Japanese movements, but possibly the White House suppressed the information or pretended ignorance. The US Archives say that the chief staff Marshall had warned the army officers that the secret will go with them to the grave. The strategic world was puzzled why the massive movement of Japanese flotilla missed the American military eye, its radars and spies. Pearl Harbour was lucky turn for Stalin. Regarding wars, the causes and consequences may give rise to conflicting arguments later, but the rationale of every decision in history's turning points is liable to be subjected to repeated re-examinations by historians and students of history, and this enquiry goes on without end. As usual, a comparison between the strategies and strengths of the winners and the losers are undertaken afterwards, but the world always show the knack to pass judgment invariably in favour of the winner, as the more daring, more gallant and wiser than the loser, but often the contrary being true. Military experts say that, if Hitler had invaded Russia some months earlier, he would have won before the arrival of 'General Winter'. Others say if, after the invasion of Poland, he had re-equipped his forces and armour with repair and additions and waited for one more year, the Barbarossa would have triumphed. The Japanese decision to choose the United States as the target has always been criticized not only as unwise but recklessly suicidal. How can Japan an island chain in the Pacific fight the economic, technological and industrial leader like the United States? No doubt the Japanese strike on Pearl Harbour, was a crushing blow to the US navy and American prestige, but that strike unwittingly was supplying all excuses, which President Roosevelt was seeking to enter the war directly on the side of the English and the French, and quite strangely on the side of Bolshevik Russia also. Who could then assume that sooner in post-war days, Stalin will mount a mortal challenge to world democracy, and he doing it by exploiting his case of partnership with world democracies in the war and reaching victory in the battle field!

52) I have already related the fact of Mao confessing later that it was the Japanese who (indirectly) helped the Chinese communists to win the Civil War. In the war against Japan, the Communist and Kuomintang forces fought many battles jointly, but the main brunt of the fighting had to be borne by the Kuomintang. Fearing the Japanese onslaught, Chiang was forced to shift his capital from Nanking to Wuhan and then to the interior city of Chunking during 1936-37. In 1945, the surrendering Japanese forces in Manchuria had left huge quantities of arms. The final post-war agreement between America and Russia was to make the latter agree not to transfer these arms to the communists, who will use it against the Kuomintang. Even while fighting the Japanese jointly, both sides were planning for the Civil War, then looking very much imminent. Deceit and breach of promise being the basic strategy of Stalinism, Russia secretly transferred a big lot of these arms to the communists, who will use it against the Kuomintang in the Civil War. But as late as during the Korean War, General MacArthur was urging President Truman for a massive American intervention in China and to restore Chiang in Beijing, but Truman, lacking any futuristic vision and bold plans, and guided by the confirmed defeatists like Secretary of State—Dean Acheson—and General George Marshall—turned this suggestion down. Acheson was mortally convinced of the invincibility of the Chinese communists, and for him, the fear of China was as bad as a vested interest. America—the democrat was already talking too much, and the country's domestic debate about the profits of surrender was rising to its crescendo. Truman could not foresee that by ditching the Kuomintang, America was surrendering the Chinese continent and 800 million free people

(then) to communism. The world policeman missed the point that not only he was losing his staunchest ally in the east, but installing her most hated foe in his seat. If through a powerful intervention, the United States had rescued the Kuomintang, the result would have been that there would have been no Korean War, no Vietnam War and no threat of Red-China against Tibet and Singiang, and the Chinese shadow over India would have vanished into thin air. But American democracy and her democrats, in the hour of danger, talks too much and do nothing. They will start to act when victory is impossibly away. Finally, calling the situation desperate, they will leave the scene abjectly, and this pattern defines America's post-war behaviour. Let the world compare the economic might, military strength and technological superiority of the free world, with that of the communist bloc (if at all such a block now existing) and see democracy's disproportionate dominance in all cases. Why the communist power continues the nightmare of the "all powerful" democracy? Is not democracy too much obsessed with her own body beauty? What the communists cannot achieve by direct action, they accomplish it through secrecy, deceit and sabotage. They fortify the totalitarian state by ruthless cruelty, fake-trials, mass persecutions, and finally by mass-murder. Against this triumph of fraud and malice, the break through for democracy came with the collapse of the totalitarian regimes of Soviet Russia and Eastern Europe in 1989. The economic decline and disorder faced by the so-called socialist dictators like Castro, Allende, Sukarno, Kim Ill Sung and their opportunistic flirts, continue to plague and defame the system. The press and the electronic media of the free world, claiming the born ally and defender of human rights, are now a days not a committed ally of democracy, and very strange they plead for the dictators and terrorists, entering the political world under socialist garb.

53) The press and the electronic media rather the fourth estate can firmly plant their foot only on democracy's soil, but their head and tongue are deeply in the totalitarian cage. This media partisanship and dichotomy continues an institutional self-contradiction in the practice of the fundamental rights of man the freedom of expression and equality. Why do the press

refuse to criticize the dictators, terrorists and saboteurs wholly endangering the rights of man? The answer comes easy. They fear the dictators and terrorists will retaliate, placing the news maker's life itself in danger. At the same time, the media-man is certain he will never be punished by a democrat like the US president, Japanese prime minister, French president or the Indian prime minister. These rulers act under the Constitution and rule of law, and they observing it, the media-man does not come under the threat of physical harm, even remotely. Under the critical scanner of the press come the democratic states. The largest quantity of 'rights violations' taking place in autocracies, fails to come under press-view, review, comment and censure. The media-man says that there is absolutely no use in criticizing dictators and communist rulers, that mission being a futile exercise, invariably meeting the rock. In spite of the very powerful 'rights-regime' of modern times, the majority of humans continue non-self-determining and they live political serfs. In Latin American states, there existed fractured democracies and shadow democracies for long, and many popular elections were rigging-celebrations. In these territories, important changes are now taking place. When a written Constitution is violated, usually that violation is suffered by the people for sometime under silent protest, and this conduct has become part of a continuing, irregular behaviour of democracies. The ruler then acts increasingly adventurous, introducing a lot of political romances to attend on his arbitrariness. Such ideological romances spoiled the experiments of rulers like Allende and Castro, who imposed their personal dictatorships on the people, the people not even remotely able to contemplate their liberation day. In Latin America the democratic process, did not become disciplined and organised, even one and half-century after the revolutions mounted by Simon Bolivar and Garibaldi. Recent developments show change, as the political romances of dictators are meeting with increasing popular resistance. Among the Latin American Big brothers—Brazil and Argentina, and in the former revolutionary territory of Chili, the forces of democracy are becoming more regulated and durable. In Africa, the former colonies of Britain, France,

Portugal, Germany and Belgium are either non-democracies or dictatorships, there being no settled democracy in the African continent except South Africa. The existing political trends in the continent give no hope of these non-democracies changing into real democracies, through a course of political reorganisation and reform, though they show 'better signs in economic development and management. The Jasmine Revolution in the Middle East is a turbulent but hopeful development for human rights in the region, till now living total stranger to democracy, though not hostile to popular government. The former states in the erstwhile Soviet Union like Ukraine, Uzbekistan, Belarus, Turkmenstan, Kazakhstan, Georgia, Estonia, Latvia, Lithuania and others are now the experimenting democracies, but they, being nascent, look irregular, bodies. A full constitutional democracy is yet to establish its foothold in these countries but matters move more hopefully. Of late China's 1350 million people, though a communist society, are getting more economic freedom to work and earn, but denied political rights, and this denial is absolute. Palestine, Afghanistan, Iran, Iraq, Egypt, Kuwait and Saudi Arabia are either monarchies or autocracies or irregular, uncertain or accidental democracies. True, there occur occasional cloudbursts of human rights in these lands, but soon recoiling back. The new forces produce thunder and lightning for a while, but then fading away into mystery. In an approximate division, the number of people enjoying freedom on the surface of the globe are around 2500 million. The remaining live under dictatorships, semi-dictatorships, military juntas, communism, monarchies, monarchic communism or under the hotchpotch of irregular, uncertain or accidental democracies.

54) By making a brief survey of democracies, non-democracies, semi-democracies and totalitarian states, it can be said that the world media, which essentially is a free-world-progeny, focusses its critique exclusively on democracy's faults and failings, while turning a blind eye on the unfree people, numbering about three-fifth of the humans inhabiting the earth. In what manner should the freeman reflect on this media-morality, professing to fight for making man free, and keep his freedom wider, deeper and enduring. In this context, I refer to the

recent example of the BBC blaring out against prisoner abuses at Abu Graib and Guantanamo. These abuses are cosmetic and peripheral when compared with the crimes committed by despots and tyrants. This world—renowned broadcaster is ignoring and eclipsing the fact that these detenus are mass-murderers, having killed hundreds of innocents in treacherous bomb attacks. Stranger that the victims of these high-criminals are not their enemies, but their unsuspecting, innocent brethren. These detenu's are committing dastardly crimes in the name of revolution, whose logic, no worldly mortal can understand. How this killing of innocents will mean revolution, the human mind is unable to comprehend. If we examine the media exposure of modern terrorism, as exemplified through 9/11, and other ghastly attacks around the world, there is reason to say that the mediaspeak generally goes terror-friendly, as their expositions are indirectly extolling these bloody crimes as great gallantry in the revolutionary game. A terror-friendly media, often unintentionally, works against democracy, human rights and human lives, and so they too deserve to be indicted as co-conspirators in the genocide, which is a crime against humanity. After exploding a bomb in a crowd of innocents and killing a hundred, what these captains of human bombers eagerly look for is how much coverage they get in the TV screen and the media is hell-bent to give maximum exposure to these ghastly crimes, and the terrorist, immensely pleased of this media endorsement, remains thankful.

55) The world is yet to digest the truth that once the communists seized power in Russia and China, they left absolutely no chance for another political motion for revolution to overthrow them through popular upheaval. Tens of thousands, and afterwards millions of political opponents, dissenters, doubters were annihilated in Soviet Russia through gulags, mock-trials, and mass shootings. The strategy of the communist system is that the state shall zealously eliminate the slightest chance of dissent, through the savagery of physical elimination of the rebel. Such wiping out of the entire opposition, up to the last opponent, is a thing which no other system of tyranny or despotism in history ever experimented with. Had any other

system practised the mass-murder of opponents, in those non-communist systems also there would have come the least chance for a revolution to break out. True, against this conclusion comes the historic and logical query, why and how there broke out counter-revolutions in Soviet Union and Eastern Europe in 1989, sweeping away communist rules through massive counter-blows. But the difference is that this counter-revolution was the making of an unprecedented economic collapse, unseen by the world. The massive surge against economic bankruptcy was aided and abetted by the Big-Brother communists themselves, feeling remorse on the horrible sins and hell-like misery they unloaded on a people, enslaved under ideological illusion and economic misery. Gorbachev—the ruler himself led the counter-assault, allowing the Soviet people to liberate themselves by throwing away the totalitarian yoke. This self-sabotage, the ruler himself masterminded because of his empathy with a people, emaciated by economic terror. Such ruler's behaviour is rare in history, but the Gorbachev move was the inevitable consequence of the terminal illness long corroding the Soviet body. The economy was collapsing, but this vaulting tragedy kept out of the know of the world, and the captive (soviet) population through misinformation and lies, was suddenly descending. The people of Russia, for 72 years, languished under untold miseries since 1917, but at the same time the propaganda machine of the state lambasting the ears of the world with the imaginary riches and pleasures of the Soviet Eldorado, which in truth was a ghost-land of groans, wants state-terror and genocides. How long can this whopping inferno be hidden behind the Iron Curtain? Inevitable that one day the peoples' anger, hatred, revulsion and outrage will burst out. In fact Lenin and Trotsky, though having only the following of a small minority in Russia, was steadfastly refusing a compromise to form a coalition government with other parties. In the usual course, such an unpopular minority leader like Lenin will go unattended and unacknowledged in a mass movement. But the First World War, going disastrously for Tsarist Russia with too many battlefield reverses and war-agonies, was giving Lenin the unusual opportunity to come in the open as saviour. Lenin can win power if only he was ready to commit treason. Really Lenin succumbed to high treason, only because of his unbridled lust for power. In early 1917, there was news that the Americans were coming to enter the war in Europe on the side of the Allies, and so the Tzar was eagerly waiting for American troop landings sooner, but they did not arrive before his abdication. Lenin, then living in Switzerland (Zurich) as fugitive, came forward ready to succumb to the German overtures. He got the guarantee that the German military will take care of his safe return to Russia, if only he will agree for an armistice on German terms. It was a surrender deal so pathetic and dishonourable that no Russian patriot would agree. If the people knew about the contents of this secret deal, then all Russia would have been rising in revolt against this humiliating deal, but the details of the deal were high secret. On the other side of the political spectrum, the Russian people were in frenzy to end to the war at any cost. Kerensky too, the socialist prime minister catapulted to the top post in July 1917, refused to withdraw from the war, as that act would make Russia a treacherous ally, betraying her war-partners. But the choice was crucial, and what Lenin wanted was power at any cost. In their mad race for victory in the battle field, the Germans were indulging in wild choices, and they met a good conspirator in Vladimir Lenin, vegetating in Zurich, when the February Revolution dethroned the Tzar. Kaiser Wilhem II was myopic or rather blind to the political consequences of a Romanov fall in Russia, as he never dreamed that the waves of the October Revolution would reach Berlin sooner than later. When Lenin promised the war-torn millions of Russia that he would end the war at any cost, the Congress of Soviet Dictatorship at Smolney went into applause. In the beginning of 1918, at Brest Litovsk the Russian delegation headed by Trotsky, signed off the major part of European Russia to Germany. When Lenin is in power so ruthlessly suppressing dissent through the fast growing Red-army of Trotsky, who will come out to protest? The Russian capitulation before Germany was dishonourable, ignominious and traitorous, but Lenin will keep his word to the German Field Marshall Ludendorff who hatched the plan to shunt Lenin back to Russia in a sealed rail coach with a forged German passport. At the same time, the Germans never hoped that Lenin had any chance to capture power. They thought that once reaching Russia, Lenin will be able to create disaffection and disloyalty among the Russian troops, and that would lighten the burden of the German war machine. But luck would make Lenin the tyrant of Russia. By this time the tide of war, with the coming of American troops, began to turn in favour of the Allies. If Kaiser Wilhem II thought that a Russian revolution and overthrow of the Czar would guarantee a Russian surrender and German victory, and victory for the Hohenzollerns, he was sadly wrong. The waves of the Russian revolution would batter the walls of Berlin sooner, and Germany's military top brass had already hatched a plan to end the war on terms permitting them to keep the German war machine almost in order, and that attempt failing, to stage a coup. The generals assumed that only by compelling Kaiser Wilhem II to abdicate, they can end the war on favourable terms, and save the war machine. The emperor himself smelt the impending threat from his own generals, and without waiting, he fled to Holland, and the Hohenzollern empire came crashing down, and the Great War was over. Lenin was again lucky that though he betrayed the Allies, still Russia would make big making gains at the Versailles Conference. Soviet Russia, having deserted the Allies midway, was not invited to come to Versailles, and so no Russian delegation was sent to Paris to negotiate. Still the Versailles powers decided to return all Russian territory surrendered to Germany at Brest Lito Vsk, and thus the wounded Russian pride was so smoothly and surprisingly repaired. This Allied generosity had the immediate effect of at once exonerating as well as eclipsing the abominable Leninist treasons against Russia. Had Russia failed to get back European Russia at Versailles, that loss would have remained a Bolsheviks in against the Russian pride and nationalism, and in future a powerful weapon in the hands of anti-Bolsheviks to beat the Bolsheviks. It is historic that in all his political gambles, Lenin was especially lucky. His call for the October Insurrection was one of the most dangerous gambles in history. The party conservatives like Kamenev, Zinoviev, Bukharin, etc. opposed it as too premature and risky. Stalin pleaded for an alliance with the Mensheviks, but Trotsky strongly supported the Lenin move. It is interesting that during this volatile period, the future tyrant Stalin was nowhere seen in the open in Petersburg or Moscow. The insurrection triumphed, and Lenin said 'Now we can begin to build the socialist state'. Before October 25, many times the Bolshevik Central Committee vetoed the resolution for insurrection, and Lenin was furious that real opportunity was slipping away because of overcaution. In protest he went underground for some time in the safety of Finland, and reports say that during these days he was keeping himself busy completing his magnum opus "State and Revolution". While his most trusted deputies Zinoviev and Kamenev continued to oppose the move, Lenin contended that the climate for revolution will stand favourable only for some weeks or months, and if that opportunity goes unavailed, that boiling climate will die down and the anxious crowd becoming despondent and wearied will disperse away. In history, Lenin will follow the strategy of Napoleon Bonaparte whom he chose as political guru and role model. Because of the refusal of the Central Committee to give the green signal for Insurrection, Lenin once resigned from the Committee, only to coerce them to endorse his demand. After several adjournments, at last the Committee gave the long delayed green signal, and the Lenin gamble paid off. His defiant courage and strategy was the force that allowed the Bolsheviks to capture power on 25th October, and overthrow the Kerensky regime. Again Lenin, who had never been a mass leader, will stabilize his power through high handedness. The October insurrection virtually sabotaged all important political forces and snuffed out all the freedoms then liberated to storm through Russia. The Russians, by accepting Lenin, were in fact embracing a Frankenstein. Immediately after his seizure of power, Lenin let loose a reign of terror, and wiped out the main opposition through mass executions, brutal terror and incarcerations—a political art which his estranged disciple—Joseph Stalin would play more thoroughly and abominably in the thirties. Lenin articulated the murderous political dogma of the dictatorship of the proletariat as the safe cover for his authoritarian power, and its massive sins against people and freedom. Under the Bolsheviks, a General Election was held in Russia in which the Bolsheviks were roundly beaten, but Lenin would not leave his throne. When the State Duma (parliament) convened, Lenin employed troops and mercenaries to disperse it by force, and Russia, instead of the age of freedom, was suddenly falling into the age of darkness. The people of Russia were confined and condemned in the dungeon of genocidal terror? To fortify the terror state, Lenin and Stalin built up the most mendacious propaganda corps and spy-ring across the world, and this machine worked overtime as the thorough instrument of lies and falsehood to feed and mislead the political society and free society. This Lenin programme was later fully copied and executed by all communist rulers in the world, who were ordered to act as agents of Russian revolution and Soviet imperialism. These agents too will feed the world with lies, and repeat these lies a thousand times to make it sound true. As Rajaji said, communism is against natural laws and therefore it will fail in the long run. When Russia and Eastern Europe collapsed thunderously in 1989, it was nothing but the fall of the tower of lies.

56) The doctrine of equality is the child of the French Revolution, which in turn was the child of the American Declaration of Independence. Equality is the fundamental plank on which the Bill of Rights of man are constructed by the coming generations of liberalists and freedom warriors. This right makes its earlier expression in the English Bill Rights. The communists propounded the theory of economic equality to divide the people into haves and have-nots, and this slogan has been mightily successful in raising the spectre of class-hatred and class war, which no dogma could resist through any kind of civil confrontation. Its bitter practice alone will expose its falsity. It took more than seven decades for the Russians to overthrow communist terror, in spite of the economic ruin, political depredation and cultural destruction caused by this hellish theory. The horrors unleashed on the people of Russia and Red China, will find no parallel in history. As a political philosophy, no theory as old as Spartanism or Stoicism or as

recent as Socialism or Anarchy would unload so much of sin on so many.

Imperial China

57) After the death of Mao Tse Tung in 1976, Deng Ziao Ping, winning the power struggle, recognised the great urgency for economic reform in order to stem the rot, and he was able to galvanize the majority of Chinese Communists to his argument for a drastic overhaul of economic policy. The party, once brainwashed by the revolution, was to be re-brainwashed by Deng. For a communist, this was change, radical, revisionist and counter-revolutionary. Still the academic dogma of communism, will not pretend the dilution in party philosophy, and therefore the red signboard continues to hang at all political portals to justify the party's despotic rule. In this context, it is important to note that a ruler like Fidel Castro, whose unelected tyranny is more than half-century old, is practising one of the worst dictatorships by calling himself communist. Nothing strange that this "communist" adjective provides a safe ideological cover to rule, through armed terror. Though the Maoist propaganda made mountainous claims on China's economic conquests, the dissidents in the party, well aware of the miserable economic situation, remained apprehensive about the future. They shuddered to look at the prosperity of the free world and its capacity to build and deliver new pleasures, which growing science and technology continuously empower. It must be true that when Deng was preparing to take the plunge, the collapse of Soviet Union, as the focal point of Marxian decay, had not happened. But no communist in China could miss the sight of the sudden take off of Asian countries like Japan, South Korea and Taiwan into economic brilliance, and the miraculous rise of the other free economies in the neighbourhood called the Pacific Rim Tigers. The humiliating episode of the flight of refugees from the poverty-stricken East Berlin, to the prosperous West Berlin was another example, throwing world communists continuously on the defensive. West Berlin was the shining showpiece of free enterprise in the midst of the totalitarian blackout of East Germany. Before 1997, when the British quit

the colony—Hong Kong, situate at the fringe of mainland China, was the most brilliant exhibit of free enterprise before Red-China not only to look and demur but to emulate and enjoy also. This British colony of seven million was a unique story of success, urging thousands of mainlanders to migrate stealthily into the island city, seeking wealth and freedom. This flight of Chinese refugees into the freedom of Hong Kong was another embarrassment for Communist China. No doubt the Russian and East European rulers too were feeling shy of the economic prosperity of neighbours like West Germany, Austria, France, Belgium, Italy and Switzerland, but they appeared not eager to see the writings on the wall. Communist rulers and ideologues went crestfallen when Gorbachev decided to capitulate. In reading the warnings of history, more than any other communist state, the Chinese leaders were prophetic and realistic. Deng saw that to suppress the prolonged groans of the people, suffering economic and political terror, would be too dangerous to be confronted by force. Had China persisted in the dogmatic Soviet path, perhaps she (China) too would have gone down the drain, as Soviet Union went down in 1989.

58) But the self-contradiction is that the Chinese communists are not willing to dilute party dictatorship on political power, as their love for power prevents them from loosening the party's stranglehold on peoples' freedom. While Chinese Communist Party's (CCP) political dictatorship continues as before, they are willing to go halfway, and this halfway programme is to liberalize the economy without liberating peoples' rights. A liberal economy with private property, is as radical a change as half-repudiation of Marxian dogma in a Communist state. Marx and Engels are dead long ago, and now the Chinese politicians have to interpret and re-interpret the theory for their continued survival in power and to strengthen the emerging communist dynasties and princelings. The CCP does not admit that they follow economic liberalism, but they showcase and project their brilliantly redone, shiny economic body to the world, and asks how differently the country's new economic face looks. While the party dictatorship continues, the liberal economy is galloping, throwing collectivism overboard through

unkind political neglect. China's neighbours, seeing the speed of her economic growth, feel scared that shortly Red-China can challenge the economic leadership of the free-world, and this rise is throwing manifest security challenges to the latter. Viewed in the background of the aggressive and expansionist history of Red-China in the Mao-Chau En Lai era, there are threatening precedents to keep her neighbours in dangerous anxiety. Even Japan—the world's second largest economy (now overtaken) become apprehensive of the fast rising power of China. The rise of China through political and geographical consolidation and economic rise renders her capable of funding a large military machine, and only usual that China's military buildup rouses the fears of neighbours. Concerns are merely negative wishes, but for the weak neighbour, there is no other remedy than to express concerns and more concerns. A mighty military machine can be confronted only by a more powerful one. In this case the behavioural contrast between pre-war Japan and post-war Japan offers the example.

59) In the beginning of the 20th century, when Japan started rapidly industrializing and building a large military apparatus following her historic success in the Russo-Japanese War of 1905, anxieties ran high not only in Asian capitals, but in the imperial capitals of London, Paris, Vienna, Copenhagen and Berlin. In Asia, the country then standing most threatened by Japan was China, and that threat would culminate in the Second World War, and more particularly the war between America and Japan in the east. Asian concerns about an imperial Japan were becoming acute with the Japanese defeat of Russia in 1905. The Japanese jump on the Asian mainland was on the plea of finding more living space for her rising population, and under that pretext she invaded Korea in 1895. During the Second World War, she embarked on the conquest of all Asia, after Germany subjugated Poland and France. Much before the war, Japan invaded Manchuria in 1931, and as the Western powers have failed to react, she could easily reduce that province into a defacto Japanese colony. Then Japan began pouring her armed forces into different parts of China, and more into the coastal cities. She occupied parts of Peking—the capital city, whose

areas were already occupied by many Western powers. But during the war, when America tightened her trade embargo on Japan, the Japanese militarists, leaped westward to attack the far distant, most powerful United States. Only after Japan struck at Pearl Harbour, the Second World War was going truly global, encompassing both the east and the west, in direct combat. Alarm bells rang in Europe when Hitler started rearming in the thirties, while her neighbours—France and Britain, were sleeping over rising German militarism. The Hitlerite adventures would heed no caution except force, and when Europe slept, the Nazi juggernaut rolled forward ruthless, leading to history's bloodiest conflict, lasting from 1939 to 1945. Political analysts say that if Britain and France had warned and resisted Germany at the earliest opportunity, the German dictator could have been stopped at the starting point itself. Strangely, it was the French army and air force which were the strongest in the continent in the beginning, but unfortunately the French politicians were living in a fool's—paradise, as Jawaharlal Nehru was languishing in his illusions during the India-China-Bhai-Bhai days. In 1939, when the world war started, then too the biggest economy in the world was the United States, who, once entering the war in 1941, could easily convert herself into the mighty military-industrial complex working as the inexhaustible armoury of the Allies. America, situated on the other coast of the Atlantic, was not immediately concerned about German armaments, she being only a distant cousin of European balance of power. But a timely ultimatum by the United States or France or Britain would have halted Hitler in 1939, but all European statesmen, instead of daring forward to check the conqueror, were flitting from place to place as peacemakers and peace-brokers. Hitler looking at these peaceniks with contemptuous scorn, the avalanche of war was irrevocably moving down on Europe. I narrate the pre-war episodes to contend that when a country is aggressively brandishing her armed might, there is no purpose served by the targetted (countries), ringing alarm bells. A counter build-up alone will check the daring aggressor. As it was usual in the twenties and thirties, Asian countries and the United States are now voicing fears about the Chinese build-up, but Red-China meeting these concerns indifferently? If the past of Communist China is any guide, it is likely that China's phenomenal military buildup shall be threat to all Asia. But even a protesting voice against this growing danger comes only from Japan, South Korea and the United States. India, the main target of Chinese imperialism right from the days of the revolution, is deeply anxious about this threat, but even after the 1962-war and debacle, she fails to record her fears and protests openly and assertively. The right of a country to build her military might to any level she wants, is unquestionable. But the other side of the question is what can and what should Asia do to check a Chinese offensive which is possible, when a weak American President like Carter or Ford enters the Oval office. In the present context, the possibility of a Chinese attack on India depends more on the severity of the response of the United States towards the crime, than on the power of Indian response. China, by modern economic standards, is still a poor country as the living standard of the common man is not enviable, though fast improving. In this respect the Indian case is worse. But India has to see that in spite of the extreme poverty conditions prevailing in 1950, the war-lords of Red-China did not hesitate to plunge the nation into the abyss of the Korean War, a war against the most powerful United States, whose option to strike China with nuclear weapons was looming large. But come what may, Mao Tse Tung jumped into the fray, and the war tied down an impoverished China for three and a half years in deadly conflict. In the war China demonstrated her grit and determination to enter a war and fight it, even in the face of the oppressive economic misery, pushing her poverty-stricken people into the agonizing low. Why a poor China entered the Korean War is evidence of Mao's imperial ambitions, while the country was in deep economic distress. Contrast this Chinese behaviour with that of the democracies, where the chances to go for a preventive-strike are rendered almost impossible by hostile public opinion, and the so-called public opinion orchestrated by the motiveless, media, and panicky demagogues. These forces rush to the forefront to malign war-efforts. These agents will condemn any attempt to make a preventive strike misbranding it as a warmongering blind leap into the inferno. That media call will be propped up by the debate of the fearfuls, styling themselves as intelligentsia and peacemakers. Such moves restrain and stop not only democracy's preventive wars, but even the talk of war. Any democratic ruler pleading for a preventive military strike will instantly become unpopular among the masses, who are tutored to believe that democratic patriotism can go for war only after the enemy has struck. Popular democracy, because of its peace obsessions, stands permanently robbed of the advantages of an adventurous military initiative, and they wait for the enemy to strike first. If there is a popular election approaching, the democratic ruler, in spite of being convinced of the essentiality of giving advance battle to the enemy before he grows unbeatable, will like to postpone the campaign to the less demagogic post-election days. During the Cold-War years, American President Eisenhower, while responding to a Khrushchev bluster on the might and readiness of Soviet armed forces, declared that America continues capable of making a massive retaliation even during a presidential campaign. This declaration was sending the message that election time in democracy is a sick period to wage war, and this period is as bad as gestation time for a pregnant woman. But will the enemy wait till the election fever is over? Such debility inhering democracy's war-making power was evident in modern wars like the Second World War, the Korean War, the Vietnam War and other local wars. In these theatres, the war was started by dictators, tyrants, and totalitarians, and responded by democrats in defence. It is true that during the Second World War, the democrats had joined hands with totalitarian Soviet Russia to fight Nazi Germany. But when the war started in 1939, Soviet Russia was in the company of Hitler, as the latter's natural ally, and together they invaded Poland. Midway through the war, perhaps provoked on the Russian demand for a larger share in the Polish booty, Hitler turned his guns against Bolshevik Russia itself, and entered the disastrous phase of his conquest. When, without provocation, North Korea suddenly pounced on South Korea in 1950, America entered the war, and that was only to defend the South and not to invade the North. Today any despotic conqueror is certain that democracy will never attack, but will defend only, and that too only hesitantly. The body-safety of the authoritarian conqueror stands almost guaranteed by this passivism of the free world.

60) North Vietnam started the Vietnam War making small scale incursions into South Vietnam through guerillas in the beginning, but the war would suddenly escalate into a bitter war between North Vietnam and the United States. Reports say in the war, America used more bombs than she dropped in the Second World War, but demagogic America did not show the resolve to fight the war to its logical end. The ultimate abandonment of South Vietnam by America to communist imperialism continues to haunt the free world as the most cowardly act of the world-policeman after the Second World War. Mc Cain who celebrated prisoner in the hands of the Yiet Cong, and later the loser in the US presidential race of 2008, asserts that it was a war about to be won, but the spineless leaders in Washington rushed to surrender. It is the new politics of Washington that the so-called rulers in the White House were all along coerced and battered by a defeatist Congress. When the Vietnam War was raging, the American communists (so small a body), and the left, once again employed their most devastating weapon—the propaganda of falsity and lies. They launched a murderous misinformation campaign within the United States, and this campaign would kick up American public anger against her own war scheme and war efforts. Democracy's freedom allows the communist parties to work free and more free even during wars, and the state allowing the latter to misuse the Bill of Rights to the advantage of their communist masters, fighting the motherland. In present day media exposure, as misused in democracies, it is very difficult for a democracy to wage a successful war in the face of an overzealous media pumping out its cowardly options and grandiose visions about the high economic profits of surrender. They do not care a damn if these suggestions help the enemy to defeat the mother country. The circumstances compelling Richard Nixon to announce an "advance-surrender-schedule" in Vietnam presents the clear example of the same mischief played upon America by the country's print and electronic

media. This media chase was zealously encouraged by an anti-Nixon Congress and the American left, who were laying siege to the White House through the Watergate. This onslaught on the White House stands out as the glaring example of the media sabotaging America's war programmes. The motive of the media may not be treason, but it is the media hubris that they are more powerful than the President and the Congress, and they want to superimpose their will on the powers that be. This kill-power they demonstrated in the Watergate hunt and the Vietnam War, and they were victorious. In the process they never cared the case that through this strategy the country was going to be humbled and mauled up by the enemy. After the Watergate, the free world media often assumes, and not unreasonably, that they are more powerful enough to command the elected rulers. If the ruler is on war with the foreign enemy, still the media will talk against the war. Finally, the media goes up as the extended arm of the political left, and this power the media majority are happy to acknowledge. The American left mounted campus revolts and campus bombings, and they designed and coordinated it through the funding channels of international communism however weak it presently is in American territory. Not only politically but strategically too, a communist fifth column in a country, continues the dangerous risk factor on national security. Strangely, democracy suffers this danger under the plausible constitutional caption called 'freedom of equality, expression and assembly' and lately this sabotage has been very cleverly concealed under the so-called "rights regime" ratified by democracy's courts International communism, though wholly debilitated after the fall of Soviet Union, does not retract from its Leninist dogma that communists are not nationalists, and their loyalty transcends national boundaries. Interesting to know what is the present political stand of the communist parties of democratic Europe like Italy or Greece or France? These reformed communists also have not ideologically renounced their allegiance to international communism, though they now care to act more nationalistic. In future, if they have to go without a communist master state to serve and worship, they will have to invent one to reinvent their transnational loyalty.

61) True, the world, including the communist world, have changed fundamentally since 1989, and this is history's compulsive process. But the loyalty of a communist during war remains suspect. That this foreign loyalty had been wreaking havoc to the party generally during the Cold-War years, does not constrain them in any way is surprising. Nationalists often fail to enjoin the communists with anti-nationalism, which in the past was indicted as 'treason'. Treason is an offence raising alarm bells during war years. Dangerous that modern democrats have come to view this revolting sin not as a high-crime, but ideological dissent. This low-key interpretation of the crime of sedition is outrageous, adding one more threat to democracy during emergencies. In the 1962 war, the Indian communists refused to support the national stand on the border, and so the leaders of the CPI (unsplit) had to be detained in prison, but still they not retracting. After 1989 also, the communists take a stand in important policy issues which, in final political analysis, will end up pro-China. But in spite of this disloyalty cloud over their head, the Indian communists gained a new respectability in 2004 when they joined as a constituent of the UPA ruling coalition. Through this power-sharing programme, they wanted to pull back the ruling Congress from accepting that big offer of nuclear technology to India by President Bush, and this left stand once again was striking the anti-national note. On this issue the Indian left wanted to bring down the UPA Government in 2008, but the move was thwarted at the last moment by manipulating a new political alignment with floor-crossings, and the Congress-led coalition was making a hair-breadth escape from the block. Political commentators contend that the left support to the UPA worked as permanent brake on the vitals of market economy, including the full liberalisation necessary to reach the take-off stage. The Marxists and the political left are still bombarding and maligning the Indo-US Nuclear Deal, and the much needed second generation liberalisation of the economy. In each move, their technique is to raise the bogey of American imperialism, but in truth it is to jeopardise the Indian potential to compete with Red-China, who is the declared enemy of India. This dangerous Marxian game of running with the hare and hunting

with the hound very often land the people in dilemma. It was the arithmetics of parliamentary majority that forced the Congress party to seek the support of the left in 2004. Even today, the two important Communist parties of Europe are the French and the Italian, but the democratic parties make it their policy not to participate the communists in government making as far as possible. They fear such partnership ultimately harmful to national interests. When the French governments were running notoriously fragmented and short-lived in the pre-De Gaulle era, then too there was no urgency felt by the French democrats to enlist the support of the communists for making the coalitions more stable. There was political surprise and uneasiness in India when Morarji Desai—that unbending Gandhian, did keep the door open for the communists to join the Janatha Government of 1977, but the communists, though an electoral ally of the ruling coalition, refused to take power. Possibly they felt it too early to commit the ideological heresy of running into the den of Gandhians, which they call as part of the political reaction. In the end, they joined hands with the detractors to topple one of the finest regimes free India ever had, particularly in popular endorsement but that was in 1979. When patriotic questions run into top-gear, usually the communists lie low and lie silent. In spite of the many major policy shifts and reforms they underwent since 1989, they could not agree with the plan of a dynamic, fast-growing Indian economy under democratic aegis. Neither can they themselves endeavour to make an orderly society, as peace and market economy are not revolution's end game. They go the violent way to fight the final class war and what is class war and what is class, Karl Marx seems to have left it for Lenin and Stalin to define.

62) How easy it is for a dictatorship to go to war, and how difficult it is for democracy to fight it are the aspects straining the power of democracies to make war. In a democracy, it is awfully unpopular to start a war unless attacked by the enemy, whereas it is smooth sail for a communist tyranny to go to war at short notice or even suddenly. Communists have an identified ideological catalogue to be fought by arms, and the causes and excuses for starting an unprovoked war always form part of their regular rhetoric. Among the cutting weapons of communism, the most powerful are the bundle of lies they throw up through merciless, malicious propaganda, and this propaganda's murderous reach is a thing to be felt, to be believed. In spite of mounting political debacles, the communists will not acknowledge the reality that a mountain of lies can conquer only for sometime or for more time, but not for ever. Every communist party's strong arm is their international propaganda brigade, working under the iron discipline of a criminal syndicate, feeding on the faults and failures of others, and never on their own work and reconstruction. In spite of continuous failures, they will push that final day of triumph further and further through violence and turmoil. In any case the fantastic lessons they supply to human psychology and logic deserve deep study, as it contains some brilliant strategies regarding the powers of collective fraud.

CHAPTER 4

Betraying Tibet—Betraying India

63) Democracy in the neighbourhood must be a constant irritant to a totalitarian state and China too will not feel kindly against India. It is a fact that India is a democracy and China is communist. A communist state not only abhors, but fears a democratic state. It is part of communist practice that totalitarian China is zealously seeking its opportunity to sabotage Indian democracy. After 1991—when India too inaugurated market economy, Indian democracy will appear potent and threatening. In 1949, the Indian Prime Minister Nehru was unable to see the communist dragon hissing. After repeated warnings, also by friends Nehru defiantly refused to see the enemy in Peking, in spite of abundant evidence coming to confirm these warnings. The Chinese heyna appearing in heyna's clothes also did not convince Nehru. Abominable self-contradiction it was that this great democrat and moralist was in conscientious company with dictators, despots and tyrants, who in the hour of danger would betray him. The NAM betrayal of India in 1962 was the most unkindest cut. Nehru committed himself to the proposition that supporting communism and socialism alone identifies him with the progressive and socialist forces. Credulous, and procommunist, he went across the world, celebrating the communist seizure of power in China. He called it China's liberation, deserving the applause of the free world. In this leap into political darkness, Nehru was ignoring all notes of caution, voiced by statesmen and nationalists at home, and friends abroad. What camaflouged his suicidal blunders in foreign policy was his image as a socialist

among the capitalists. His grand standing as the spearhead of the liberation of Afro-Asian colonies from Western colonist made him a world celebrity. But the great liberator was refusing to see the new colonies and new imperialism launched by the totalitarian country like Soviet Russia and Communist China. True, Soviet imperialism and colonies vanished all on a sudden in 1989, but the Chinese colonies of Tibet, Sinjiang, and Inner Mongolia survived the 1989 storm.

64) While Chiang Kai Shek (Jiang Jeshi) and Nationalist China honoured India as the great companion civilization, Mao Tse Tung, was taking the thoroughly hostile, view declaring ideological war and armed war against independent India. As is usual for a communist, Mao started by misrepresenting and maligning India, but who knew then that this was to prepare the ground for his imperial expedition on Tibet and Aksai Chin. When, for the first time, the Kashmir question came before the United Nation's Security Council in 1948, it was the beginning of India racing into communist embrace, even at the risk of undermining her relations with the west. Because of Nehru's unreasonable and vituperous outbursts against the Western democracies as a class, America, Britain, many Commonwealth countries and European powers had already started to drift away from India. While the democracies were driven to the opposite camp, the pro-communist and anti-American tirades of India, particularly before the United Nations were making this estrangement with the west complete. In that critical moment, a negative vote against India in the UN Security Council would have demoralized Nehru to the point of abandoning Kashmir into the kitty of Pakistan. In that crisis, it was the veto of Kuomintang China that saved India from embarrassing capitulation. At that time, the fact that Chiang Kai Shek himself was in the pro-American and pro-Western camp may look a paradox; neither was he hostile to Pakistan. Chiang wanted to defend free India, and uphold the Sino-Indian cultural bonds existing through ages. It was risking the displeasure of the west and the pro-American Pakistan that he cast his veto in favour of India. But this fund of goodwill vanished into thin air, when the communists, overthrew the Kuomintang and drove Chiang into

the wilderness of the Formosa Island. Thereafter things would turn upside down in Peking. Why Communist China, was suddenly turning into the deadly adversary of friendly India? The dragon saw the weakest ruler in Nehru. Having no territorial or imperial conflicts in between during the past millennia, what was the reason for this murderous malice of the communists, coming to power in Peking, just two years after Indian independence? This was sudden change India never expected? The policy shift shall be connected with the anti-democratic philosophy of the Chinese communists. Communism is permanently at war with the freedom of man. Being the world's largest democracy, India is Red China's main target in Asia. Before the imperial Mao, India lay there the debilitated, isolated, and friendless territory. He was sure this golden opportunity would not present itself again after the dreamy era of Jawaharlal is over. Kuomintang China did not consider her objections on the McMahon Line worthy for making a provocative border dispute with British India or free India. The Kuomintang concern was to make China's uncertain suzerainty over Tibet, more real. Emerging victorious in the Second World War, Nationalist China was settling many border disputes with Soviet Russia at the earliest opportunity. Chiang was euphoric when he got back, the expansive territory of Manchuria, the large islands of Formosa, Hainan, other large occupied in land areas, in the mainland and the many pockets in the east coast, from the Japanese invader. During the pre-world war and the world war years, the Chinese claim for suzerainty over Tibet was uncertain vague and unrecognised and such claims were staunchly fought by the Tibetans. During the war years, the attempts of Chiang to encroach into Sinjiang were stopped by the Britain and the United States. The McMahon Line was the accepted boundary, and Nationalist China and British India had no doubts about the place through which it ran. It was bilaterally accepted in all transactions afterwards. In a totalitarian society, popular will and popular voice are the monopoly of the communist party elite, and the Goebellian official media. When popular voice has been driven out from the voice of governance, what is the meaning in saying that the people of China are friendly. War-lords go to war, not because of the people, but in spite of them. To have war or not to have it is the will of the tyrant.

65) Communism's political fantasy is in non-stop war with the non-communist world, and this doctrine is held on, in spite of their programme of world conquest becoming increasingly improbable every day. Historic to say that more often the creation as well as the destruction of states and empires had been the result and consequence of wars. Communists continue the ideological war with the non-communist world, even after this war has become a Quixotic zeal in ideology's war theatres. As part of their strategy in the battle field, any communist ceasefire had only been opportunistic or farcical. When the communists came to power in China, what they did first was to declare history nonexistent as history is not pro-communist. In 1950, just after the communist-revolution, China presented before India her 'ideal programme' for the 'peaceful liberation' of Tibet. In his licentious poetic enthusiasm and diplomatic irresponsibility, K.M. Panikkar, the Indian ambassador to China, certified to New Delhi the honest intentions of China behind this crass imperial programme. But it very much seemed that Nehru was waiting for such a pro-China report to come, only to be seized and accepted. By doing so, Nehru was overruling Indian public opinion national leaders, media warnings and the advice of the high officials in government. Sad that from this reckless and irrational pursuit he could not be stopped, by arguments. What did China mean by 'peaceful liberation', Nehru never bothered to get it clarified from Peking. By this time the Korean War had broken out, and the attention of the world was wholly focussed there. Utilising this Korean tumult and drum-beat as the red herring, China sent troops to storm the reclusive land of the Lamas. Under the slogan of "peaceful liberation" the war-lords of Peking launched the naked conquest of Tibet. The Tibetan resistance was fierce and gallant but it was crushed, though Tibetan blood flowed freely across the plateau. Was this the 'peaceful liberation' promised by China and hurriedly happily approved by Panikkar? Nehru and India were appalled and the world stood shocked. But Nehru, who ought to have alerted the free world and called for immediate withdrawal of

China, simply lay low, only to capitulate later. Why did Nehru agree for this crude armed liberation, which actually was the rape of Tibet, spilling Tibetan blood abominably? After all, what was the need for liberating a people, already freed from the "suzerain" shadow of Peking? 'Peaceful liberation' was merely a camouflage for brutal conquest, and China could foresee that the weak ruler he was, Nehru will do nothing to stop her, once the dragon locomotive is set to roll forward. All the British sabre-rattling and ian muscle-flexing on Tibet during colonial days were coming to naught in 1950. In betraying squeamishly friendly India, Communist China never paused and hesitated. A Nehru objection in the beginning would have stopped China at the starting point itself, but as done in Kashmir he would surrender even before the enemy will ask for it. Certainly this Chinese fraud on Tibet was the start of the violent estrangement of the two future Asian giants. When war descends on them, the once friendly people of the fraternal states too are forced to come face to face with swords drawn. Hitler, in 1939 set the war-weary Germans suddenly against the European breathren. True, the Germans had a cause—they were bitter about the terms of the Versailles Treaty, but in 1939 they were not ready to go to war. Once China slapped her imperialism on Tibet, then inevitable that any war turns into a patriotic war once the guns begin to shoot.

66) Finding a soft target, the communists hasten to strike at, but where the job is hard and risky, they wisely turn back. The Chinese Communists won the Civil War only because of the indifference and irresolution of the Truman administration. The President was refusing to rescue the Kuomintang, already battered beyond repair by the hammer blows of Japan during 1931-45, and worse during the Second World War days. Communist China won the Sino-Indian war only because the Indian ruler Nehru was in his strategic fantasy land. Why China did not rattle her sword against the United States, but for whom she could have bulldozed across Asia with absolute impunity? Peking targets India because India is again a soft state, paralysed by Nehruvian Non-Alignment, and living isolated and friendless. In spite of these outrageous Chinese betrayals and frauds, free

India is failing to evolve a strong policy to challenge and explode the myth of Chinese invincibility. Pre-world war history says that the Chinese communists were never valiant fighters their general strategy being hide and seek, retreat, and sabotage. The Communists begin war that starts always, but ends never until they make the final win against the non-communist enemy. In the battlefield, unfortunately post-war democracy appears in a great hurry to end a shooting war at the earliest, be it victory or defeat, and that obsession inviting uncalled for setbacks to human freedom. In all her post-war battles with communism, as said above world democracy is in unseemly haste to reach peace, but the consequence of these half-fought and half-won wars, has been more wars and more defeats for democracy afterwards. The Cold War and post-Cold War years saw many battles, and in many of these conflicts, the communists were pitted against democracy. In the battle-field, the former adopts unexpected and unusual strategies and tactics hitherto unknowns. The red-brigade enters into negotiations, settlements, ceasefires and treaties, but before the ink is dry, they start violating the same through well planned and phased breaches. For them, the ceasefire ending one battle is the beginning of its renewal, and these peace intervals had been the time for them (communist forces) to regroup and remobilize and they never allow a peace situation to stabilize in favour of the enemy. This communist treachery the world witnessed in Eastern Europe in the immediate post-war years, and afterwards in Korea, Laos, Cambodia and Vietnam in the fifties, sixties and the seventies.

67) Is there a war under the sun which can be won or lost according to a timetable unilaterally charted by one opponent? The breach-regime had been the basic strategy of communists in Korea, and Indo-China and more ruthlessly in Vietnam. In Tibet, they were playing fraud more openly. Because of battle fatigue and the habitual laxity constraining the battle morals of the demagogues at home, the democrat in war is fleeced by the (so-called) public opinion very often manipulated by the leftist media. Such media clamour in the United States for withdrawal from Vietnam would turn intimidatory at one stage, leading to America's pull out, and to the abhorrent genocide in 1975 by the

communists. Recent reports say that American public opinion had supported the Vietnam War, and those who opposed it were only twenty per cent. But the leftist, anti-war American media misinformed the world that the whole of America was up in arms against the war. To purchase domestic peace, and to end the turmoil and tumult of populism damaging the ruler's election prospects, democratic rulers buy abject defeat in the battle field. This is new sickness afflicting the morale of post-war democracy. While the fighting goes on in the battle field, the communists wage their parallel propaganda war in the territory of her (democratic) opponent, and more effectively through their international brigade. They do it through the leftist media, and this has been ably coupled with their negotiation-war and war through treaty-breaches. These breaches are followed by vehement remonstrations and denials and with these cutting-edge weapons, the communists corner the more powerful democratic opponent, who becoming tired of fighting the barrage of the war of attrition, finally falters. Surprising that these defeats and debacles are suffered by democracy, in spite of her superior economic and military power. In an open war, the military power of the communists is no match for the power of the free world, but strangely, the communists emerged winners not only during the Cold War, but in the post-Cold War days also, when ideologically, they are fast on the decline. The triumph of the much less-powerful communists over democracy shows how badly the demagogic free world has lost their will to defend human freedom by arms. The democrat is yet to know that human freedom cannot always be defended through the ballot box.

Communism on the Decline

68) In the twenty-first century, communism is a shrinking political ideology, and now it is the convenient ideological weapon seized by many dictators and despots to legalize, legitimize and moralize their illegitimate power, like the powers of Castro and Kim Ill Sung dynasties. True, under the armour of communist ideology, they hope the monstrosity they commit would appear less illegitimate and more defensible. Another

unfortunate development in the post-war years is the free press and the electronic media speaking for despots, totalitarians and terrorists if not directly, then indirectly. When North Korea was on her way building the nuclear bomb, the world media was over-looking its calamitous impact of this bomb on human life and life on earth. At the same time, the same media would come down heavily on any plan for a preventive military strike on North Korea's bomb-making plants. The left media, as a matter of policy, fails to complain that Saddam Hussain slaughtered 1,50,000 political innocents point blank, and massacred enmasse 5,000 Kurds in a single poison gas attack. This gassing was reminiscent of the gas chambers of Hitler at Austwitzch and Treblinka. The leftist media again refuses to criticize the thousands of political executions taking place every year inside Communist China now liberalised. They wholly sweep under the carpet the human rights of 1,350 million people, held hostage under totalitarian dictatorship. They miss to refer to the 1,20,000 political prisoners detained in Cuba's prison cells without trial. At the same time, they make vociferous cry about the cosmetic Guantanamo 'rights-violations' committed on those genocidal criminals who massacred hundreds of innocents in cold-blooded human bomb-attacks. Only vaguely the media complain against Pol Pot killing millions of innocents in Cambodia, in the ghastly experiments of social engineering. At the same time they bash George W. Bush overthrowing the murderous regime of Saddam Hussain, and call it an unpardonable breach of international law. The leftist media felt no shock when Chinese tanks, in 1989, rolled over the protesting students in Peking's Tiananmen Square, killing thirteen hundred students. They fail to indict the human bombs and their wealthy patrons killing thousands of innocents in terror attacks in Iraq, Pakistan, Afghanistan, India, Indonesia, London, Madrid and where not. The media, while covering up and concealing the violence and persecution employed on people by terror-regimes, project and highlight the minor, silly, rights-violations taking place in democracies, who already are in the work of repair and correction. Political mystery, why the media is shadowing the interests of democracy, while defending the horrors of tyranny? Like Communist China, are the media also in search of soft-targets? Is free media committed to do disservice to human freedom and human rights, is a bad question, but needs to be asked.

69) For the man permanently in search of the perfect and rights-friendly state, democracy holds out evident and natural hope and promise. The cost of freedom is permanent vigil, and the peoples' urge for more rights is the essential part of democratic living. Democray's strength is that it needs no protective wall against popular assault. When an un-democratic system fails, then without prodding and brain-washing, the people go in search of democracy as the automatic and natural front-runner in their choice. But it is democracy's lack of discipline which is its Achilles Heel for non-democrats to strike. The enemies of democracy are the demagogues inherering the system.

1950—Aggressive China Climbs the Himalayas

70) In 1950, India was suddenly sighting the communist foe climbing atop the Himalayas, breathing fire. Nehru, who saw it with his own eyes, did not want to believe it, and strangely he chose to call the demon an angel. I refer to the history and behaviour of communism and communist states, to highlight the ideological deceits and betrayals employ as their murderous political tools. Man and civilization never witnessed the horror and dastardliness unleashed by the communists for upholding a political philosophy which was fancied by a man hating humanist. Who can then say that Karl Marx the humanist contemplated the terrors and butcheries of Stalin—when he wrote the Communist Manifesto? All political, religious and cultural morals built up through man's civilised life and learning, and more fundamentally through rule of law and orderly society, were rudely overturned, through the weapon of madding human hatred. This was to win the class war. The blood-thirst and savagery unleashed by Leninist, Stalinist and Maoist terror, was born out of the mortal fear of these tyrants losing the arbitrary power they got into their hands. The communists, to seize power promise heaven to the have not, and who will not want to reach heavens, if any divine agent would lift him up bodily to that land of ecstasy, so dramatically? Why they promise the fantasy land

they cannot build? Only because they are certain that once they seize power, they will at once turn the state into a monstrous terror machine, setting people run for life from the reach of its murderous jaws. "Where is the heaven you promised" no human being will dare to ask the totalitarian tyrant staring at him with gun in hand? What stands in the way of the Marxians promising heavens, when that promise need not be fulfilled. In the rights-friendly, rights-conscious world, it is only usual that any inhuman political system will collapse under the weight of its own sins, but that process taking a very long time, as in the case of Soviet Union. Finally the world had to witness how the Soviet behemoth and its East European satellites moving to the brink, tottering, and finally collapsing. In spite of they constructing the most murderous terror-state in history, the collapse became inevitable. Certain that this terrible fate of Soviet Union and Eastern Europe sends it danger signals to Beijing, Pongyong and Havana, but doubtful whether the message has made any impact on them. After China, now it is the turn of Havana to confess its failure. The Castro dynasty is now vigorously thinking of economic reform. The more vital question is when will political reform come to Havana and Pongyang.

71) Looking at the high crimes Communist China slapped on an unsuspecting, and credulous India, the latter can see the diabolic enemy in Beijing. Even after her 1972-détente with the United States, China thinks she is above political, diplomatic and international discipline. Her "peaceful liberation" of Tibet turned out a horrible blood-bath, but she went home unpunished. In 1947, Free India saw her close ally and friend of the Indian democracy in Nationalist China, but after 1949, India's mortal enemy is Communist China. To meet this deadly adversary, it is pitiable that India consistently and continuously fails, and sad that even after 1962, the latter looks like a Chinese underdog in the diplomatic world. Will China continue defiant in the event of India turning defiant, and going for a military alliance with Japan and the United States? India making an anti-China alliance with democratic Asia is the other powerful option, but it is a complex scheme to materialize immediately. Thousands of tons of printing ink has been poured over the world newspapers

regarding the transfer of power in 2012 November in Beijing. But the new Chinese leadership is yet to make its policy spelled out that the new masters hold any political reform that they will soften their stand on Tibet, the Indian borders and Singiang. If the developments in the South China Sea is any indication, the new leadership of Xi Jinping and Li Kuquang is likely to be harsher though they speak more generous.

72) The policies of the new Japanese Prime Minister Abe shows serious Japanese thinking on her military policy forwards China. China's claim on the Senkoku island in the South China sea which is in the possession of Japan has kicked up new controversy in the Pacific. Post-war Japanese regimes were ignoring Chinese imperialism in South Asia and South East Asia and they were leaving the whole of Asia to Red China as her free turf. A change in Japanese policy is visible only now and that change is the opportunity for India to make use. Japan is a rich country and Asia's technology leader, whereas India is a fast growing economy facing grave military threat from China and it is time India seize this opportunity to bolster up her economic and military might against China. The Sino-Japanese tensions in the Pacific Sea board and the South China Sea are growing. Japanese technology and economic cooperation will help India the powerful way to rebuild the Indian defence forces. The other countries in Asia like Philippines, Indonesia, South Korea and Vietnam are eagerly waiting for making a new balance of power in Asia and the India—Japan alignment will not only be a new boost to their assertiveness, but it will help them to put through the claims before China more assertively. India Joining hands with Japan will be an effective check on Chinese aggressiveness.

CHAPTER 5

Why India Fears War?

73) Very hesitantly, India now reach judgement that Communist China threatens her existence and in the near future the former cannot escape that frightening shadow. Even after the 2012 transfer of power in Beijing, the policy utterances from Beijing indicate that Chinese imperialism is set to bounce forward as the two-headed monster, territorial and ideological. True, with the Dragon imperialism on the march, the ideological head has lost much of its cutting edge, but not yet going blunt. After the Second World War, the world witnessing the marvellous economic recovery and reconstruction of Japan, was fearing the revival of Japanese militarism, but despite the titanic rise, Japan lives through her post-war pledge towards total democracy and total peace. During the sixties of the last century, was it not possible for post-war Japan to wriggle out of the Yankee embrace and go rearming for a new imperial role? It was possible, but she opted for peace, leaving the wide Asian space free for the dragon to predate and run over. Because of the Japanese retreat, Communist China could easily rustle her imperial feathers and storm into the wars in Korea and Indo-China for expanding the totalitarian empire. It is not only India's misfortune but Asia's too that the new leadership of independent India was sympathetic to the Socialist imperialism of Red-China. Soviet Russia, the godfather of Chinese communism in the fifties and sixties (of the last century) was speedily drifting away from the Chinese ward, and soon the guardian and the ward would be bitter rivals. Nikita Khrushchev, the reformist

Russian ruler, opposed the Maoist vagaries like the "Great Leap Forward", and 'Let Hundred Flowers Bloom', as non-Marxian and anarchic. This Russian indictment angered Mao violently, and from this point on, Russia and China were pulling apart to fall out. This Sino-Russian quarrel reached the explosive point, and the two communist big brothers were re-discovering their state boundaries, though this discovery was un-Marxian and uncommunist. The collapse of communist order in Russia and Eastern Europe during 1989-91, was the anti-climax of the Marxian call for world revolution, but through the counter revolutionary (economic) reform movement of Deng Ziao Ping and comrades, China was able to stand the storm. Russia and Eastern Europe, from the ruins of the fall, are now rising up, and mostly through the democratic path, leaving China alone to battle for world communism. After 1989, China is fighting a loner, carrying on the burdens of world revolution on her own shoulders. Defocussing from her bland rhetoric for a (Trotskyite) global revolution, she is now concentrating on a capitalistic, and corporate economic build up. If Karl Marx, seeing his revolution being hijacked by Adam Smith, Malthus, Keynes and Ricardo, turns in his High Gate grave in London, let him turn. China is the country of Han Chinese, relentless on the drive to become a capitalist super-state.

74) That Richard Nixon's launching of Communist China into the main-stream of world affairs in 1972, and the withdrawal of American economic sanctions, was preparing the ground for the fast-pace economic reconstruction of China, has been wholly missing in the noisy world debates on the Chinese economic miracle. That legendary hatchet man of Nixon-Henry Kissinger is alive to witness this transformation of Marxian China into the capitalist hot-house. The economy of China has already overtaken Japan, and she is on her way to wrest out the first place from the United States in the short run, and if not in the long run. When China rises, what worries her Asian neighbours is her growing military muscle and the madding arms race she engages in, challenging the Asian neighbours like Japan and India. The Sino-Pak axis, contracted in 1963, then looked a big diplomatic and strategic puzzle, but was it really so much of

a puzzle? In a policy about-turn, China, executing an about turn swiftly moved to strike a military companionship with Pakistan, who strangely has been the committed ally of the United States, then China's enemy number one in the cold war. Rawalpindi thought that between Pakistan and China, this apparently self-contradicting military logic is stunningly realistic. In 1963, Pakistan, being the military ally of the most powerful United States, China could not lay hand on her without provoking Washington, which China did not want to do head on. Instead she sought the hands of Pakistan as her second love, as the latter was already in love with her powerful paramour—the United States of America. Pakistan is playing a dazzling game in flirting with both.

75) The free world and more particularly free Asia regrets that the United States could have resisted Pakistan from joining the Chinese camp in 1963. But America was apprehensive that by pushing Pakistan too hard, she runs the risk of losing an ally, and thus losing the military bases in Pak territory. In that context, who will compensate the loss suffered by the United States? Will India step in to fill the strategic gap? No, because that would be against India's neutrality—a self-imposed diplomatic and strategic blunder, India once ran into and thereafter wrestles with so wastefully. For Nehru, India's self-appointed moral leadership of the world was more important than the security of the country's and territory. That this political mischief in military strategy had cut at the root of Indian security, did not concern him even after the 1962 debacle, is depressing. What was the patriotic moral standing higher to the nation's existence!

76) At the risk of displeasing and estranging the United States, Pakistan was going resolutely ahead in her pro-China gamble. The Pak-army has already developed a vested interest in keeping the Kashmir question burning for ever. The army top brass believe that once the Kashmir question is resolved, its political dominance and ascendancy will go on the decline. The Ayub proposal for an Indo-Pak joint front against China came at a time when the rulers and leaders in Washington, and particularly in the American Congress were daring Cold-Warriors, anti-communist chasers and McCarthyist hunters.

When Nehru rebuffed the Ayub offer for an Indo-Pak joint front against China in 1963, the latter, getting offended, did not pause, and executing an about-turn, threw his lot with India's committed enemy-Red China. Reinforced with this new friendship with imperial China, Ayub, in 1965, launched his invasion of Kashmir. In the war, China threatened to intervene on the side of Pakistan, but Lal Bahadur Shastri was able to call the Chinese bluff. Ayub did not win the war, neither was he punished at Tashkent for the crime of invasion. Tashkent turned a tragedy when in the midst of negotiations, Shastri passed away in the Uzbech capital. After 1965, India was witnessing all Pak rulers and demagogues leaning more and more on the shoulders of Beijing, and often on Pongyong also. In 1971-72, this Sino-Pak honeymoon played a vital role in making the Sino-American détente and rapprochement, resulting in the hot embrace of two-deadly adversaries—Richard Nixon and Mao Tse Tung. This historic reconciliation was launching an estranged and isolationist China into the bosom of the comity of nations, and the launch would lay the foundation for the miraculous economic rise of China as we see today. With the liberal Carter coming to office in 1976 America established full diplomatic relation with China in 1979. In the UN Security Council, Nationalist China (Taiwan) was replaced by the Peoples Republic of China (mainland). Communist China, now freed of all shackles can prepare for her economic take off and madding arms race. Without this détente, any radical move by Deng Ziao Ping would not have been able to build a laissaize-fare corporate economy, integrated with the economy of the world. With the Soviet economy in shambles, and the economies of Eastern Europe also running sick, any Chinese liberalization into market economy would not have made a big difference, unless China's political isolation from the free world and the international trade-sanctions had ended. The economy of the free world—the most powerful and voluminous part of the world's goods and services, was being thrown open to China after 1972, and fully after 1979. But Mao Tse Tung, who died in 1976, failed to seize this great (economic) opportunity, and thus China's market revolution had to wait until 1978, when

Deng—the pragmatist would emerge supreme in the post-Mao power struggle.

77) For safeguarding national interests, Pakistan is making timely shifts and realignments in her foreign and military policies. Assume the strategic position of Pakistan in her wars and the struggles, had not she allied with the United States. In 1948, India could have easily reconquered the whole of Kashmir and resolved the Kashmir question, once for ever as she settled the Hyderabad question the same year. But Nehru, a stranger to military strategy and war, was always moving defiantly against the realities of human conduct. He wanted to impose his dreamy illusions over the rules of pragmatism. In 1948, General Kariappa was heading the Kashmir operation, and the Indian forces were evicting Pak Razakars fast. But Nehru, supposedly on Mountbatten's persuasions, gave orders to the army to ceasefire and turn back and the generals were appalled. Nehru took the Kashmir question to the United Nations. Later, when Kariappa asked Nehru the reason for calling the ceasefire, the latter said that things have come contrary to his expectations, and in 1948, he should have given some more days to the army to evict the Razakars, Nehru was regretting his stand in 1948. Kariappa, on seeing the Chinese maps showing Indian territory as part of China, warned Nehru against Communist China's intentions, but Nehru pooh-poohed it. Often it looked Nehru entertained a vested interest in distancing himself from battles and wars under the guise of hating violence and wars. Did he ever think that he was abdicating two-fifth of Kashmir to Pak Razakars and terrorists to gamble over? In 1948, Kashmir was not an international question, but only the internal problem of an undivided India, divided a short while ago. The smaller power she is, Pakistan after independence acted realistically, and opted for a military alliance with Washington and she regularly received large quantities of military hardware and economic aid from the latter. When the Pak-rulers read or misread this US alliance as not enough and effective, they made an about-turn and went over to Beijing, which move, evidently looked a strategic gamble, challenging the fundamental interests of the United States in South Asia. Protests from Washington did not

cut any ice in Islamabad, and Pakistan moved ahead to play the role of a double-agent in alliance politics. To counter this move, what did India do to safeguard her interests? She did nothing except riding the moribund NAM bandwagon and hooting her concerns about Pak belligerency from diplomatic roof tops. In the 21st century, India feels encircled by China and Pakistan adjured at by Sri Lanka and Maladives but again she is refusing to enter into a military alliance with any country including the United States and Asia's powerful democracies like Japan, South Korea, and Australia. Regarding India, the threat scenario has only worsened after 1962, whereas China strides along as the committed opponent. The strategists of New Delhi pretend ignorance of the obvious, they not yet getting tired of chasing for the most dangerous enemy in Pakistan.

78) Under Narasimha Rao, very slowly and hesitantly India executed a paradigm shift in her relations with the United States but this violent shift again slows down half-hearted and faultering. In the event of a new war with China, whether America as in 1962 will again come for India's rescue, is the vaulting question facing 21st century India. That certainty of 1962 is now uncertain. Every Indian now asks this blank question again. President Obama is more a compromising demagogue, than a chief executive possessing the will and stomach for prompt military response, and therefore it is unlikely he will respond mightily to an Indian S.O.S. as in 1962. Obama did not make a clear and powerful military response in any theatre of conflict or conflict zone during his last five years in offices. The chief magistrate sitting in the Oval Office, being a man of dilemma, he exposes the world democracy to dangerous risks. India's policy of self-reliance for the defence of the country is another blundering obsession very dangerous to national security. Is there any country in the world, except perhaps America, capable of defending India against Communist China? In an immediate India-China War, the Asian nations, as in 1962, will not even plead India's case, much less joining India in the war. Russia, who stood with India during the Bangladesh War (1971), is no longer a big power. The above events point to the fact that the possibility for a powerful military response from America, as

in the Kennedy days of 1962, is now sadly missing. Amongst these concerns, another aspect is whether the Indian defences can be left to the whims of the mercurial politics in Washington? But still it is a fact that even in the event of a weak President sitting in the Oval office, India enjoying the status of a military ally of America will bear its deterrent value with the enemy. Was not Nehru forced to throw overboard Non-Alignment and Panchasheel overnight, when the Sino-Indian war in 1962 was going disastrously for India? In a strategic tussle with China, the stand of the Indian left cannot but be anti-American and pro-China, that being the irrevocable Marxian discipline. Under the present balance of power existing in South Asia, so long as India refuses to enter into a military alliance with the United States, Indian security remains the most uncertain thing.

79) The moment Pakistan entered into a military alliance with China, India ought to have gone for an alliance with the United States and the west, offering them military bases also on the Himalayas. Some US bases near the McMahon Line would have ended the Chinese threat not only presently but almost permanently. Once India enters into this alliance, it is possible that American interest in Pakistan may decline, enabling India to challenge the Chinese mailed fist from a position of strength. This suggestion, no doubt the Indian left and the left-intelligentsia in the country would hasten to condemn even prime facie. The Indian intelligentsia as our experience shows, will defend only the ideals and ideologies doing no good to the country. The political left will oppose any scheme that goes against the wishes of Communist China, and they will start to play the politics of hide and seek, very cleverly camaflouging the question of Chinese threat. These spokesmen of China are to be condemned, through popular indictment but always escaping. The Indian worries about the military power of China is rising, but at the same time the former is failing to make any effective and realistic counter move. Those opposing a Indo-US Alliance are to be told that a military partnership with America is not a new thing for India. When China attacked India in 1962, a pro-communist Nehru himself feeling unguilty of welcoming American C-130 Hercules planes with American pilots and

arms into the land of Panchasheel, was a (Nehruvian) about turn to be retold many times. It was in these planes that Indian troops and arms were ferried from Chandigarh to Leh for the successful Chusul counter-offensive. Nehru was summoning squadrons of war-planes also from Washington and London to bomb the Chinese concentrations in Tibet. But sensing danger, Mao Tse Tung suddenly declared a unilateral ceasefire and withdrawal from the territory now called Arunachal Pradesh. Unwisely but avidly, India succumbed to this Chinese bait once more, and that was India's biggest blunder in the war. Many decades after, India is again coming under the nightmare of a dangerous Chinese offensive, when the latter has risen as a world power armed with thermo nuclear weapons. In the face of this mortal threat, why India is not moving and taking steps to guarantee her security by radically changing her military options, when such options are clearly there? The Indian communists can look back to what Stalin did in 1941 (during the Second World War), when Hitler suddenly turned his guns against Soviet Russia, often called as a naked and shocking act of betrayal by Hitler. In the beginning of the war, Stalin was guilty of joining Hitler in the brutal conquest of Poland, exposing himself to the charge of committing ghastly crimes against humanity in the campaign, and later during the Warsaw Ghetto. When Hitler suddenly turned his guns against Russia, Stalin did not hesitate to somersault into the Allied camp, headed by none other than that imperial bourgeois—the United States of America. No surprise, the communists the world over turned overnight Yankee—friendly, and the Indian communists, perhaps more loyal than the king, embracing the suicidal policy of condemning Gandhiji's Quit India Movement, from which guilt, they never could extricate themselves. For a communist, America till then was the reactionary capitalist renegade, standing the stumbling block against the onward march of the Marxian juggernaut on the super-highway of world revolution. Was it strange that after winning the war and seizing the victory trophy, Stalin would suddenly repudiate his partnership with world democracy, and from Potsdam he would go home to start the Cold War.

80) While considering the question of India making a military alliance with the United States, I will say that India shooting an S.O.S. to the White House, as in the 1962 war, will not make much sense with the American rulers and people in the 21st century. America, still being the world policeman, different strategic opportunities are unfolding before India. America fought many wars in Asia like the Korean War, the CIA sponsored Khampa Revolt in Tibet, the Vietnam War and so on. In these wars India continued a harsh critic of US role and policy, whereas an American victory in any of these theatres would have strengthened the security of India more than any other country. As one writer suggested recently, if China can equip Pakistan with nuclear arms, India can counter balance the Chinese threat by coming forward to nuclear arm Vietnam against China. China is scary that in spite of her gallopping economy, she fails to gain the good will and confidence of any Asian country, perhaps excepting North Korea and Pakistan. What prevents India from entering into a Nuclear agreement with Vietnam and seek missile bases for India in that country? Domestic criticism of the left will come that India is irresponsibly and recklessly following the same dangerous Pak policy in underworld nuclear trade, but the question is will this be more dangerous than China nuclear arming Pakistan and Pakistan nuclear arming North Korea and engaging in nuclear trade with the terror-friendly regimes of Libya and Iran? China furtively endorses the roguish North Korean nuclear dance. To counter the Chinese threat, India has only dangerous options before her, and among these the safer option is she allying with the United States through a security treaty. India entering into a nuclear pact with Vietnam, can be the secondary option.

81) To join in a military alliance with the United States, the proper, and good occasion will be normal times and not war times. When India knocks at the door of America while she is at war with an enemy like China or Pakistan, that request will receive only a humanitarian consideration. On the other hand, had India made even a token involvement in the Korean or Vietnam or Afghan Wars, she thereby would have earned the right to get American good will and more importantly the

American liability to assist. In Korea and Vietnam, India not only missed this opportunity but stood against America. Again she missed the new opportunity to take part in the wars in Iraq and Afghanistan. In the Iraq War, India is an innocent spectator. But the NDA Government under Vajpayee, was set to adopt a more active policy in Afghanistan by participating in the economic reconstruction of the country, particularly in strengthening the transport infrastructure of the war-torn nation. This Indian involvement certainly has invited the wrath and hostility of the Taliban, Al-Qaida and Pakistan, but the Manmohan government stood the ground. The Indian role in the reconstruction of the country is appreciated in Afghanistan and in the United States and the former. President George W. Bush, referring to the Indian role, had only warm words of praise. Symbolic to her role, India is building the majestic parliament building in Kabul. No doubt India's economic role has made a public impact in Washington and Kabul.

India and the Afghan War

82) Why not India, the second most powerful military and nuclear power in Asia play a military role in Afghanistan as prelude to she making a military alliance with the United States? India, though fighting many wars against Pakistan and China after 1947, is still a country of defenders. How did it became possible for a smaller Pakistan to invade India several times? China the bigger power invaded and defeated India in 1962. India was fighting almost alone except in the Sino-Indian War of 1962, in which Anglo-American help proved critical. By examining the consequences of Indian involvement in the Afghan War through any angle, it looks a safe campaign and a great opportunity for India to flex her muscles. Why India does not come forward for a military alliance, and what is the logic behind this soft policy? Her illusory idealism brought her ignominy and defeat in 1962. President George W. Bush sent clear request to India to join the Afghan War and the NDA government, for sometime, was toying with the idea, but as usual, the unadventurous, unstrategic, fearful India would finally back off from that opportunity also. With India joining the war,

suddenly there would arise a new strategic situation giving the new image of India and the United States jointly pitted against China, and if necessary against Pakistan. Such a compact would throw the existing balance of power in South Asia haywire. But who can draw the diffident New Delhi rulers out of the dungeon of defeatism into which they lie self imprisoned! Again and again India misses her opportunities to change the balance of power in Asia in her favour. India is a growing economic giant, but when will she be the military giant showing her profile in courage?

83) As related above, in Afghanistan, India is missing her safe opportunity for exercising her muscles held idle for long. She got the call to induct a contingent of troops in the Afghan theatre, and fight the war on terror, standing shoulder to shoulder with the superpower the United States of America. For sometime India was mulling this option seriously. For the Indian left, such an Indian move was not only adventurous, but a reckless and immoral breach of the rules of Non-Alignment. At the same time, these critics pretend not to see the setbacks India suffered through Non-Alignment and now its pervading hangovers. It is history that very often adventurous decisions alone are safe-decisions during crises in politics and war. Pakistan has been adventurous in Kashmir, China is adventurous in the Indian borders, reckless and bloody in Tibet and Sinjiang and acted genocidal in Indo-China and Vietnam. Then, why India cannot go adventurous in Afghanistan? Can India—the emerging big power go on for ever a manufacturing and trading corporation? The war-skeptics and critics will vanish from the scene, the moment India wins the war on terror in partnership with the United States, and returns home with the victory trophy. Already India is heavily involved in the civilian rebuilding of Afghanistan. When India is waging America's war in Afghanistan, there will be no threat to her security from China or Pakistan as she is on the side of the most powerful country in the world. Why India hesitates to enter such a safe campaign, which in future will guarantee her security more certainly? Americans feel that they fought and are fighting a lonely war in Iraq and Afghanistan for the sake of distant Asia, and that too without any Asian participation and approbation. Once India enters the Afghan War, the American, European and

Asian perspectives about the war itself will undergo a vision change, enabling to gear up the war on terror, more resolutely. Once the Afghan War is won, the chances for India to settle the cancerous Kashmir issue through dialogue also will suddenly brighten. Participating in a shooting war will bring recognition and respect for the military credentials of India already battered irreparably since 1962. The strategic importance of the Afghan War is that by winning the war, not only India but Pakistan also will become terror-free, and in a terror-free Pakistan, democracy can sink deep and stronger routs. The most important gain for India through the Afghan campaign will be the friendship of the people of the United States, who are anxious about the rising power of Communist China, and the confusion and disunity prevailing among the Asian nations in meeting the Chinese threat. Pakistan playing the China card against India and the United States, has to be forced to choose between Communist China and the United States. Pakistan opting for China to replace America will be damaging her economy and defences, as the American void cannot be filled by the rising China in the near future. Another India friendly change will be the strategic realignment of forces in South Asia. India committing forces in Afghanistan would have produced a 'win-win' situation for the 'Estranged Democracies', and this making a new watershed in the Asian balance of power. That India caring the arguments of the communists and left intellectuals, will be all risk for the country's security has been evidently established already on many occasions. The 1962-war also says that the security of the country can be guaranteed only by blood and arms, and not by the phantom of illusory ideals. In 2003, the Vajpayee governments move to send troops to Afghanistan was vetoed by the isolationism plaguing free India's policy, and now when America in fact winding up her engagement in Afghanistan, these thought are fast becoming redundant.

84) The world would like to call the 21st century as the century of Asia, and India and China are the competing symbols of emerging, Asia. China strides along as the Big Brother but India follows with her rising concerns about China. To counter the Chinese threat, one alternative, but immediate Asian option

can be to remilitarize Japan, but the Asian thoughts in that direction gain only slow momentum. The world assumes that though they are nuclear powers, India and China will be forced to fight a non-nuclear war only in spite of the Maoist bluffs to the contrary. After Hiroshima, there broke out many battles and wars, but any war has been a war with conventional weapons, as nuclear war leads to the termination of life on earth.

85) Considering the economic forces at work, India reaching economic parity with China is not a nearby or probable prospect. Economic power builds military power, and for military power to reach its high point, it needs to be supported by high technology also. The annual military spending of India, is about 35 billion dollars. The declared figure for China for 2012 is $119 billion, but Western observers guestimate that the real figure will go beyond 150 billion or more. The United States suspects that China's military spending, whose many departments are concealed under false heads, can be much more than what is officially admitted. In a present war, human courage, generalling and conventional strategy plays a subordinate role to technology and weaponry. But man's vested interest for survival urges him to hope against hope that there will not be a nuclear-war in future. But India is yet to prove her will and determination fight a conventional war with Red-China? The Chinese fortifications in Tibetan Himalayas are fast expanding to reach every corner of the plateau. As follow up China pumps out propaganda, bloating and demonizing her might and resolve to smite her opponents into smithereens. Though she lost the 1962-war with China, the fact remains that India failed to fight a full war with China even with conventional weapons, and common knowledge that the 1962 defeat was more due to panic and breakdown of command and political leadership. Out of India's half million troops (then), only 6000 were sent to NEFA to be mauled by the dragon and the weak-state syndrome haunts India ever since. This image of India has to change and India got several occasion to make the image change over, but again and again she hesitated stepped back. In that context the Afghan participation, more particularly would have been the apprenticeship for India in

a future war in counter-insurgency and guerilla war. The most important strategic gain because of this engagement would have been India preventing many future encounters, skirmisher and battles with her traditional enemies, India and China. Adventurous India alone would stop the daring enemy. At the same time, there may come the barrage of questions about the reverse consequence of an Afghan War being lost, and India returning home empty handed and humiliated. The Afghan enemy constitutes guerillas and terrorists, who can terrorise, but cannot conquer and subjugate, but can strike terror. They are not a conquering force. If India loses the Afghan War in the company of the most powerful superpower, then what other option is there for India or for any country in crises. By 2012, America has abandoned Iraq in full turmoil to its fate. In 2012, America wants to get out of Afghanistan because it is Obama's electoral platform in 2008. Was there any powerful Asian voice supporting Uncle Sam in Afghanistan and Iraqi? In post-war years America suffers defeat, because in the age of conspicuous consumption she gets easily bored and tired in the battle field. Having lost the moral certainty of the World War years America has become irresolute, fearful and diffident. Only wishful thinking to say now that a direct military entry by America in the Chinese Civil War would have prevented the communist takeover of China in 1949, and thereby have prevented the Chinese conquests of Tibet and Sinjiang, and the wars in Korea, Vietnam, and India-China. Chiang Kai Shek winning the Civil War would have ended the reign of communism wholly from the face of the earth after 1989. The 21st century military threat to Asia and free Asia is from Communist China, a regime born as the child of American dilly-dallying in the Chinese Civil War. In the moment of judgement, Truman ran into his "American Dilemmas", and this dilemma only worsened as the war turned more bitter and bloody. But strange to see Truman shocked and frustrated by the final loss of China to communism with a heavy heart. Regarding India a similar mistake has been she keeping out of the Afghan War. To go to war in Afghanistan, India needed a Sardar Patel in New Delhi, whom the Indian capital has lost long ago in 1950.

86) On the India-China border question, the policy of the Indian Marxists is clear and emphatic, and they can only uphold the Chinese arguments. In the February Revolution in Russia, it was the Russian Socialists who captured power, and this revolt was the popular uprising against Tzar Nicholas II. But due to Luvov's and Kerensky's generous, liberal and incautious approach towards the bloodthirsty Bolshevists, Kerensky himself (Prime Minister) was preparing the ground for his own downfall. He was allowing the minority Bolshevists who stay underground to come to the surface to suddenly reorganize, into a rebellious body. True, the October 25 insurrection was a very dangerous gamble for Lenin, but the gamble won to the great surprise not only of Lenin himself, but of all Russia and Europe. The Bolshevik moderates like Kamenev and Zinoviev—the two Lenin disciples and the majority of members in the Central Committee persistently cautioned their leader against a premature putsch. During the insurrection, Stalin was seen nowhere in Petersburg, presumably hiding to escape arrest. In future history this Leninist gamble and victory was throwing open the great moment for Lenin to found the first socialist terror-state on earth. The Indian Socialists, like the Russian Socialists, standing between the antinationalism of the Leninists and the patriotism of the democrats, do provide an ideological buffer for communists to cover up and hide their anti-national card. Come what may, the Socialists are happy to call themselves anti-American in the twenty-first century also, because anti-Americanism alone will entitle them to be ideologically loyal, but there were differing voices among the Indian Socialists also. Jayaprakash Narayan, the Socialist Titan and the almost Prime Minister of free India after Nehru, was not anti-American, but turning violently anti-China after the war of 1962. George Fernandez—the Socialist radical and spear-head, is calling China India's enemy number one. Acharya Kripalini was a Socialist, but turning anti-communist and anti-China after the Chinese rape of Tibet and the invasion of India. Politically fashionable that during peacetimes, a section of the Indian Socialists are both anti-American and anti-China, but vehemently, anti-American. Though shrunk in size, the anti-American Socialists

in India provide a safe buffer for the powerful pro-China faction (of Indian communists) to bury their head of disloyalty during Sino-Indian crises.

87) While looking into the consequences of the military rivalry between India and Communist China, it becomes necessary to refer to the history of communism in general and particularly in their flagship states of (erstwhile) Soviet Union, Communist China, and their satellites. Focus on their political strategy of deceits, lies, and their murderous false propaganda, and even Joseph Goebbels would go desperate before them. A skeletal survey of the false alibis in communist practice has been made and this is to explain how totalitarian rulers misrepresent universal truths only to disclaim man's history. Once they reach power, how crudely and cheatingly they trample over their own promises, and how through bloody suppression, they ensure total immunity for themselves from public scrutiny. Why the communists fail to look into the fake trials and mass killings of Stalin, through which he established the complete terror-state, has been referred to incidentally and this is to explain the violent breach of promises committed by communists. China's breach of faith against Nehru was reckless, thankless and monstrous, and this betrayal was committed against a person, who till 1962, was the leading Asian democrat appearing as patron, spokesman and defender of Chinese communism and its imperial crimes. Still Communist China thought it politically moral to cheat a camp-follower, credulous enough to invest the security of his country (India) itself, with the communist trustee in Peking. Nehru's blunt reply to General Thimmayya's warning against Chinese activities in Tibet and the Indian border bears testimony to the suicidal trust.

88) The arguments made here will be termed as confrontationist, and running in conflict with the Indian attempts to reach a political compromise with Beijing. But the real question is whether there is any meaningful step by China for compromise and settlement. For the last six decades or more, India could see no softening in Peking, except the enemy playing the game of blowing hot and cold, and hide and seek, but still blatantly aggressive. After making certain occasional and

tactical softenings, suddenly she dares violent and aggressive. As in the past, China wants India to stand down a silent accomplice to her naked conquest, of Tibet, and Sinjiang and the massive repression going on in these places. On the question of Tibetan autonomy, the Indian policy, even after 1962, continues abject, compliant and submissive. India's moderation impels China to challenge even the legitimacy of the Indian president and prime minister travelling to Arunachal Pradesh. The dragon responds to the Indian claims and arguments in the contemptuous, confrontationist way, and why? Because India fails to catch the dragon by its horns. To meet the Chinese threat, what other option is there for India, than making a military alliance with the United States? Why do India fear establishing US military bases in the Himalayas? The George W. Bush era was good occasion to execute these policy changes, but as usual, India missed that opportunity also, in spite of the Indo-American-Nuclear Deal being successfully negotiated.

89) The post-1962 leadership of India, including Indira Gandhi, were groping in the dark in evolving a strong and pragmatic policy against China. Certainly China is bigger, stronger and more dangerous than Pakistan but India's dithering and doubting as demonstrated during the NAM celebrations, needs to be ended, if India is to regain her confidence to fight the enemy. In the prevailing political atmosphere, when India announces an alliance with the United States, the ordinary Indian will be surprised, he being brought up brain-washed and misinformed under the overhanging, over-whelming defeatism of the Nehru era. In the Asian political scene, Indira Gandhi appeared a strong leader, but it looked a self contradiction that she was more anti-American than anti-China, in spite of America having no territorial dispute with India. This Indo-American mutual suspicion during the reign of Indira was for different reasons. America refused to condone Indira's dictatorial policies, and this US stand making her furious, she was going anti-American and anti-China in the same breath. Significant that she never came forward to make an open call against China. During the Emergency (1975-77), there was no question of totalitarian China opposing a dictatorial and authoritarian Indira, and this

political endorsement by Peking was giving a favourable climate for the dragon to fish in the troubled political waters of India.

90) The main fear of China is the day when India will withdraw recognition to Chinese suzerainty over Tibet. Recently, Dalai Lama dropped from his absolute power, his temporal authority on Tibet, and on 8th August 2011 a prime minister (Lobsang Sangay), from the Tibetan diaspora was elected. Lobsang Sangay is now the Prime Minister of the government in exile. A secretariat for the Tibetan government in exile also has been inaugurated in Dharmasala. But again the question is whether a dithery New Delhi will allow a Tibetan government in exile to be free enough to impart new vigour to the Tibetan war of Independence. The new prime minister has made a call to the world, telling the story of Chinese rape of Tibet, and the resolve of the Tibetans to fight communist imperialism with determination. By conquering Tibet in 1950, China, has trampled upon the body and soul of the monastic land and thereby she was tearing the Simla Convention also into pieces. While contemplating a military alliance with the United States, India has to redouble her efforts to persuade Japan to go for full rearmament, and this campaign for rearmament will have go in top gear. To execute this violent change-over, the Japanese need the open endorsement and support of the United States, as this conversion will be wholly overturning the Japanese policy in the long Cold War years from 1946 to 1989. India is bound to launch a diplomatic offensive, calling upon Asian democracies like Australia, Indonesia, Philippines, Malaysia, Singapore and South Korea to unite against the dragon. The Asian powers joining hands to construct a separate Asian military alliance to meet the Chinese threat itself will open a new era in Asia's balance of power, and a purposive start in the direction will force China to look at her neighbours with concern and anxiety. These steps not yielding results, India and the United States will have to declare support to the Tibetan war of Independence and the Uyghur revolts an independence these people very much had till 1950. Against this move, China will not hesitate to make even a nuclear blackmail, but such threats are mainly to balance the terror.

91) After 1989, Communism is a shrinking political ideology, and China is the only powerful redoubt in the ideology's battle for world conquest. But what the world fears is not the military power of China but her determination and daring to go against desperate odds. Compared to world communism, how much more expansive, entrenched and powerful are the democratic world, comprising the most powerful superpower also! To add to the powers of the United States is Canada, Britain, France, Germany, Poland, Eastern Europe, the many seceded Russian republics, India, Indonesia, Philippines, Turkey, Greece, Italy, South Africa, Brazil, Argentina, Australia, Mexico, Chile and so on, and these countries spread over the continents of Asia, Europe, Africa and Latin America. Among the powerful democracies and upcoming democracies in Asia are India, Japan, South Korea, Taiwan, Philippines, Indonesia, Malaysia, New Zealand, Australia and the small countries like Israel and Singapore. Israel, though small territorially, is militarily powerful, upbeat and gallant. Singapore is a jewel in the Indian Ocean, and though a guided democracy, human rights are reasonably protected. Though a majoritarian state of ethnic Chinese, Singapore stands informally allied with the free world. Now the unexpected shot in the arm for world democracy is the stormy advent of the Arab Spring, and the people in that region rising gallantly against the dictators of Libya, Tunisia, Egypt, Syria, Yemen and others. The Arab uprising is so unprecedented an event that the dictators of Egypt, Tunisia and Libya are already overthrown. The tyrant of Syria engaged in a killing spree, is tottering, and now very much isolated from people when this is written. The Arab Spring though unsettled and undisciplined as in Libya and Egypt gives big warming to China, and looking at the rebellious uprisings, and counter revolutions, the China looks at them in puzzle. Strange to note that this expansive world of democracy, possessing a many multiple of the economic and military might of China, is living in fear and scare of China, who under her liberated economic regime, also stands isolated in the political world. The world admires China only for the goods and services she produces, and her bulging foreign exchange belly. The increasing political isolation of China could not be breached even

in 2011, as her ideological imperialism and political malice still run high. The disunity prevailing in the free world, and the non-coordination of their very large economic and military resources, are the big constraints in their battle against communist tyranny. Democracy's obsession with the comforts of peace throws her permanently into the defeatist mode. Mightily united during the Second World War to wage war against Nazism, Fascism, and Tojoism, why the same democracy cannot once more unite in the 21st century to make war to defend human freedom? Similar to the pre-world war conditions existing in Japan and Germany, the power of the Chinese economy is very much dependent on her massive trade with the free world. True, a rising China imparts economic benefits to the non-communist world also, as much as she is benefited in return. The world saw how the Chinese economy was languishing during the period of economic sanctions, imposed by the Western world, and how surprisingly she was making her spectacular recovery after Richard Nixon, lifting all sanctions, launched her into the storm centre of world affairs. Well-known that it is the economic reforms introduced by Deng and comrades that resulted in the making of China's economic miracle. There is no doubt that the Deng reforms gave China the basic economic expose and momentum for rapid growth; but had these trade sanctions of the free world continued after 1972, these reforms would have succeeded only in part, rather limited to her domestic market and the communist markets then in shambles. The historic step was America recognizing Communist China, and the latter replacing Taiwan in the UN Security Council with power to veto the world. When Deng decided to take the reform plunge in 1978, the stage was already well set for China's economic take off go international, whenever she wanted.

92) Military equations frequently change, and countries have to redefine their security concerns in accordance with the fluctuations taking place in the world's balance of power. Changes in balance of power are caused by the combination and recombination of power blocks also. Twentieth century witnessed the frightening militarism of Germany, Soviet Russia, Japan and Italy during its first half, but now these makers and shakers of history are peace entities, living in good conduct. The same world, rid of the German and Japanese militarisms, are now asked to see the emergence of new pretenders to the imperial creed, and in the east, China enters replacing Japan with more ominous portends. In Europe, Soviet Russia came to replace Germany in the post-war and during the Cold War years, subjugating the whole of Eastern Europe. Soviet Union suddenly vanished in thin air in 1989, leaving America alone as the superpower. Democracy's non-adventure, and her internal checks and balances imposed by its constitutionalism, human rights, and rule of law pulls her back from the brink. During peace times, democracy is celebrative and successful, but in war her capacity to confront the enemy on many occasions is found as lost in demagogic platitudes. To conquer a country is easy, but to consolidate and mop it up in the long run is the difficult, and complex job. Today, it is America's police-actions, half-hearted, hesitant and irresolute, that invite the contemptuous reaction of her enemies and friends alike. The rise of post-war American defeatism is giving a free-hand to the shrinking, and debilitated, communist savagery to reign high and mighty over the much superior power of democracy.

93) A dangerous feature of balance of power is the absolute inability of small states to defend themselves. Generally, this had been the case throughout history, but in the age of weapons and engines of mass murder and mass destruction, this incapacity come more exposed. Till the beginning of the First World War, balances of power remained more regional than global. The First World War was almost localized within Europe and the Middle East, and its Asian and African engagements were in pockets and corners. The Second World War was going truly global, and its battle theaters ran from Europe, to Russia, to South Asia, South East Asia, the Far East and North Africa. The battles in the Atlantic, being only naval engagements, the continents of North America and South America did not yield battle grounds, in spite of the air and naval operations going almost global. But after the Second World War, no corner of planet-earth stands away from arms and battle and the 21st century makes every home and every human threatened by the next apocalypse. Lately balance

of power is slated to go not only global, but spatial and cosmic. When Hitler attacked Poland in 1939, America seemed far away from the reach of German guns, and the people of the United States did not feel threatened by a Trans-Atlantic invasion. This 'battle-field immunity' was rather absolute for the American continents, but the wrong side of this immunity is Americans looking at any war anywhere as somebody else's war, but she forced to fight, and therefore developing the despondent desire to quit the battle field on wrong occasions, or half-way through. The safety belt of geographical distance has vanished and today the American citizen feels threatened by the tirades of that small, and sickly state called North Korea. In conventional wars also modern technology allows a division of well-equipped soldiers and arms airdropped at any point on the earth surface within hours, and the first test was carried out by the United States in Lebanon in 1959. Lately missiles and nuclear bombs target the furthest corners of human habitation very pointedly. This global mobility of arms and troops makes a new war universally fearful. Under global strategic scenario, a small power readying to defend herself is certainly in the world of fantasy in spite of the ideal that a state, however small, is having the absolute right to exist. But how this right can be made a reality is the question? International law upholds this right, but how to accomplish it militarily? For this rule, there are rare exceptions like the state of Israel who is small in size, but big in military power, or rather big in military adventures, though the Jewish state also hopes to be rescued by American arms ultimately. At present, a country like the United States alone can say that she can defend her national territory with her own power. Another question exercising the strategic thoughts is whether China, single handedly can meet the armed power of the United States in a future war? This question will invite different answers, in the context of China (Civil War), Korea and Vietnam. But in spite of these American debacles, it is a fact that the armed power of America remains superior to all other powers. A small country, can guarantee her own security only in alliance and company with another powerful country. See how the big powers like Britain, the United States, France, Germany, Austria-Hungary, Russia, Japan, and

Nationalist China fought wars and world wars. They fought in combinations as power blocks, called the Allies, Central Powers, Axis Powers, etc. Disclaiming and denouncing this universal strategic reality, Nehru invented the Non-Aligned Movement (NAM), which in practice, was to challenge the fundamentals of human behaviour with fantasy and illusion, and NAM destined to fail in real politik. Philosophers themselves could not defend their philosophy, let it be Plato, Aristotle, St. Augustine or St. Thomas Aquinas or Kant or Hegel and for doing that job, there shall be a state. It looks a self-contradiction that great religions also fought their way by arms, and survived through the armed power of their faithfuls and the patron states. The danger of the NAM philosophy was that Nehru was not a philosopher, but a ruler burdened with the high duty of defending his country with arms. Through Panchsheel, he was preaching the world that moral rearmament was going to win not only the battles of arms, but all battles of peace. Nehru, riding high on the wave of his NAM rhetorics, was envied and hated by Mao, and in 1962, he came forward to smash that Nehru myth, and his guns, smote it into smithereens. India, still holding up the NAM flag in hand, lay there battered, bruised, shattered, unsung, and unhonoured. But in spite of that abject fall, no NAM follower came forward to give that body an honourable burial, and many protagonists were doubting that still there is life in it. The echoes of NAM platitudes still haunt New Delhi's foreign-policy corridors. India going to fight China single handed will once more be a fail option, if there is a new war.

94) Twenty-first century India maintaining high alert on her security. She is making new arms and more arms, conducting researches to build tanks, guns and missiles, and nuclear bombs. But the big question is whether she can defend herself against China by her own arms and men even with the best of resources in her command. An atomic arsenal, after 1945, has not been for use in the battle field, but it is very much there to threaten and deter, though not to shoot. A future war with China also is hoped to be fought with conventional arms. Japan, South Korea and Taiwan in the Far East, got rid of the Chinese threat by entering into security treaties with the United States. Why not

India follow suit and get rid of this killing worry? Remember, India has no common border with the United States, and no territorial dispute with her. Neither India has a like dispute with any Western power. But New Delhi, unless reaching the brink as in 1962, looks at the option of military alliance with shame, surprise and feeling of moral guilt. Can India allow her illusions and ideals to veto her security concerns? Even after her tragic defeat in 1962, if India feels it dishonourable to breach the Panchasheel commandments she preached from roof tops, so much so she is not out of Nehruvian myths. So long as the Indian rulers continue to wonder at hard military power, the country will remain the soft target of the dragon.

95) To the rising Indian economy, the economy of China stands at least three times larger, and China's military forces are more unequally powerful. Both economies are growing fast, but India's inequality gap unlikely to be bridged in the near future, even in case the Indian economic miracle would outshine the dragon. The basic question facing India is how will she defend herself, if a new war with China breaks out immediately? Having no military allies and committed partners, India will have to fight it alone, and the result, in all probability, will be a repeat of 1962 and clear rout. The Chinese foot-army, 2.3 million strong, cannot be matched by India. In the age of high technology, man cannot find solace by pointing to the dramatic turns accomplished in the epic battles of history because of great generals and generalling. History will cite the examples of the exploits of the Carthaginian general Hannibal or the French military genius Napoleon Bonaparte or the German desert-fox Valery Rommel. Rommel's exploits in North Africa, during the Second World War, seemed magical even to the enemies. But that German strategic genius also had to bow before the quantitative superiority of the American war production. With new challenges confronting her, what is the winning route for India in the next war with China? Though not entering into an open military pact, as it exists between Japan and the United States, the Asian democracies like Australia and New Zealand are already under the American nuclear umbrella by strategic assumption. The advantage India will enjoy by allying with the

United States, is she getting rid of the fear of China overnight, and if so what stands in the way? It is free India's political irresolution and the heavy ideological and idealistic baggage she voluntarily carries on her shoulders. In spite of much of water going down the Yamuna since 1962, India's anti-Americanism and anti-westernism, entrenched in the socialist philosophy of Nehru, is still alive to take its toll in India's strategic initiatives. The NAM protagonists will know that had India persisted in her self-destructing harangues of the NAM, the Nehru S.O.S. to Kennedy and Macmillan for immediate dispatch of arms would not have been sent in 1962. Nehru, the political romanticist, idealist, demagogue, procommunist and the anti-American was suddenly waking-up to see his country under the threat of a Chinese take over. The Five Commandments of NAM (Panchasheel) could not stop his patriotism from making a total appeal to the imperial United States and colonial Britain for a rescue mission, and with unprecedented promptness, such aid was flowing in in-spite of the Cuban Missile Crisis. Rather strange and accidental that it was when America herself was suddenly caught in the Missile Crisis and her armed forces placed under high alert across the world. That was in 1962, and those days are now history. That total American commitment in the Cold War years to save the world's largest democracy at any cost, is now not only not total, but optional, shaky and ambivalent. Will Obama and Kerry will make the same thunderous response John Kennedy made in 1962? Regrettably, after the seventies, that guardian commitment of the United States to the free world has worn off to the point of a bad dilemma. Today's America, in the moment of danger, may come or may not come, and that is the American climb down coming through her post-war moderation. The British response looks more uncertain, its effectiveness depending on the person then sitting in No. 10—Downing Street. For example, India can expect a helpful reaction from a leader like Tony Blair, but not from a dithery Gordon Brown. It is bad tiding that the once bitterly anti-communist and McCarthyist American Congress also is becoming conciliatory, mellowed and cost-conscious. Compare this congressional stand-down with the McCarthyist political onslaught and saber-rattling launched from the Capitol Hill against the American communists and world communism in the early nineteen fifties. The same America now allows Communist China to admonish President Obama not to have a rendezvous with the Tibetan spiritual supremo-Dalai Lama, though this Beijing fiat was rejected by the America only after much hesitation and haggling. Can the world think of Mao Tse Tung issuing a similar admonition to Harry S. Truman in 1949? The increasing Sino-American, Sino-European economic bonds are a vital factor shaping the China policy of Britain, America and Europe. All these said and done, what is the highest morality in war? It is victory and nothing else, and to reach that patriotic end, any change of policy or even the wholesale dumping of the so-called political morals will be justified. The political ideals recklessly introduced by Nehru in his foreign policy initiatives all turned out strategic blunders, and these blunders are India's permanent self-inflicted wounds. Nehru moved through the dangerous route, only to please himself, to please the anti-Indians, and to please the Chinese fifth column infiltrating his court. Always his sympathy lay with the political left and the left intellectuals, who were India's merchants of treason, but appearing under the banner of intellectual race horses.

96) It is now the national urgency for India to place the security of the country above the mischief of ideological wrestling matches. India is working to strengthen her defences, but things are not moving fast enough, and this is because of lack of pragmatism, and vision, and due to the absence of proper strategy, ideological prejudices and policy vagueness. To strengthen her defences, India has to build a deterrent air force, and that project will get high priority. She has to upstage the missile defences, and construct theatre missile systems in the northern and western borders. The North Korean nuclear gamble and suicidal ultimata and manoevres may look silly and childish and dishonourable, but the world is apprehensive that she has a number of bombs in her armoury. North Korea may be terror state or rogue state, but she has to be confronted and how? High time India instal antimissile defence. Upstaging missile technology is not immediately possible through indigenous

R&D, and therefore the import of Western technology is the possible alternative to build a missile defence system. A technology leader like the United States may be willing to pass this technology to India, but only with India's deeper commitment to the former's security interests. It is true that the Narasimha Rao, Vajpayee and the Manmohan Governments have made a definite tilt towards the United States, but that tilt falls far short of a military alliance, much less a meaningful military partnership. Only by changing into a more clear prodemocracy and pro-US policy, India can obtain the state of the art Western technology to meet her defence needs. America, as the military ally of Pakistan, is still giving large quantities of arms and money to the latter, including modern fighter aircraft. It remains an American policy contradiction that with these weapons, Pakistan targets not the appointed enemy China communism, but Indian democracy. American strategic aims on Pakistan are mostly missing, except perhaps in the case of Osama Bin Laden.

97) Big mystery for political pundits, why in the 1960's, America could not dissuade Pakistan from gate-crashing into her double-edged military alliance with Communist China, when China was the hated Cold War enemy of the United States? Later and even after the 9/11, the Pakistan military is happily utilising the services of terrorists and human-bombs, ignoring the American calls and commands to the contrary. As explained already, the Pak military has a vested interest in keeping the Kashmir question boiling. The military's logic is that it can call the shots in Rawalpindi, only so long as there is a violent Kashmir. In spite of this military paramountcy going perverse and taking a suicidal turn during the East Pakistan rebellion of 1971, and half of Pakistan breaking away to form the new state of Bangladesh, the army top brass remain unfazed. As on many past occasions, Pak democracy is limping back to Rawalpindi again, and in June 2013, Nowaz Sherif is again sworn in as the new prime minister, but again the terrorists and the ISI are calling the shots. How much and how long Pak democracy will survive under the goodwill and command of the ISI, the army, and the terrorists? The recent history of war on terror in Pakistan declares that the government can wage

only a see-saw battle against terror, even under American vigil and drone attacks political observers say that the elimination of the terrorists alone will pave the way for resolving the Kashmir dispute, which is a time bomb, ticking continuous.

98) The Obama administration, faithfully obeying the post-war American dilemma, wants to quit Afghanistan also on a prefixed timetable and 2014 is the final date. Under worldly strategic calculus, who under the sun will be able to fix a timetable for winning a war or losing a war? Or, perhaps a timetable can be fixed for losing a war, because in all wars the option to surrender is always there, as the patriotism of the dishonourable. America lost the Vietnam War because of she prefixing a time table for withdrawal, a scheme never reciprocated by the enemy. Time table was precursor to military disaster and it finally led to her abject surrender in the war theatre, causing the biggest blood bath of innocents in post-war history. She almost lost the Iraq war also under the theory of timetabling, and she is now ready to lose the Afghan War also, which she so thoroughly won in the beginning. About the timetable theory, Nixon was the pioneer, and its architect was Henry Kissinger. Nixon's policy of a prefixed timetable for the Vietnam pullout was the first instance of America's unilateral surrender. This timetable enabled the Yiet Cong guerillas and terrorists to make all advance arrangements for accepting American surrender on a platter, and they waited impatiently to conduct the victory celebrations through the horrendous massacre and bloodbath, its grand finale being the flight of two million refugees of which one million drowned in the South China Sea. After Vietnam, this timetable strategy is becoming an American obsession and fetish, and for the world policeman, time has become the essence of wars, let it be victory or defeat.

Part II

Chapter 6

Border Dispute—The Result of Nehru Deserting Tibet

99) The running sore between India and China is the latter's conquest of the Indian territory Aksai Chin—an area covering 38000 sq. kms. This territory became part of British India in 1846, when Kashmir was annexed by the British. After the 1949 communist capture of power, China invaded and reduced Tibet into possession, and this was with notice to New Delhi, and New Delhi merely stood down. Without wait, China invaded Aksai Chin during 1950-54. After the invasion it is usual she will be advancing arguments to justify aggression and to make it legitimate and legal. When she could cross Tibet like knife cutting butter, China saw Aksai Chin lying undefended and unguarded before her. She felt she can occupy it, without firing a single shot so long as Nehru is the ruler in Delhi. China argues her Tibetan case with reasons, but the argument is the argument of guns, only to camaflouge history and events. Students of history want to know the reasons and facts of history, though these arguments are going to make no impact in Beijing. Here is a brief look back into the history of the recent past. India-China border dispute is said to encompass the whole length of the border, running for more than 4500 kms, but the real area of dispute with India is Aksai Chin. While examining the general theory of Sino-Indian hostility through political, ideological and strategic angles, Sinologists contend that resolving the dispute on Aksai Chin will remove the bone of contention, enabling both sides to reach agreement.

100) While searching into the causes the real stumbling block before China is neither the border nor the McMahon Line, but China's domain and suzerainty over Tibet. She fears what will be the future stand of India on (Chinese) Tibet. Till 1950, Tibet had never been a tributary or province of China. Only Communist China invaded the plateau and annexed it in 1950, and the world calls it China's rape of the Roof of the World. For the invasion of Tibet, China met no military opposition from non-violent India, and this Indian acquiescence and passivism was real surprise to the word. Mao was massing his troops on the border and waited for India's reaction and reports from his informers in New Delhi reported that Nehru has taken the final decision not to make any military intervention and he was confident to go ahead and Tibet fell in no time. Then his troops occupied part of India itself which is Aksai Chin and thereafter he was becoming confident of more encroachments. Nehru's war mettle has been tested by Mao in Kashmir, where the smaller Pakistan was able to challenge India—the bigger power successfully. The Pak challenge itself decimated the world image of India. For Mao, Aksai Chin looked a no man's land and he occupied it, while New Delhi was sleeping.

101) It is history that for more than a century, China was moving heaven an earth to get her suzerainty on Tibet accepted by world powers, but the world was sitting over the demand equivocal. Then all on a sudden Nehru would surrender Tibet without China asking for it so unconditionally and Mao and Chau En Lai were surprised regarding the Nehru surrender. Because of the Chinese conquest of Tibet in 1950, the suzerainty question has become irrelevant so far as China is concerned. Ancient India or British India did not have a common border with China, but had a common border only with Tibet. China had a common border only with Tibet, and Tibet remained the buffer state between India and China for thousands of years. So far as China's title over Tibet is based on naked conquest, what is the meaning in China saying that she has a border dispute with India? The real worry of China is not Aksai Chin or McMahon Line, but Tibet. China conquered Tibet in 1950, reducing Dalai Lama a virtual prisoner in the Potola Palace and latter fearing his personal safety and life, he fled Tibet and escaped to India, where he is the celebrated exile.

102) About the causes of the border dispute between India and China, the important modern events are the relationship between British India and Manchu (Ming) China during 18th and the 19th centuries. How the Sino-British relationship influenced the Sino-Tibetan relations during the end of the nineteenth and early twentieth centuries can be seen as more important. The border dispute, since the 1962 war, drags on and on, and now the mediators ask why India cannot accept the much internationally canvassed position of give and take. That is the real part of diplomacy and statecraft, but regarding India the border raises sentimental as well as emotional questions, blocking the move for a compromise through the transfer of Indian territory to China. The real dispute is expected narrows down to the strategic Aksai Chin in Kashmir and many believe that once that part of the dispute has been resolved, it is possible that the India-China border dispute will come to an effective end. They say the sparrings about the alignment of the McMahon Line and the question of Arunachal Pradesh can be pushed to the background, once the claims and counter claims on Aksai Chin are resolved.

103) To make the Aksai Chin territory more possessed and secure. China constructed the new highway to Sinjiang from Tibet, and now this is said to be China's strategic artery to the rebellious province and this is said to be the main concern of China. She considers possession by Tibet as possession by her, and she claims she is the legitimate successor to the Tibetan title through the conquest in 1950. Kashmir state was delimited and fixed in 1846 between the Kashmir King and Tibetan authorities though no map is available and some vagueness remained. Ladakh (including Aksai Chin) being the area of the old Punjab state, where the writ of the king of Ladakh ran until India became independent. But before the Chinese conqueror, the only deterrent in 1950 was the capacity and readiness of India to strike back and check her. As no Indian guard was seen within sight, China easily trespassed to occupy Aksai Chin, a conquest that was completed and consolidated during

1953-57. China was certain that Nehru had neither the will nor the sword to strike back, and so the former, without firing a shot, annexed about 38000 sq. kms. of Indian territory. She is making more encroachments. China did so, assuming that already Tibet has become the settled part of the new communist empire. After the invasion, she built the Aksai Chin road and following that, the Karakoram Highway also, which is now China's traffic artery to Sinjiang. After the invasion, it is only usual that the aggressor will put forward arguments justifying the conquest, which in fact are the arrogant summonses of an aggressor to the victim to accept a fait accompli. All conquerors in history had had their own arguments, justifying naked aggressions, and in this respect the modern example is Hitler. Hitler, after occupying Sudetenland and Austria through lightening operations in 1937 and 1938, presented his fantastic excuses before the world justifying these crimes. If Aksai Chin looked a 'no mans land' or disputed area, a peace-loving China should have raised the issue with India, who was in actual possession of the territory, and in the deliberations, both countries would be free to reach agreement. But a plain surrender to aggression through a feigned negotiation, in addition to territorial loss, tells upon the patriotism and honour of the victim, and so India, as the loser, finds any compromise option hard to swallow and the India-China standoff is likely to prolong till the conqueror comes willing to vacate.

104) While considering the totalitarian practices and precedents since 1917 it is certain that China will accept only the arguments of guns and never the arguments of reason. But before dismissing the Chinese arguments as the haughty summonses of an aggressor to the victim to come to the negotiating table only to sign on dotted lines, it is necessary to make a look back into certain incidents highlighting the relations between China and Tibet, Russia and Tibet. Russia and British India, British India and Tibet, Britain and Russia, and more particularly how the balances of power changed in between those powers during the second half of the 19th and the beginning of 20th centuries. The border dispute and the possibility of another war being the theme of the book this question has been generally discussed also.

105) After annexing Aksai Chin, China declares the territory as belonging to Tibet whose sovereign successor is China, and therefore her occupation is absolutely a legitimate act. It is history that India was defeated in the 1962 war, and in consequence, India's national honour self-respect and pride stand seriously offended, turning public opinion in the country furious against Red-China. The people of India consider the 1962 Chinese invasion not only an aggression but an outrageous betrayal and back-stab. How can naked conquest be legalized through negotiation is the Indian negotiator's dilemma.

106) For more than one thousand years, China and Tibet have been maintaining very deep religious bonds. There existed a patron-priest relationship between these country. Tibet was the chief priest of China and China the Patron. Bogle, the English visitor and emissary of Warren Hastings to Tibet in the 18th century would compare this relationship to the ties that existed between the Roman Pontiff and the Eastern Roman Emperor. From the 16th century onwards, Dalai Lama continues the temporal as well as the spiritual head of Tibet. In the 13th century Tibet was conquered by the Mongols but the Khans, fascinated by the divine scholarship and powers of Buddhist Tibet, hesitated to destroy the divine culture of the Roof of the World. One Khan even converted himself into Buddhism and he invited lamas to Mongolia to teach and preach Buddhism. This divine and religious connection between Mongolia and Tibet gradually strengthened and Mongolians came to respect and honour the role of the lamas and the Dalai Lama in the religious life of Mongolia. This religious connection even now continues and when the 13th Dalai Lama fled to Mongolia to escape the Chinese invasion of 1909, the Mongols received him with much fanfare and honours. It was the Mongolian Khans themselves who later took the initiative to make Dalai Lama the temporal as well as the spiritual head of Tibet, and from the 16th century on, the latter continues the spiritual as well as the temporal ruler of Tibet. Thereafter he presides over Tibet as its ultimate priest and King. In spite of China making attempts including the invasion of 1909. Tibet could never been reduced into a vassal of China paying tribute to the emperor. But in spite this history and

politics of the long past, what happened in 1950, reduced Tibet as the defacto part of the communist empire. The Second World War changed the political map of Asia and after the war Tibet is under China's physical possession, and China now argues that Tibet is part of China.

107) After the Bogle Mission, Governor General Warren Hastings (at the end of the 18th century), sent the Macartiny Mission to Lhasa and McCartney toured Tibet during 1788-92. He reported back that there is strong Chinese influence over the plateau, but Tibet enjoyed full autonomy not only in collecting tax from regions as far away as the Ladakh border, but also in conducting foreign relations directly. The independent status of a country is decided mainly on two parameters, who runs the foreign relations of the country and who is responsible for her defence and even in the 21st century these are two fundamental planks. No incident in history tells that the foreign affairs of Tibet was ever taken over by Peking, though in many negotiations and transactions, China was the medium as well as the intervener on behalf of Lhasa. The principality of Ladakh, prior to her coming under the British India with the forming of the state of Kashmir in 1846, was conducting her foreign relations directly with Lhasa and not with Peking. In 1846-47, the boundaries between Kashmir, (the Sikh territory) and Tibet were negotiated and redefined, and the defacto condition confirms Ladakh as part of the Kashmir state. It is true that in some maps the British have shown the Ladakh border as undefined, but physical occupation was with the Kashmir state. If border is not marked, it is a dispute regarding the border, and not broad, wide territory. Aksai Chin had never been in the possession of Tibet.

108) As said already, India's main dispute with China is Aksai Chin. Kashmir was part of the Sikh Kingdom, and in 1846 through the Treaty of Amritsar, British India annexed Kashmir. But immediately, the British government in Calcutta, more in need of money than the large territory of Kashmir, sold Kashmir to Gulab Singh for a price of ₹ 75 lakh. This sale was on condition that Kashmir will accept British India as guardian and protector. Jammu, Kashmir and Ladak were the land regions comprising the state of Jammu and Kashmir. Kashmir

and Tibet lie adjacent. Disputes regarding the boundary between Kashmir and Tibet often arose, and eventually Britain proposed a boundary commission with China also participating. But the Qings, as part of the empire's Fabian policy, avoided any direct commitment, and remained silent. It is history that during the 19th century, China was in political ferment, and her strategy was not to resolve any dispute with neighbours and give it finality. She was feeling insecure and harassed by the west. The British proposed Boundary Commission never materialized, but status quo continued. Because of this Chinese policy of postponement, many disputed situations came to stabilize as fait accompli, and when India became independent in 1947, Aksai Chin was the integral part of the state of Kashmir. British India was one of the pioneers in adopting scientific survey and boundary fixing. The issue before free India is whether there is any legitimate justification for the Chinese occupation of Aksai Chin. In 1950, Aksai Chin was a place with sparse human habitation or rather nomad traversed, and therefore looking a 'no-mans-land' for any attempting aggressor. It was not a 'no-mans-land' but it was the unguarded territory of India. China invaded and occupied Aksai Chin during 1951-54. On the surface of the earth, there are vast tracts of land which are un-inhabited and unguarded, but owned by particular countries. The human tracks, pathways and caravan routes in Aksai Chin were regularly used by international traders, tourists and pilgrims of many countries, including Tibet, China and India, but these were human tracks within the Kashmir state. For example, the Silk Route passes through China, Afghanistan, the Central Asian countries and the Middle East, and this route was used by international caravans for centuries. Who ruled the specific areas in the route, who collected tax from the people, the caravans and traders, and who looked after law and order in particular segments of the route, were the facts deciding possession. Aksai Chin assumes importance because it is now disputed territory. India claims Aksai Chin territory up to the Kun Lun Range—which otherwise can be called the Johnson Line, and this area was shown in the official maps of India as her own from 19th century onwards. But China objects and claims land further west up to the Karakoram pass in the north and the Pongyang Lake in the South, which includes the 38000 sq. kms. she invaded and occupied during 1950-57. In the meanwhile, the Macdonald Line was suggested by mediators as the compromise line, in order to protect China's claim up to the Aksai Chin Road. To prove the Indian claim up to the Kun Lun Range, there shall be proof that the writ of the Kings of Kashmir and Ladakh ran up to the Sahidulla Check Post. China could not produce any archival, old or ancient records to show that Tibetan power ever extended up to this area. In negotiations, China produced two maps showing Aksai Chin as part of Tibet, but on scrutiny it was found that China never published these maps officially, and these were documents fabricated after 1950. The records of the Kashmir King will establish that the King's authority extended up to Sahidulla Check Post. The Chinese contention is true that during the 19th century, British India had allowed Sahidulla post to be occupied by China for the purpose of checking a threatened Russian assault on Tibet. This arrangement ceased after Russia's defeat in the Russo-Japanese War of 1905, when Kashmir reoccupied the post. After the fall of the Manchus in 1911, Chinese power and authority suddenly collapsed all over Tibet. The 13th Dalai Lama declared Tibet independent, and this proclamation was made with great pomp and publicity. The restored position up to the Sahidullah Check Post continued until the Chinese invasion of Aksai Chin in 1950.

109) During the middle of the 19th century, British trading interests in China were constraining her activist imperial policy on Tibet. The British concern during the closing years of the century was the fear of a Russian attack on Tibet, when Russia advanced very near to the Tibetan border, through her Central Asian drive. Lord , the Indian Viceroy was alarmed, and he declared that while British India does not want to annex Tibet, neither she wants it to be annexed by another power (Russia). He asserted that it was Tibet and not Nepal which is the buffer not only between India and China, but, between India and Russia also. It was then very easy for to make Tibet a protectorate of British India like Sikkim, but the White Hall opposed the move, and 's Young Husband Expedition to Tibet in 1903 was able to perform only a half-job. But British India was coming to the new realisation that to stop Russia, the Chinese power, then on the decline, cannot any more be relied on. It was then part of British diplomacy that in every transaction, British India was honouring and recognizing the age-old influence of China over Tibet, but this British favour was because of Britain's growing trade interests in Canton and the east coast of China. The conflicting interests anyhow will to come to a head during the year. Young Husband was a 28 years old young man and an adventurous traveller. He was a bureaucrat in the service of the Government of India, who had earlier undertaken a hazardous, long trek from Peking to Lhasa. It was this mountainous trek that made him eligible to head the new military expedition to Lhasa. Young Husband headed an army of 5000 well-armed soldiers. Camping enroute at several places he reached Gyantse, the middle town enroute to Lhasa. May be on wrong information the Tibetan soldiers stationed there tried to resist the Indian expedition, and before the negotiations began, the Young Husbands army had to shoot down more than 600 Tibetan soldiers, causing much fear and resentment in Lhasa. From there, the army proceeded to Lhasa but before they set foot on Lhasa, the 13th Dalai Lama fled the capital and escaped to Mongolia where he was received with honours befitting a head of state. The lamas and the National Assembly in Lhasa were left behind to negotiate with Young Husband, and both sides signed the 1904 Treaty with the Lamas and the National Assembly. Through the Young Husband Treaty, British India secured new trading rights and military privileges, and the right to appoint a trade agent at Gyantse. Of these gains the more important was the right to station an Indian garrison in Lhasa. The rights and privileges India secured later through the Simla Convention of 1914 were in addition to these rights.

110) After the fall of the Qings, the efforts of the KMT government to assert China's suzerainty over Tibet were not successful. Even before the fall of the Qings in 1912 China was locked in war with the marauding Japan. During the Second World War, Chiang Kai Shek raised the suzerainty question with the Allied powers, but no final decision could be reached. In 1943, in the Washington Council Conference, Churchill would admit Chinese suzerainty over Tibet, but immediately the officials in New Delhi informed Anthony Eden (Foreign Secretary) that China, not having signed the Simla Convention of 1914, cannot claim suzerainty until she signs the document. They contended that suzerainty was conditional on China signing the convention, and she accepting all clauses in the conventions including the division of Tibet into Outer Tibet and Inner Tibet. During the Second World War years and before also, the British were persuading and pressing the Chinese Government to sign the convention, but every time China evading. Even after refusing to sign the convention, China was raising the plea that the convention already has accepted her suzerainty over Tibet. The British were of the view that China shall accept the autonomy of the Tibetan Autonomous Regan (TAR), and the boundaries of Outer Tibet and Inner Tibet as demarcated by the convention, and then alone she can claim suzerainty. Well-known that, the British were in favour of China's suzerainty, because of her growing trading interests in China. During the Second World War Kuomintang China was her war ally, and therefore deserving to be favoured but due to domestic political pressures, China was evading the signing she had various excuses, but her main objection was regarding the boundaries of Outer Tibet and Inner Tibet. A matter of concern was that China from the 2nd half of the 19th century was growing weaker and the Russian threat against Tibet was rising. Britain wanted to foil the Russian advance and they thought it would be wiser to allow Chinese suzerainty over Tibet so that a Russian attack on Tibet will be considered a direct attack on China, and Moscow may not be ready to take that big risk. It was not only apparent, but real Russia and the world considered Tibet an independent country on whom no other country including China has any superior dominion. Tibet is a large territory comprising half a million square miles, but militarily, she was thoroughly unequipped. A thousand years ago Tibet was a strong empire extending up to Central Asia and parts of Mongolia and China, and it was after the Mongol invasion that that power began to decline. In the 16th century, under the authority of the Mongolian Khans the Dalai Lama was made the temporal as well as the spiritual head of Tibet. It was religion and divinity that ruled Tibet thereafter, and the country was going more and more into the monastic culture and faith of Buddhism. Gradually Tibet ceased to be a military power, permanently needing a protector and military guardian China filled this guardian role very often. From the 17th century onwards China kept a permanent garrison also in Lhasa. Between Tibet and China, the patron-priest relationship was growing, persuading the British missionary Bogle to compare this bond with the relationship between the Roman Pontiff and the Eastern Roman Emperor.

111) In this context, it is relevant to note that during the debates in the Simla Convention, the Chinese plenipotentiary raised no objection regarding the alignment of the McMahon Line. To be emphasized that China and Tibet came to the conference table as equals, and Tibet not as a protégé or lackey of China. Finally Tibet and British India signed the convention, and in the signing stage, the Chinese delegate walked out. In theory, the convention will bind only India and Tibet. Tibet, had declared her independence in 1912, and till the Chinese invasion of 1950, the country was jealously maintaining that independent status. A historic fact is that during the Second World War, Tibet asserted her neutrality, and defiantly refused to change that policy under heavy Allied pressure. Even Allied war-supplies to Kuomintang China through Tibet were blocked for years and this rigorous Tibetan neutrality continued, in spite of American, British and KMT warnings on Dalai Lama to change policy.

112) The developments taking place in Nepal and Sikkim during the 18th century are of particular importance, to set the record straight on Sino-Indian relations. In 1769, the traditional Newari rulers of Nepal were overthrown by the Gurkhas, and the latter established the Hindu Kingdom in the Himalayan state. In the war, the Newari King was supported by the British, and therefore later the inimical Gurkhas turned against the British and closed the traditional trade routes from India to Tibet. The British were forced to seek alternative routes through the North East, Bhutan and Sikkim. This rivalry led to the Anglo-Nepalese war of 1814-16, which ended in the defeat of the Gurkhas. In the armistice, British India acquired the territories of Kumaoun and

Garwal, and for the first time, India was acquiring a border with Tibet through the United Provinces. In a different development, Sikkim would become a protectorate of British India. After 1775, Sikkim came continuously under Gurkha attacks, and to protect Sikkim, British India intervened and the defeat of the Gurkhas was the result. The war would make Sikkim a British protectorate later. After becoming a protectorate, Sikkim opened her trade routes to Tibet from the Bengal province, she handed over her foreign affairs to British India, and consequently the former became a protectorate of free India after 1947 (Later Sikkim would join the Indian Union). To reach peace, Britain was entering into the Treaty of 1817 with Nepal, and that position in Indo-Nepal relations continued.

113) The event enlarging the Indian areas in the North East was the Burmese conquest on Manipur and Assam. The invasion led to the Anglo-Burmese war of 1824-26, and that war also ended in victory to British India. In the Treaty of Vandabo (1826), British India got the whole of Lower Assam and parts of Upper Assam (now Arunachal Pradesh). To establish control over the tribal areas of Assam, hitherto remaining autonomous or a 'no man's land', British India sent an expedition to Rohit Valley (now in Arunachal Pradesh) and the rebellious tribes were either suppressed or they were won over. In the tribal areas, Britain adopted a pragmatic policy of non-interference in tribal autonomy and traditions, and this policy was very successful in speedily integrating these areas into British India. At the same time, the rebellious Khasis, Garos, Nagas, Monpas, Mishmis and Manipuris were suppressed by arms. The province of Assam expanded in area, and the introduction of tea and discovery of oil caused a dramatic increase in British investments in the province. New investments urged them to give more attention to the area, especially to protect their large plantation and oil firms. It needs mention that in the newly annexed areas of Assam, no administrative control had been exercised by China or Tibet, except over certain pockets, over which Tibet later raised claims Tawang was one such area. Before 1950, Lhasa had raised claim for Tawang and certain areas of Arunachal Pradesh also when Tibet was being threatened by Chinese invasion. Political commentators say that Tibet, in that context, making a claim against India was most unstrategic and undiplomatic. Others point out that Tibet had no diplomatic experience and until the advent of the 13th Dalai Lama, the plateau remained essentially a monastic territory not knowing anything about the outside world and their diplomatic nuances and power plays. When Communist China was preparing to invade Tibet, such Tibetan claim against India had caused a cooling in India-Tibet relations, and Jawaharlal Nehru himself was a bit dismayed of this untimely Tibetan demand. It is a different thing that whatever be the Tibetan policy, India defending Tibet by resisting China through arms was totally out of question so long as Nehru was the Prime Minister of India. Indian concern ought to be about the loss of Tibet as the permanent buffer between India and China and not to see whether there was diplomatic or behavioural misconduct on the part of Tibet. In any case Nehru was not a warrior and will not go for war in defence of Tibet and this Nehru policy was diametrically opposite to the strong policy followed by British India. See the case of Sikkim. In 1861, it was after repudiating her Tibetan tutelage, that Sikkim entrusted her foreign affairs with British India. For re-establishing her tutelage, Tibet made several attacks on Sikkim, but at last in 1888 Lord Dufferin expelled the Tibetans by force, and the British protectorate on Sikkim was re-affirmed.

114) Historic that during the 19th century, the Manchu empire was on the decline, and this drift and decline did not stop until 1911-12, when the Qing empire abdicated. Since the middle of the 19th century, Manchu China was in ferment, and the nemesis was the revolution of 1911-12, overthrowing the monarchy. The fall of the emperor caused a sudden vacuum in Chinese power in Tibet also. The Sino-Japanese war, which ended in the defeat of China in 1895, was the watershed, enabling Tibet to emerge free and independent with Dalai Lama and the Tibetans loudly pronouncing Tibetan independence. This Tibetan claim was challenged by the Qings by arms many times, and the final attempt was in 1909, but that attack had to be abandoned midway, as the Qing empire collapsed all on a sudden. In 1904, came to the view that the Chinese power to resist Russia was no more there, and therefore the security of India has to be reassessed. Russia, which was 2000 miles away, came as near as 20 miles from the Tibetan border. This policy-change led to the Young Husband military expedition. The expedition was bitterly fought by the forces of Dalai Lama, and some reports say that in the encounter, nearly 2000 Tibetan troops were killed and not the 600 officially reported. Fearing the arrival of the Young Husband military mission, the 13th Dalai Lama fled to Mongolia. Through this expedition, Young Husband secured several trading rights, and privileges. The expedition imposed a war, indemnity also on Tibet, which was paid by China, through Tibetan officials. The plea for a British protectorate over Tibet was vetoed by the White Hall, and thus Free India lost the vast territory of Tibet because of the White Hall, but in spite of . How better it would have been for the Tibetans to have changed into a protectorate of British India, and then become part of free India, is now wishful thinking.

115) Government of India called the Simla Convention in 1913. Already China had changed into a republic in 1912. Frequently disputes were arising between China and Tibet on the question of boundary, and on the suzerainty claim. The declaration of Tibetan independence in 1912 gave rise to new tensions between Tibet and China, and one major issue was the border between Tibet and China. Regular clashes were occurring between Tibetan rebels and Chinese troops particularly in the Amdo and Khan regions. The Simla Convention was called by British India primarily to discuss the border between China and Tibet and to settle the question of China's suzerainty over Tibet. The British wanted to recognise China's suzerainty, whereas Tibet, since 1909, wanted to repudiate it once for ever. The McMahon Line was not a subject then controversial and in negotiation the Line was accepted by the three sovereign nations. But at the last stage China refused to sign the convention due to differences about the boundary between Outer Tibet and Inner Tibet. In the conference, the deliberations went on for one and a half years. The major issue certainly was the question of Chinese suzerainty over Tibet, followed by claims on the areas and boundaries of Inner Tibet and Outer Tibet. Outer Tibet was set as absolutely autonomous where the writ of Dalai Lama alone shall run. In the final stages, the deliberations went into dead lock and that was because of China's sudden change of policy. Tibet was represented by Lochen Shatra, China by Ivan Chen and India by Sir Arthur Henry McMahon. McMahon was Secretary in India's Foreign Office, and considered an expert in survey and boundary fixing. Earlier, he had served as member of the boundary commission demarcating the Durand Line in the North West Frontier area, and the job was expediently executed by the team. Under his direction the boundary line between India and Tibet was surveyed, which line now known after him as the McMahon Line. In the map, the red line showing the boundary line was drawn by a thick nib, and so the line itself, by the scale of the map, would cover a width of 8 miles, and therefore adjustable and recognizable by clear, geographic features. In the conference, neither the Chinese delegate nor the Tibetan representative expressed any serious objection regarding the correctness of the line. The map was prepared by the Army Survey Corps, who undertook spot-verification of the topographic, ethnic and tribal features of the area around the line. The recent Chinese challenge that the line is vague, unclear and imaginary appears wrong and deliberate as it is not the product of the arm-chair imagination of some Indian bureaucrat.

116) About the Simla Convention, the Chinese government, after 1957, has been blowing hot and cold on different occasions. Chau En Lai, several times would approve the Convention, but after 1959, he found it convenient to question the McMahon Line also, in order to suit his arguments on China's aggressive plans. The fantastic theory he invented was that this line was the impost of British imperialism. If so pleaded, can't every issue be challenged as the product of British imperialism including Indian independence and that India recognizing Communist China? This new argument of Chau was the fore runner of the 1962 invasion. At the same time, the pro-China British scholars like Alistair Lamb and Maxwell were advancing technical pleas to support the case of Communist China. What these scholars consistently fail to emphasise are the turning points in history since 1895, when the Chinese power over Tibet suddenly vanished, Tibet turned an independent state. If she was not independent, what made it possible for her to maintain neutrality during World War II, against the wishes of China, and against the most powerful Allies? In 1949, when China was about to invade Tibet, New Delhi restarted arms supply to Tibet. How can India supply arms to Tibet if Tibet had been a part of China? As Lord said, China's suzerainty over Tibet had been a vague constitutional fiction. When the Chinese army massed on the banks of Yang Tse on its way to Tibet, Britain and the United States came ready to supply arms to Tibet. But it was Nehru—the biggest victim of Chinese invasion, who cold-shouldered the idea and left Tibet to the mercy of the Chinese predator. K.M. Panikkar, during his first tenure as ambassador (when he was still an anti-communist patriot) had reported to New Delhi that in case the communists win the Chinese Civil War, there exists the dire possibility of the communist invading Tibet. He suggests that to prevent that tragedy, the Tibetan are going to declare their independence and he urged Nehru that in that contingency India should recognise Tibetan independence, and America and Britain will follow suit. He advises that India may support Tibetan membership in the United Nations also. In 1948, Nehru was favourable to the policy of Panikkar, but thereafter he began to vacillate, and then dither and then execute a full retreat. Except the vague shadow of Chinese suzerainty, Tibet was an independent country in 1950. After the capture of power by Mao in 1949, India was the first free country outside the communist block to give recognition to Red-China over the objection of the Iron Man of India—Sardar Vallabhbhai Patel. As discussed in another place it was the American opposition that prevented other foreign powers from colonizing China during the 19th century. In the face of US opposition, countries like Russia and Britain did not have a free hand to invade China. At the same time, Britain and others were fearing a Russian take over of Tibet, and that was the difference between British India and Free India. The world then considered Tibet an independent country and not as part of China, and therefore Great Britain and Russia were treating Tibet the independent state. Historic that after the fall of the Manchus in 1912, the 300-year old Chinese garrison stationed in Lhasa was evacuated through Calcutta. Thereafter the Chinese nationals and soldiers found in different parts of Tibet were either decimated or forcibly expelled. After the Young Husband mission came in 1909 the armed invasion by China to restore her authority again but that attempt also failed, because of the general anarchy prevailing in China due to the abrupt fall of the Last Emperor. Tibet participated in the Simla Convention as the political equal of China, and not as China's vassal or lackey. Communist China's latest plea that Tibet, without the permission of China, had no right to sign the Simla Convention on her own, is a plea against the ground realities existing in Tibet between 1895 and 1914. True, in the beginning China was reluctant to sit with Tibet, but the former too had her special rights and privileges to be protected through Simla. Why did China participate in Simla with Tibet sitting along with as her equal? China could have easily objected and kept off. But it was very much in the interests of China to participate in Simla, as she herself wanted to restore at least a semblance of (Chinese) authority over Tibet, after her complete loss of face in the plateau after 1895. That British India favoured these Chinese claims, and that the Chinese delegate depended much on English goodwill during negotiations, is to be restated. But in any case, the Tibetan delegate would not concede the Chinese demand, even after several weeks of negotiations between Lonchan Shatra and Ivan Chen, closetted together. Regarding the other clauses in the convention, the three parties agreed, and the point of clear consensus was the McMahon Line. What urged the Chinese plenipotentiary to boycott the conference finally was the new instruction from Peking that the First World War was about to start in Europe, and China too was moving to join Britain and Russia, and therefore the British interests in the convention would vapour off immediately. Ivan Chen's reading came true. The First World War broke out in Europe, and the Simla Agreement had to be kept in cold storage until the thirties. Government of India did not even publish the accord until 1934, when Olaf Caroe, an Under Secretary in India's foreign department, advised the British Foreign Office to publish it to the knowledge of the world. In 1937, the Survey of India also published the map showing McMahon Line as the boundary between India and Tibet. Though Tawang lies south of the Line, that place was not physically occupied by India till 1951, when India established control over the town. Important to note that as per tribal culture the Monpas of Tawang are a race distinct from the Tibetans. True, the present Dalai Lama also was raising claim over Tawang, and it is only recently he gave it up. In the map, the McMahon Line extends up to the edge of the Tibetan plateau. In the 1930s' also, the British Foreign Office was pressing China to sign the Simla accord, but as usual the latter shied away again. The British wanted China—her war-ally to re-establish suzerainty over Tibet, but China will secure it only after she signing the convention which she did not do hitherto. Kuomintang China also, due to domestic pulls and pressures refused to sign, and that fundamental default even now continues. During the Second World War, Chiang Kai Shek raising this suzerainty claim before Churchill and Roosevelt in the Washington Council Committee of 1943 has already been adverted to.

117) About the Simla Convention, controversies and political myths are making their rounds, engaging endless public debate, and on this account a lot of Chinese puzzles and disclaimers were also traded off. The Chinese representative took part in the once and a half year-long deliberations, but he, taking advantage of the impending First World War, refused to sign, though agreeing on other vital points except the boundaries of Outer Tibet and Inner Tibet. It was only reluctantly and under British pressure that Tibet was brought around to admit Chinese suzerainty. India will remember that in the convention, the McMahon Line was not the point of controversy. The written convention was initialled by Tibet and India, and at the last moment China abstained. The Tibetan plenipotentiary signed it, instead of initialing it, because initialing was not in the Tibetan practice. Below the initials of the Tibetan delegate, the British delegate certified (by signature) that instead of initialling, Tibet chose to sign. When three parties negotiate, and only two of them sign, the agreement is assumed to bind only the two signatories, who in this case are India and Tibet. According to the rule of the

League of Nations, and later of the United Nations, the Chinese argument that the agreement is void in the absence of the full signature of parties, appears wrong. In fact, in 1914, Tibet was a sovereign independent state, and so the agreement between two sovereign states—India and Tibet shall absolutely bind the two signatories. At the same time, China will get any right to question the Simla agreement only as successor (by conquest) to Tibetan power, and she claims title through aggression. According to international law, armed aggression in any case is illegitimate, but law or no law, aggression establishes its own law—the law of the jungle. Going to the question of the law of initials and signatures in international relations, the League of Nations rules make it clear that initials of parties are as good as signatures. Ignoring these rules and precedents established by the League, the pro-China English historians Maxwell and Alistair Lamb, are questioning the initials in the agreement as legally bad, and on that reason they term the document void. When three parties are deliberating, it is the fact and the result of deliberation which are more important than the signatures placed on paper. Communist China wants to question the McMahon Line one way or other, only because she committed aggression, tresspassing over the line. Kuomintang China also was concerned about establishing suzerainty over Tibet. If China does not accept the Simla Convention, thereby she may forfeit all claims over Tibet, including the claim of suzerainty. In 1950, she came Tibet, to the McMahon Line and beyond, through conquest, and she blasts these arguments of law and history by the argument of guns.

118) As cited earlier, Chau En Lai, in several meetings before 1959, had accepted the McMahon Line as valid and effective. Regarding a legal document, one cannot blow hot and cold at the same time, and that is law's basic fundamental including international law. After the flight of Dalai Lama to India in 1959, the Khampa Revolt and China's notorious crackdown of the same, the Chinese attitude towards India began to harden dramatically. Sinologists contend that China came to believe that the Khampa Revolt was India—sponsored, abetted and aided, and therefore in retaliation she wanted to teach India a lesson.

But circumstances speak that China was hunting for an excuse to humiliate India and particularly Nehru and Mao was specific about making the strike. While a wounded and humiliated India was again condescending to condone and collaborate in the latter's bloody rape of Tibet, it was worse tragedy that a betrayed India, through the 1954 treaty, was again succumbing to endorse China's over—lordship over Tibet. Nehru will not stop there. He will surrender India's special rights in the plateau, secured through the Young Husband expedition and the Simla Convention. Having completed and consummated the conquest of Tibet, China demanded the elimination of Indian presence on Tibetan soil, and Nehru was only ready to capitulate before any outrageous demand. For what gain he did do so again? Why was he fearing China so apologetically? It may be a fact that any Indian presence in Tibet after 1950 would have been a hindrance and embarrassment to China planning to commit crimes against humanity upon the unarmed, monastic lamas. India's special rights, in addition to various trading rights, included postage infrastructure, telegraph lines, guest houses, the right to station a garrison in Lhasa and many more. This second surrender in 1954 also was executed only to restore the goodwill of the betraying and aggressive dragon and the Mao's goodwill was coming back in 1962 in the shape of naked, unprovoked aggression. When the dragon found Nehru too soft to be taken for the free ride, she wanted a pretext for aggression, and the pretext she invented was to question the legitimacy of the long accepted McMahon Line. After 1949 all the outrageous demands and ultimata by China were unconditionally accepted by Nehru one by one and this was simply to satisfy China's expansionist voracity. The world saw Chau En Lai taking the poor Nehru for a ride. After 1914, all diplomatic, trade, and strategic transactions between India and Tibet were carried on, in accordance with the terms of the Simla Convention. Internationally the convention was a settled fact among the three countries, though China was not a signatory on paper. During the Second World War, Tibet stood 'neutral' between the Axis and the Allies. More emphatically this neutrality points to the fact that, during world war years, Tibet remained an independent state, and Chinese suzerainty as termed by Lord remained a constitutional fiction. Today all these (legal) arguments smash on the rock of China's conquest. After conquering Tibet, China conquered parts of India also and why? Because she, more than her military might, owns the will for risk taking and adventure. In the battlefield, adventure often acts more decisive than guns. Against an armed conqueror, the arguments of law are as fragile and funny as the arguments of the lamb before the wolf in the folklore. In the present circumstances, if the Tibetan diaspora wants to re-take Tibet, they have to re-conquer it by arms but an impossible task by any accounts. If India wants to get back Aksai Chin, the only way is to re-capture it through force, as all diplomatic moves and negotiation-dramas during the last half-century has been wasteful. If India cannot do it by arms, let her call off these farcical, humiliating negotiations.

119) Now it is generally accepted that the Khampa Revolt of 1958-59 was CIA sponsored, but as it has been the usual policy of post-War America to make such sponsorships half-hearted and hesitant, the revolt was destined to end in mass tragedy. It was put down by China, killing tens of thousands of Tibetan patriots and soldiers. From Nehru's performance in Kashmir, China could read that here is a leftist sympathizer, and communist apologist whom China can mould between her fingers like a ball of clay. If the Khampa Revolt had been India-sponsored and armed, certainly that campaign would not have ended in summary suppression. India could have easily sent arms and supplies to the beleaguered Khampas through land-routes speedily and in large quantities. It was a time when China's military power and infrastructure in Tibet was poor, primitive, and sparse. In fact, it was India's non-cooperation with the CIA and her merciless abandonment of the Khampas that caused the revolt to fizzle out mid-way, and end in an unmixed tragedy. The Chinese knew well that Nehru was incapable of war or guerilla war, and when he was found unready to wage even a defensive war for his native territory Kashmir, his poor fighting mettle stood tested by the dragon. But India's China apologists and partisans make the charge that Nehru giving asylum to Dalai Lama was the cause provoking China to attack in 1962. If that was the cause, what was the cause provoking China to conquer Tibet in 1950 and Aksai Chin in 1954-57? This is adding insult to injury. Nehru, who should have challenged China through armed defence of Tibet and Dalai Lama, is accused of making silly provocations and childish irritatants. After Kashmir, the enemy saw in him the poor man and 1962 she struck India, and she went home with absolute impunity. The misfortune of patriotic India, is that this defeatist tradition is very much entrenched in her national psyche, though she is on economic takeoff.

120) Large country sides, many cities and Treaty Ports in China were occupied by Japan between 1931 and 1938, and it is claimed that 80 per cent of Chinese Railways and 170 million Chinese came under Japanese occupation between 1931 and 1945. Chiang Kai Shek had to shift his capital three times. From Nanjing he had to go to Wuhan and then to the interior city of Chunking in 1937. But in 1945, when Japan was defeated in the world war, all these places and territories were returned to Kuomintang China by the Allies, as if on a platter. The Treaty Ports, provinces and beachheads occupied by other Western powers like Germany, Britain, The United States and France were also returned during 1945 or earlier. For economic reasons China was allowing the leases of Hong Kong and Macao to continue to run its full lease period. The Middle Kingdom had territorial disputes with Tsarist Russia involving large territories. In 1946, Chiang Kai Shek, by ceding many cities, ports, land areas and a number of rail roads in Manchuria, settled a large part of Sino-Russian dispute with Stalin, but the sparrings about on the Ussuri, Amur Basin, etc. remained (These disputes were settled by Vladimir Putin and Wen Jiabo in 2005, dramatically ending the centuries old border row).

121) China had a complex border problem with Burma (Myanmar), but that also has been resolved, by offering generous terms to the friendly Myanmar junta. China's border problem with Pakistan also was settled, with Pakistan ceding about 5200 sq. km. of (Indian) territory in Pakistan Occupied Kashmir (POK), allowing China, safe passage through the Karakoram Highway. The Pak job in this case was easy, as she was robbing

India of so much of land under her illegal occupation. Even after settling these disputes with the other neighbours, China continues to adopt a different and defiant stand against India. Sinologists point out that this is because of China feeling totally insecure about her claim over the expansive Tibetan territory, permanently besieged by the suzerainty controversy and the accelerating Tibetan revolts and protests for liberation from the Chinese yoke. Presently the mass self-immolations by rebellious lamas seeking independence opens a new harakiri war front against China. The Tibetan Torch Revolt of 2008, and the Tibetan diaspora electing their prime minister in exile in 2011, adds to the Chinese worries. Incidentally, it is important to note that after the Simla agreement also, the long-claimed Chinese suzerainty remained illusory in real practice. But China's luck and high advantage was that till 1962 Nehru could not be convinced that Red-China is India's treacherous foe.

122) Again critics ask why Nehru, while negotiating the 1954 Agreement, did not insist on China accepting the McMahon Line as the boundary? This is a wrong plea. That Nehru was accepting all the voracious and imperial demands of China is true, but how can he or any other ruler will guard against the treacherous designs and demands the enemy is going to invent in future? The McMahon Line remained the non-controversial border line for long, and that being the case, how Nehru himself need kick up controversy on a non-controversial issue? China dared to question the authenticity of the Line only after she found in Nehru the pliant horse, to be taken for rough ride any time any long. The McMahon Line being internationally accepted, there was no necessity to include it in the 1954 Agreement. Communist China, by challenging the line, was once again battering the dreamer in Nehru. The real trouble was that the weakness of Nehru was that Communist China was his weakness. Immediately after the communist takeover of China, the Chinese Vice Premier met the Indian Ambassador. K.M. Panikkar (reappointed to Beijing for a second term) and placed before him China's new imperial scheme deceptively named "peaceful liberation" of Tibet. Panikkar in Nanking in 1948 was the ardent Indian patriot, but Panikkar in Beijing in 1950 turned a Chinese partisan speaking against India. Diplomatic experts assign different reasons for this overnight conversion of Panikkar as the clandestine China apologist and admirer in 1950. Many will accuse that by 1950 Panikkar's daughter Devaki Panikkar has become part of India's Communist intelligentsia. Devaki Panikkar in 1952 married M.N. Govindan Nair a Communist Party of India top brass. Was this courtship and marriage the reason for the chameleonic change in Panikkar's political philosophy? When the State Reorganization Commission Report was submitted in 1955 there was the flurry of political gossip in Kerala that Panikkar (a member of the SR Commission) was instrumental in ceding the Congress—strong hold of Kanyakumari district in the then Travancore Cochin State to the Madras state (now Tamil Nadu) so that the political party of M.N. Govindan Nair may come to power in Kerala earlier than normally possible. Exactly this happened in the 1957 general elections. I can say that with Kanyakumari district in Kerala, the Communists would not have come to power in Kerala at least for were more decade. Some other Panikkar baiters and bashers argue that the Communist regime in Beijing treated Panikkar lordly through lavish dinners and pep talk and converted him to Marxism overnight. Closer people say Panikkar has been heavily bribed by Beijing, as bribing and influencing foreign statesman and diplomats is a Chinese way of life right from the days of the Qing empire. Of course China is not alone in this dubious game. To the Vienna Congress of 1815, the French delegation included the famous French beauty Madame De Camier—whose duty was to wrest out favours from the Russian Tsar, and historians record that she was abundantly successful in her mission. She returned to France a heroine.

123) Poor Tibetans! If they pick up the names of the betrayers of Buddhist Tibet, certainly Nehru, Panikkar, Krishna Menon and B.N. Rau will top the list. Or, if Panikkar and Menon advised Nehru to go to war against China in defence of Tibet, was this advice having any chance of being accepted by Nehru will reject any advice to fight as he was always afraid of the battlefield. There were thousands of patriots in India ready to advise Nehru to fight China, but they will not over gain admission to his courtyard Panikkar knew Nehru well and knew what the latter wants and from Peking he notified New Delhi that the Chinese plan (for liberation of Tibet) need not be opposed, as their intentions appeared honest, harmless and peaceful. The fact that Nehru—the democrat, was one of the ardent supporters, spokes persons and admirers of the totalitarian takeover of China, played the fatal role in shaping free India's China policy and he got the advice from Panikkar which the former was very much desiring to get. To be loudly remembered that India's national interest and security are ultimately the responsibility of the prime minister and not his bureaucratic advisors. As the elected leader of the Indian masses, how Nehru missed and neglected the fact that Tibet stood the buffer between India and China for ages? An alert and responsible Nehru ought to have dismissed Panikkar from the job at once and sent armed forces to Tibet to resist China. But instead Panikkar, got a pat from Nehru, for this treasonable advice. The two were joining hands to throw the Tibetan lamb to the Chinese dragon to tear off. If the Nehru retreat was an unmixed tragedy for Tibet, it was strategic disaster for India. By 1959, the agency reports estimate that 86000 Tibetan freedom fighters were slaughtered by the Peoples' Liberation Army point blank, and abominable that this massacre of the innocents was condoned by Nehru the most idealistic democrat and anti-colonialist in the world. Nehru sought refuge in the arguments of the Indian left who pleaded treason.

124) In April 1959, Dalai Lama fled to India and India granted him asylum. Along with him, more than two hundred thousand Tibetan refugees also fled Tibet to escape mass slaughter, and they are now dispersed across the world. Such betraying and murderous conduct is nothing unusual in communist practice, but Nehru after 1962, would call it a case of total betrayal by a fraternal China. Unable to read into the diabolic designs of the Communist dragon, he felt shocked and agonized when China, in the name of liberation, was committing the rape of Tibet, destroying the pastoral, saintly civilization of a thousand years. Instead of fighting to defeat this ghastly crime, Nehru was meekly acquiescing in a strange conduct by the ruler of a country. Was not this Nehru zeal to appease the dragon worse than Chamberlain's notorious entreaties before Adolf Hitler in Munich?

125) K.M. Panikkar, the royalist, aristocrat, and conservative was turning a communist overnight in his second innings in China. In 1948, Panikkar was accused of writing poetry in his embassy residence, unaware of the violence and tumult of the civil war, raging outside finally calling the communists storm into power in Peking in October 1949. While Nehru wanted to play down and camaflouge the Chinese rape of Tibet, the Indian parliament was going into turmoil. Members were challenging the dubious role Panikkar played in misleading Nehru. After the communist takeover of China in 1949, many unfortunate events overtook India's foreign policy which mostly were self-inflicted wounds. Nehru led by his communist advisers V.K. Krishna Menon and K.M. Panikkar caused these wounds permanently disabling India. Strange coincidence that both Menon and Panikkar hailed from the communist dominated state of Kerala. Critics of the soft and cringing Nehru policy would put the blame for our failure in Tibet on these two confidants of Nehru. Krishna Menon was a well-known communist and a shameless spokesman and defender of communists imperialism. For him the Chinese invasion of Tibet was socialist invasion. Well-known that whenever Krishna Menon contested for parliament from Bombay under Congress ticket, communist stalwarts like Dange, A.K. Gopalan, Ajoy Khosh, EMS, M.N. Govindan Nair and others would descend in Bombay for his election work. Though found in the wrong political company, still Nehru was very much pleased of the Menon misconduct of disarming and purging India's armed forces to the point of impotency and this was done before the 1962—India-China war. But K.M. Panikkar's background was different. He was a conservative statesman serving India in different capacities. He was a historian and poet, and the chief executive of many Indian princes. He was a member of the Indian delegation to the United Nations and he was a member in India's Constituent Assembly. He owns his rise in free India was as a Nehru pick and favourite. In 1948, he was appointed ambassador to Nationalist

China, and he was called back when the Kuomintang regime collapsed in October 1949. Again he was appointed ambassador to Communist China in May 1950 and presented his credentials to Chairman Mao in Beijing (With the communists coming to power, the capital of China was again shifted from Nanking to Beijing). For Panikkar this was rare recognition that after a revolution and change of regime, he was reappointed to the same diplomatic post in the same country which was unusual in world diplomatic practice. Mysterious and surprising that Panikkar will undergo a revolutionary conversion into the communist philosophy after May 1950. What was the reason for this change that would convert him overnight into a spokesman and defender of Chinese imperialism? In 1948, he was unduly worried about the possible loss of the Tibetan buffer to India but in 1950, he showed no qualms in turning the political assassin of the peace-loving, monastic. After one and a half years he was ready to eat his own words? Most Tibetans did not know who the real assassin was. The political surprise was that the more anti-Indian and pro-China he became, the more closer he became to Jawaharlal Nehru—the Indian Prime Minister and foreign minister. Why did Nehru go against India's vital national interests and went along with the anti-Indian lobby headed by Panikkar and Krishna Menon? Many reasons are cited but the real fact was that Nehru was not a fighter and in military strategy he was a stranger. He wanted to covers up this inability and incapacity as a man of peace and an anti-warrist. He pooh-poohed able generals and overruled and snubbed military chiefs who were warning him against the impending threat from China. At the same time, he maintained top vigil against the imaginary threats from the west. He will call a devil an angel and that was his failure. Always he embraced the defeatists who will advice him not to go to war. But very intriguing that none surpassed his patriotism, and its moment was when he appealed for Anglo-American military help in 1962, and detained all the leading communists imprison.

126) The correspondence of Panikkar from Nanking (while ambassador to KMT China) will show that his views were realistic and patriotic raising serious concern about Indian security in the event of China falling to the communists. He told New Delhi that Tibet, after 1912, had been enjoying defacto independence and if the Kuomintang administration collapses, it is likely that Tibet will declare their independence. In that event, the Tibetan Government in Lhasa would desire to get the immediate recognition of countries like India, Britain and the United States for the new status. But Nehru himself warned Tibet against going forward with such declaration. He told Lhasa that such a move would provoke China further and the Tibetans dithered only for want of India's support, and their declaration of independence was postponed. When the Tibetans expelled the Chinese in Lhasa in August 1949, just before the communist takeover of Beijing, Nehru intervened to caution them and he himself intervened later to smoothen it out. As many commentators point out, the main responsibility for the Chinese conquest of Tibet was on Nehru but he bungled at as the Kashmir problem had been compounded by taking it to the United Nations on Mountbatten's advice and against the advice of his right hand man and cabinet colleague—Sardar Vallabhbhai Patel, the Indian Bismarck integrating the princely states of India into the Indian Union.

127) Why did Nehru appoint K.M. Panikkar for a second time in China when such practice was unprecedented. It was evident that Nehru liked Panikkar's anti-Indian counsels, which allowed the former to act the man of peace ignoring the country's security. Panikkar had not been a communist prior to 1950 as Krishna Menon had been, but only after May 1950, Panikkar was a new man. Ignoring the Nehru instruction that India accepts (Communist) China's 'suzerainty' over Tibet, Panikkar wrote to the Chinese foreign ministry that India accepts China's "sovereignty" over Tibet—a treasonable breach in favour of China. China being newly 'sovereign' over Tibet, she can make a legal invasion of the land of the lamas through the good offices of Panikkar. In 1948, Panikkar was anxious that only by recognizing the independence of Tibet by the United States, India and Britain, the Chinese communists can be kept away from the Indian border. But after becoming the new ambassador of Red-China in May 1950, he will turn suddenly red, showering praise on China's crimes against humanity and her rape of Tibet and Singiang. Suzerainty is a vague, uncertain term whereas 'sovereignty' has imperial, overlording sound bites. How did Panikkar muster courage to change the word 'suzerainty' into 'sovereignty' against the clear instructions of his prime minister? He was confident he can find excuses before a credulous pro-China Nehru even after committing treason. Later a high official in the Indian embassy in Beijing would confirm that this treasonable word-change had been deliberately made by Panikkar himself against the advice of his officials. Think about the fate of the Chinese ambassador in New Delhi saying that China is merely 'suzerain' and not 'sovereign' over Tibet? He will immediately be dismissed and court-martialled. With the credulous Nehru, Panikkar—the Nehru protégé and favourite can play any game and he knew it. This was fantastic conversion for Panikkar belonging to a landlord family in Kuttanad who all along was a political conservative. Hereafter many diplomats would call Panikkar not as 'ambassador to China', but as "ambassador for China". Nehru simply looked on for two more months before the message was hesitantly and fearfully corrected into 'suzerain' but the damage is done. It was a different matter that the CCP had already taken the decision to invade Tibet and the plan and scheme have already been laid, provided there was no military intervention by India or the west. China knew that Nehru's India will only stand down militarily and in any case Peking had nothing to fear from a Nehru, perpetually afflicted by war-fear.

128) When Chinese troops were massing in Eastern Amdo to march towards Lhasa in 1950, Panikkar sent message to New Delhi that there is scant evidence regarding the presence of PLA troops in Tibet, and an Indian protest at this juncture would jeoparadice the Indian efforts to get Communist China admitted to the United Nations. Very strange that when China was conquering Tibet killing thousands of lamas and freedom fighters and destroying monasteries, Nehru was strutting across the globe to get China admitted into the world body of peace. On Tibet, the United States wanted to follow the lead of India in providing arms aid to the Tibetan fighters, but India the main security victim of the Chinese rape of Tibet, again advised America not to do anything against the threatened Chinese invasion. Even Chamberlain will not commit this blunder of fawning before the openly betraying foe. When Chinese troops were committing massive crimes in Tibet, Panikkar was inventing excuses and justification for these crimes which prompted Sardar Patel to complain that Panikkar has undergone conversion as the spokesman of communist imperialism in Asia. Again Nehru will ignore Patel and encourage the Chinese spies and partisans inhabiting his court. What is the reason for Panikkar's overnight conversion? Many in India believed that Panikkar had been lavishly treated and heavily bribed by Communist China and they bought him off. India was the first country outside the communist block to accord recognition to Red-China. Reports say the Chinese top brass received Panikkar with pomp and hospitality and he was over whelmed. Panikkar in Peking changed into a Chinese commodity, and that was real. The Indian public will never know the truth of these allegations, but it is logical to speculate this way, when a patriot, without reason, suddenly turns against his own country, and that too eating his own past words.

129) It was the fuss and talk in New Delhi that during 1949-52 the Indian policy towards China was decided by two persons—V.K. Krishna Menon and K.M. Panikkar. The majority of Congress leaders, state chief ministers, and union ministers opposed Nehru's pro-China moves, but he being the unquestioned leader and political supremo, who will dare speak against him? To oppose Nehru point blank would have been political suicide for any Congress man. The famous diplomat and Foreign Secretary General Girija Sanker Bajpai wanted to oppose China and supply arms and money to Tibet but this advice was spurned by Nehru. When things of national importance are being debated, a prime minister takes into confidence his senior political colleagues and top leaders of the country, and not his cronies, and courtiers. The job of the bureaucrat is to help implement the leaders' instructions. A diplomat, as Oscar Wild said, is a person who remembers a woman birthday, but forgets her age. The great visionary and the iron man of India—Sardar

Patel advises—and Nehru ignores, his foreign ministry advises—Nehru ignores, a famous diplomat like G.S. Bajpai advises, Nehru ignores. The whole parliament, except the communists, are on their legs denouncing Red-China and calling for military intervention in Tibet, but Nehru ignores. In 1950, Mahatma Gandhi was no more there to stop Nehru; Patel tried to stop him, but in vain and if at all Patel could do anything, he will be dead in the next month (December) after sending the long letter of warning to Nehru about the new China who is chauvinistic and imperial. Patel was gone, and after December 1950, Nehru was absolutely free to run amuck into his world of illusions and dreams. He was surrounded by droves of sycophantic spies who swarmed around to exploit things to their own advantage.

130) Though not so badly similar, there arise the vaulting question why the American President Truman heeded the advice of the defeatists and weaklings like George C. Marshall and Dean Acheson and threw the Kuomintang and Chiang Kai Shek to the communists? The fact was that Truman was not ready for the adventurous programme of direct intervention in the Chinese Civil War. He wanted to mediate between the treacherous Communists and the corrupt and invalid Kuomintang, and at last he will find fault with his ward the Kuomintang, and this was the Truman excuse to wash his hands. In any case, Truman bears little resemblance to the dreamy frailties of Nehru. As the leader of the Allies in the Second World War, Truman had no hesitation to bring Japan to heels by employing the apocalyptic destructive power of the atom bomb. After bringing Japan to heels, why was he going back in the Chinese Civil War and how the strong man has gone weak after 1945 in the mysterious post-war American puzzle. There come a bundle of theories, but Truman alone knew the real reason. He called the Kuomintang a bunch of thieves and rascals but was it good reason to abandon China to Communism when the United States was bound to defend the free world against communist imperialism. Was not the United States capable of defeating the Communist in the Civil War. On this question America was deeply divided. The Republican wanted to save the Kuomintang at any cost, but the Democrats remained vague and undecided. When a nation is deeply divided

on the question of war, certainly defeat will be the result and in China it was Truman and not Chiang Kai Shek who was really defeated. Still Harry S. Truman daring to employ the atom bomb against Japan deserves no comparison with Nehru, the perennial non-fighter and peacenik. Strategists are unanimous that Nehru could have easily stopped the Chinese invasion of Tibet by employing Indian military. Communist China had just come out of the Civil War and her hold on the mainland itself was loose, shaky and thoroughly unorganised. Chiang was to be unleashed on the mainland, if Truman cared for the advice of MacArthur. Was it incidental or purposeful that the invasion of Tibet and the entry of China into the Korean War occurred simultaneously? China was wise enough to fore see the future of her present adventure. PLA had a large number of soldiers in Tibet but being ill equipped, they feared an Indian entry in Tibet. In 1950, the Indian army as party to the victory of the Allies in 1945 was waxing under that glory, and its equipment and man power were sufficient to check China. If not sufficient the free world was really to help in a big way. The Krishna Menon purge and disorganization of the armed forces were a decade away. The democratic world was full of sympathy with the fate of the people of the monastic Tibet, who fought with their blood. Had India ventured to support the Tibetan resistance, America, standing furious at Red-China and more because of her callous entry into the Korean War, would have liberally supported the campaign with arms and money. India could have easily committed soldiers in Tibet, and while engaged in war in Tibet with American support and participation, Pakistan would not dare to make trouble in Kashmir. Strange to say that in 1950 Pakistan had no love lost with China, and Karachi came forward ready to intervene on the side of Tibet. But Nehru was the real obstacle as he was interested in picking up quarrels with the west, and particularly with the United States when they were well on retreat from their Afro-Asian colonies. When China was conquering Tibet to make it her new colony Nehru found it more urgent to fight Western imperialism. The country most threatened by the Chinese invasion of Tibet was India, and when India was found in silent collaboration with the Chinese project of digging India's grave in Tibet, the United States, Britain and Pakistan were absolutely taken aback. Sweeping the Chinese rape of Tibet under the carpet, Nehru was proceeding to Korea as the celebrated arbiter and peace angel. When Nehru abandoned the poor Tibetans to their dismal fate his tongue lashing about the dangers of the Korean War was rising to its crescendo. Through his throwing Tibet to its tragic fate, Nehru was suddenly losing the Afro-Asian acclaim as the defender of democracy and crusader against colonialism. The words of a ruler who never showed the capacity to fight armed battles attracts not even the weight of religious gospels. Unaware of his loss of recognition, Nehru was plunging into the Korean negotiations and China sympathized with the credulousness of her innocent rival. India saw the difference between Nehru and his protégé Shastri in the 1965 Indo-Pak War. In the war Shastri coolly called the bluff of the Chinese Helmsman Mao Tse Tung. Mao saw that this tiny Indian was determined to fight. Mao triumphed against Nehru, and America's Harry S. Truman. Again a tough question? Has Mao fought any big war after Korea? No. Has China succeeded in conquering South Korea? No, because it was costly and it was dangerous to push further. Mao's total victory was over the poor monastic Tibet and the undefended Muslim Singiang. In Korea, he was thoroughly mauled up and he lost millions of PLA troops as cannon folder. After Korea, what is the big military campaign under taken by China—Nothing. There are always careful not to lose.

131) Nehru went to numerous war theatres and for a plead the case of India's enemies. He went to Korea, he went to the Suez Canal, he went to the African and Asian anti-colonial wars, but did he send a single soldier to any of these battlefields? His high gallantry was India's UN peace-keeping missions. His wars were mere tongue lashings and nothing more and Mao Tse Tung and his super-diplomat Prime Minister Chau En Lai knew it. China conquered Tibet like knife cutting butter. How did Nehru continue anti-west, pro-China, and pro-Socialist even after the Chinese invasion of Tibet? Simply it was India's suicide march. The scriptural statement goes, "Vinase Kale Viparutha Budhi (At the time of ruin your mind decides against yourself)". Nehru

was a true patriot but never a strategist and warrior. He was philosopher preaching to the wild bull. The only patriotic move he made while in office was his call for American arms during the 1962 war, and that call became possible only after dismissing the pro-communist defence minister of India—Krishna Menon.

132) The Tibetans, cut off from the tumult and din of the outside world went into tizzy, when they knew Red-China was about to attack. In 1950, it was festival time in Tibet and monks and lamas were on celebrations and tours. Panikkar had clear information that China was going to invade Tibet immediately. When PLA troops poured into Ambdo, it was surprise in Tibet, though Lhasa had news that the Communist have the plan to invade. But once they got wind of the impending attack Tibetans and Lhasa swung into action, and preparations to resist the impending aggression went in full speed. The country very much to take the initiative for the armed defence of Tibet was India, and the Western countries were waiting for the Indian initiative in this respect. As already pointed out, China's military power in Tibet then was not quite enough to fight a full war with India. If Truman, during the Korean War had unleashed Chiang Kai Shek on the mainland, the PLA would have scattered across, but to accomplish this feat America had to make a direct intervention, if necessary with nuclear threat in America failed to do it. Interesting to remember that Stalin, during the Korean War was not ready to enter directly, but promised help only afterwards as he wanted to wait and see the course of the war. For Russia, Tibet had been a coveted prize lost by Tsarist Russia and Stalin was not happy with the Chinese invasion of Tibet. As demanded by the Tibetan authorities, India had supplied a large quality of arms and ammunition to Tibet in 1949, but refused to commit soldiers. Even if well armed, what can a small number of Tibetan soldiers do? When China began to move forward, Nehru moved backward and he continued his retreats from his original position one by one, and he was preparing to accept the Chinese conquest of Tibet as a fait accompli. Again to emphasize that, not being a fighter, whenever faced with the situation of a shooting war, he will invent excuses to avoid the battlefield. For beating the retreat he will turn to those advisers who will talk for the enemy and talk against war and battle. Nehru was the Prime Minister of India for 18 years, and after December 1950 (After Patel death), he was able to rule India as the democratic dictator. Then what failed him? He was afraid of war and he never fought a war to the end and much less to victory. During 1948, when the Pak Razakars trespassed into Kashmir, what stood in the way of India winning the war and recapturing the Pak occupied Kashmir? Russia and Nationalist China were not to interfere in Kashmir. Though driven to the wall by his anti-west utterances America and Britain did not want to enter Kashmir. Indian army was confident of throwing out the Razakars and they were fast doing that job. But Nehru, because of his personal jealousy, to Patel removed Kashmir from the Home Ministry and placed it under his foreign Ministry—already infiltrated by pacifists, anti-Indian intellectuals and communist spies Patel threatened to resign, but Gandhiji stopped him. Thereafter how many wars India fought with Pakistan because of Nehru stopping Indian army in 1948? All subsequent battles had to be fought only because of Nehru's Utopian thinking as the peace umpire of the world. But when compared with Tibet, Kashmir pales into in significance in India's security perspective. Nehru the ruler of India wanted to be the arbiter between India and the enemy, and what a strange fate for India. When arms begin to clash, Nehru will lose all nerves and he goes about seeking the advice of weaklings who will recommend only retreat and surrender which was his favourite theme. Then it would be ridiculous to say that Panikkar and Krishna Menon misled him. How did Nehru override the huge body of patriots who advised him to resist China by arms? A born non-fighter, he will reject any advice for gallantry. After Kashmir, he will surrender Tibet and this time the recipient was Red-China.

133) Himalayan Tibet stood through ages as the long and high fortress and buffer guarding India through ages. Even a colonist like wanted to keep Tibet the permanent buffer between India, Russia and China. Critics leveled a thousand charges against the non-patriotism and war-fear of Nehru, but these charges he ignored. After suffering defeat in the 1962 war, he was indiscreet enough to sit in power till his death in May

1964. Will any other country tolerate such abominable security risk except India? After defeat in war, which democratic leader whatever his popularity will sit in the seat of power after such ignominy? Thank about the fate of India if China did not order a unilateral ceasefire and withdrawal from Arunachal Pradesh? If China continued to proceed to the lower plains of Assam and Bengal let India fancy that nightmare! Menon and Panikkar acted against India, but the real culprit was Nehru. Assume these two advisers also recommended to fight China resolutely. Nehru would have bypassed them and gone for somebody else who will advise surrender. He repudiated and discarded the mass of patriotic demands and advices within India which a war leader alone can accept. Nehru was not a warrior much less a strategist, and that sealed the fate of Tibet as the case of Kashmir. The greater danger of Chinese Tibet is that it entirely jeopardized the security of free India. While fighting the imaginary enemy in the west, he was mauled from the back by the real enemy in the east.

134) War commentators contend that at the time of the Tibetan invasion, China had no big war machine or war infrastructure in Tibet. The Communist Party's hold on the mainland itself was loose and shaky, but China knew that Nehru pretended an anti-warrist because he feared war. He fought the Kashmir war in 1948 and unnecessarily surrendered 2/5 of Kashmir to Pakistan. When Tibet was going to be attacked by China in 1950, Nehru had no plan to resist it, though he knew it well in advance. India in 1950 could have easily stopped China militarily in Tibet. The Communist party's-power unconsolidated on the mainland, China was in hot waters in Korea. To open a new war front against China in Tibet a lethal arm supply from the United States was certain, as such diversion will certainly weaken China in Korea, but India was always arms shy. To forfeit the Tibetan buffer was suicidal for Indian security but Nehru's interest was in celebrative international conferences and meets to build his image as mediator between the democrats and the communists. While he was arbitrating anxiously between the United States and China in Korea, he ignored the poor Tibetans and by ignoring the Tibetan agony he was apparently and really going to the side of the aggressor. It is time that during the beginning stages of the invasion Nehru was deeply concerned about the breach of promise of China, but he was unable to think of any scheme to resist China. Strategists say it was eminently possible for India to stop China and with that stoppage India would have risen to the status of a big power honoured by the entire world. Who will care for a leader lying in the battlefield thrashed and lynched? As remarked by a journalist, with India stopping China in Tibet, she would have got the status of a world power and the threat of Pakistan would have disappeared from the radar. By surrendering Tibet, Nehru was establishing his impotency as a national leader. At the same time, he was appearing as a communist fellow traveller which angered the west, again and again. The Chinese rape of Tibet, reduced India into a third rate power cared by none. Nehru had only brand enemies. The west alone were his imperialists and for him the communists were merely socialists. Krishna Menon declared that a socialist country cannot go imperial. For their Nehru illusions and dreams, India had to pay the heavy prize of Aksai Chin and Arunachal, but the heaviest prize was paid by the defenceless people of Tibet. As a British newspaper commented, Nehru invited the Chinese soldier standing on the Sino-Tibetan border to the Indian border. The tragedy was that even after China's conquest of Tibet and the destruction of that civilization, Nehru was flitting from capital to capital arguing for the admission of China into the United Nations. Ignoring China's rape of Tibet, he will journey to Bandung to welcome that Chinese betrayer—Chau En Lai. Bandung was causing more international scorn and amusement than admiration Nehru continued to sing the song of India-China-Bhai-Bhai, and sinister tragedy that Nehru will not disclaim that hymn even after the back-stab of 1962, which devasted him mentally and physically. After the 1962 defeat, Nehru survived only for 18 more months. The poor man was betrayed by that Fox of Beijing—Chau En Lai.

135) Except that Mao could betray a gullible Nehru and conquer the unarmed, helpless Tibetans what are the strategic initiatives and achievements of Communist China? After 1949, has China entered any big war and won it? True she won the

Civil War because Tom Dewy failed to win the 1948 American presidency and Truman the retreatist returned to the White House with his defeatist team well in tact. In the Korean War, China was mauled up by MacArthur and she suffered heavily. Millions of PLA soldiers went off as cannon fodder for MacArthur and Ridgeway. An armistice was agreed to because of lackadaisical Eiesenhover whom Truman will call the president of surrender. China got the Vietnam War fought by her proxy North Vietnam, and the main assistance for North Vietnam came not from China, but from the Soviet Union. During the Bangladesh War, Mao threatened to intervene on the side of Pakistan, but Shastri who was not Nehru, boldly called the Mao bluff and Mao quietly backed out. Communist China has been more careful in assessing the enemy psychology than the enemy power. Acting a bully she achieved most of her aims, but when there is the prospect of a big war and long war she simply backs out. What did she gain from the Korea? She was pushed behind the 38th parallel, and South Korea reemerged to become a big economic and military power. Even now China's major military victories are the isolated, weak territories of Tibet and Singing—and in Tibet she escaped the block only because of the Indian philosopher king and pro-communist partisan—Pandit Nehru. Was not the India-China War of 1962 sabotaged by the communists infiltrating India's war room far in advance? What was the end of the Chinese invasion of Vietnam in 1979? After making a tempestuous entry, China pulled back. She seized Tibet when the world was focussed in Korea and she could subjugate it only because Nehru was a non-fighter. China's conquest of Tibet was less gallant than India conquering the Maldives. For centuries, China was the protector of Tibet, but in 1950, when the protector suddenly turned the assassin, Tibet could only succumb. It is no credit to her military power that she conquered these poor, weak nomadic territories. Why Mao did not intervene on the side of Pakistan in the 1965 war? He like Bismarck was a great strategist and he was a votary of the concept of gaining the maximum by fighting the minimum. Very often China is making good use by setting up North Korea against South Korea and the United States to play the ridiculous game of nuclear dance. The North is (April 2013) threatening nuclear war against the South—but without firing shots. North Korea bullies its neighbours to the brink but only to beat a retreat when the opponent is ready to respond. What Germany and Russia did in Poland, or Japan did against the Allies during the Second World War were total wars exercising its muscle and arms to the ultima. Communist China never waged a full war after the state came into being. After 1949, she did not face a full invasion by an enemy as Kuomintang China faced from Japan during the thirties and forties. Red-China's major testing grounds are the poor, rather monastic people of Tibet, the unprotected people of Singiang and Non-Aligned India. Certainly 21st century China is militarily big and economically and territorially huge, and she wants to maintain that power without that being wasted in risky, reckless adventures. India's foreign office opposed the Chinese move for liberation of Tibet as fully suspect, and it was through this "peaceful liberation" (of Tibet) that Nehru's disastrous love affair with Red-China was hitting the road-block. Not only that Nehru agreed for peaceful liberation, but urged the Tibetans also to go along the suicidal path, but the Tibetans could not be held back and they rose up in revolt. Unable to defend themselves, the Tibetan lamas looked to their benign neighbour India for rescue. But what they found to their horror was their defender and saviour joining hands with the assassin in grand conspiracy. What was the motive behind programme of 'liberation' by a totalitarian state, who condemned democracy and trampled over human rights? Nehru himself had asked from whom are the Chinese going to liberate Tibet, but doing nothing militarily to stop the outrage. Nehru was thinking how to save the Tibetans, but without any military action on his part. As quoted already, Patel said in 'Kalynga, Ahimsa should be met only by Ahimsa', Nehru was sacrificing national security by hiding behind the smokescreen of non-violence. He wanted to undo the Chinese invasion of Tibet through preachings and gospel and he will prevent the west also from taking any armed action against the Chinese conqueror. He will attempt to defend his inability through ideals, and step by step, he would leave the Tibetans to the sad fate. What was the reason? Nehru was a dreamer and not a fighter. Gandhiji never knew that Nehru was a China apologist and Marxian ideologue who will expose Indian freedom to be ravished by the dragon. Several times in the past Millennia China wanted to invade Tibet and failed every time. Now she succeeds because Nehru always decided against himself. Why did Nehru succumb to the false plea of liberation, when Tibet, after 1895, had become a fully independent state? Was not this concession the Nehru blank-chit to China to steamroll and decimate the Tibetan civilisation? China was achieving naked conquest through two misleading words "peaceful liberation". Nehru, looked upon by the world as the champion and defender of universal human liberation, was in this case acting as collaborator and accomplice of totalitarian terror and genocide. For the messiah of world peace, this was monstrous self-contradiction, but he will ignore that indictment. His demonstrated zeal to ride the revolutionary bandwagon of China turned out India's race towards political alienation and isolation from the democratic world. Unfortunate that during the Nehru rule there was no political force in India to restrain and pull him back from the bear-hug. After Gandhiji, Sardar Patel alone could apply brake on him, but Patel died in December 1950, leaving him absolutely free to start his unbridled sojourns into his policy fantasyland.

136) Well-known that for hundreds of years, Tibet was maintaining her theological dominion over China and Chinese emperors were honouring and respecting Dalai Lama as their spiritual guru. Often Dalai Lama travelled to Peking as China's chief priest. This Tibetan status is in sharp contrast with the Chinese plea that Tibet had been a province or colony of China. When China assumes that when she invaded Tibet, all previous treaties and conventions fell to the ground, and her argument of guns has put a full stop to all arguments of diplomacy and history. So thinks Beijing and correctly too. But even after committing armed invasion, China argues that her conquest is not conquest, and she cites the rules of international law to rename her conquest as liberation. When China argues her Tibetan case with the haughty, and blunt excuses of an aggressor, is there any use of the Tibetan agitators or India repeating their legal arguments before the dragon. Abraham Lincoln said 'when arms clash, the law falls to the ground', and so the Chinese argument runs.

137) As related above a unique historical aspect in Sino-Tibetan relations is Tibet maintaining her high priest status over China, and the Chinese emperors themselves showing their esteem and honour towards the spiritual eminence and religious paramountcy of Tibet and Dalai Lama. After the 16th century, Tibet had been a country not able to keep a large standing army of her own, and therefore when threatened by any foreign power, she was calling in Chinese forces and many times the Chinese emperors sent forces to drive away the invaders. It is history that before a thousand years, Tibet was a sprawling empire extending up to Central Asia and parts of China and she was an imperial giant threatening China also. The Tibetan empire declined and thereafter, and particularly after the Dalai Lamas became the religious and temporal head of Tibet, Lhasa was calling in Chinese troops for her defence. On some occasions the latter could not or did not send help. In the 21st century also, there are many countries having no powerful defence force of their own, and depending on bigger powers to ensure national security. Kuwait, though a rich country, has no powerful army of defence. There are many islands in the India Ocean, the Pacific and the Atlantic whose defence is the duty of their guardian allies. European gambling dens and tourist paradises like Monaco, San Marino, Liechensteine, etc. do not have their own defence forces, but they are neither the vassals nor colonies of the guardian allies. Vatican—the seat and home of the Roman Pontiff has no standing army to defend the highest seat of the Holy Sea. India, during the 1962 Sino-Indian war, called for American arms and troops, and that help came immediately. Will that call be reason to say that India has accepted American overlordship? The religious bonds between China and Tibet were unassailably deep and strong for hundreds of years. Ask the question who is supreme between the Pope and the Holy Roman Emperor? For centuries the Dalai Lama acted the chief priest of China.

138) Regarding the political status of modern Tibet, the recent turning point came through the political developments in China at the end of the 19th century, causing a new equation in Sino-Tibetan relations. During this period the British Empire in India was reaching its high point. London's trade relations with the closed door policy of China during the middle of the 19th century, was compelling British India to adopt conflicting postures in her Sino-Tibetan policy. During the second half of the 19th century, a closed China was suddenly opening to the world, and Britain, like many other Western powers, was becoming actively engaged in the development of trade with Peking, and large opportunities were unfolding both ways. These trade interests were constraining as well as conflicting with British India's general imperial policy on Tibet and this British dilemma would reach the crisis point during the Years. —the indomitable viceroy of India (1899-1905), apprehended that because of the decline of Manchu power, more particularly exposed through China's defeat in the Sino-Japanese war of 1894-95, Russia, (in league with the young Panchan Lama) was planning the invasion of Tibet, and he thought that if unchallenged, a Russian takeover of Tibet was imminent. This apprehension of British India, in the back-ground of the Russian advances into Central Asia and because of the impact of Indo-Afghan relations, resulted in sending the Young Husband military expedition to Lhasa in 1903. If the Viceroy had his way, he would have reduced Tibet into a British protectorate, but the White Hall was opposing the plan, because of London's apprehensions on how the move would impact on Britain's growing trade interest and the land leases like Hong Kong, which China had already granted to London. For the British Government, the development of trade with China was more important than the territory of Tibet, but this policy was to undergo a change under . The Young Husband mission, made successful only in part, resulted in the signing of the Indo-Tibetan Treaty of 1904, opening Tibet for Indian trade in a big way. The treaty was allowing India to appoint a trade agent at Gyantse, a town situate in the middle of the trade route between the Indian border and Lhasa. (This trade agent was later upgraded as Consul General of India, and shifted to

Lhasa.) Incidentally it needs mention that on hearing the news of the Young Husband military mission, the young Dalai Lama fled to Mongolia. He ran away fearing the military expedition, and left behind his regent and monks to deal with Young Husband. It was the intervention from London that prevented from taking over Tibet and make it part of the British Empire in India, and in this respect the ultimate loser shall be Free India.

139) The fall of the Manchus in 1912 shattered the Chinese authority over Tibet, and this turn is historic, opening a new era in Sino-Tibetan relations. The defeat of China in the 1894-95 Sino-Japanese war was the watershed, urging the world to look down upon the Manchus, and this defeat emboldened Tibetans to declare their independence, challenging the suzerain claim of China upon Tibet. A Chinese garrison was stationed in Lhasa from the 17th century onwards, but the new developments in Peking and the decline of the Qings will give Tibet equal status with China, and this was cause for new strains in Sino-Tibetan relations. In the Sino-Indian quarrel, the important and the decisive question is whether any kind of Chinese suzerainty was ever accepted by the Tibetans after 1895, in spite of the British attempting to impose it through the Simla Convention of 1914. The collapse of monarchy in China in 1912 would drive the last nail on the suzerainty claim.

140) One incident needs special attention. During the last phase of the 19th century, British India, in connection with her trade talks with Tibet, sought the permission of China to send a trade team to Lhasa under Macaulay. The Chinese were unsure whether a Peking authorisation would be honoured by the Tibetans, and therefore China evaded the issue for a while. In 1876, Tibetans made it clear that they would not welcome a British delegation under Chinese authorisation, and consequently, British India had to disband the Macaulay Mission, already armed with Chinese passports. This Tibetan refusal, makes it again clear, that the Chinese writ did not run in Tibet during the last phase of the 19th century. The incident shows the vague nature of Chinese suzerainty assumed to exist at the time of the aborted Macaulay Mission. But the historian Alastair Lamb argues that regarding Tibet, on several occasions, the British were negotiating with China and not with Tibet, and this is clear proof of Chinese suzerainty. Whether China is suzerain over Tibet is a question, first to be recognised by the Tibetans themselves, before it being recognised by third parties. Whether there is admission of this claim by Tibet herself has been the logical thread running through the diplomatic dialogues after 1895. The recognition of Chinese suzerainty by other countries is only of consequential importance, as such recognition generally follows, when the Tibetans accept that dominion. Again to be emphasized that till 1950 there was no successful Chinese invasion of Tibet, and suzerainty was a see-saw relationship. In the long history of the empire, China never exercised exclusive, uncontested physical possession over any part of the Tibetan plateau until the invasion of 1950. The stationing of Chinese garrison in Lhasa has been pointed out as indicative of Chinese suzerainty. In 1912, that garrison was evacuated by China under military pressure from Tibet. In post-war years, American garrisons are stationed in Japan, South Korea and Western Europe and presently in Eastern Europe and Poland. Before 1989, Soviet garrisons were stationed in Warsaw-Pact countries. Does this garrison-stationing speak of US sovereignty over Japan, South Korea, and Western Europe or Soviet sovereignty over Eastern Europe? Communist China advances these arguments only after she invaded Tibet, and forced its supreme ruler Dalai Lama flee the country and seek asylum in India. Revolting for Indians to know that Nehru will again attempt to discover a socialist content in the Chinese rape of Tibet. It is true that Nehru and the Indian rulers were taking care to distinguish the Tibetan territory as fully autonomous, but the plea was producing no impact in Peking. Where has gone Tibetan autonomy, when Dalai Lama and Tibetan protesters were forced to flee the homeland, and the Khampa rebels and other revolters gunned down enmasse? The Khampa Revolt, turned out the mass hara-kiri by Tibetan rebels before Chinese machine guns. The big impediment in Sino-Tibetan negotiation is China's brutal crackdown of the Tibetan freedom fighters. There is absolutely no Tibetan voice in governance since 1950, in spite of the repeated claims of Beijing about the reformist and socialist storm raging through the plateau. Half-century after his flight to India, Dalai Lama, the people of Tibet, and the Tibetan diaspora across defiantly refuse to accept Chinese overlordship over their homeland. The question continuously asked but never answered is whether at any point of time, Tibet was part of the Chinese empire during the last three thousand years? It had never been. But the history of thousands of years has been breached and buried by the dragon through the violent seizure of the land of the lamas and monasteries. The attempts of China to legitimize her naked conquest (of Tibet) is the new affront to international law and diplomatic morals. China's new arguments produce more scare than dialogue. While China argues for legalizing and legitimizing her conquest, the world terms her arguments as legal-terror.

141) Not only the British, but the Russians and the entire Western world and Asia, were seeing Tibet as the exclusive territory of the Tibetans and Dalai Lama, and never as a province of the Manchus. Tsar Nicholas II was planning to attack Tibet, because Tibet lay before him the undefended Kingdom of Dalai Lama, and not part of the dragon empire. In the event of a Russian thrust on Tibet, the most that Moscow had to fear was a rescue mission from China, but under the political disorder and confusion then prevailing in Peking, that move was unlikely. What deterred the Tsar was the opposition of the British empire, and in this case the power of British India. The British were intending to slap Chinese suzerainty over Tibet and this was Britain's clever move to prevent the threatened Russian conquest of Tibet. In Simla the British were thinking that Chinese suzerainty over Tibet would dissuade the Russian Tsar from laying hand on the plateau. Neither the Russian Tsar nor Lord would ever have ventured into Tibet, had it really been part of the Manchu empire like Yunnan or Xianxi. In this context America's China policy during the 19th century was another decisive factor. During the 19th century, it was due to American opposition that the other Western powers were stopped from invading and partitioning the Chinese empire into many colonies. In the face of American objection, was it possible for the Russian Tsar or the Indian Viceroy to go for the conquest of Tibet, if Tibet had really been a part of the Chinese empire? and the Tsar considered Tibet the Kingdom of Dalai Lama, who, they thought, could be dealt with, without dangerous military consequences. Because of her stakes in the growing trade, Britain was asking for the permission of Peking for any transaction with Tibet, but at the same time the Tibetans resolutely opposing such moves. Even any border negotiation directly between British India and China was opposed and repudiated by the Tibetans, for whom their independence was the paramount factor in every transaction particularly between British India and China. Looking through these events, the 1954 Treaty between free India and China, cannot bind the Tibetans, as Tibet is not party to the document. Thinking the opposite way, what was the authority of India and China to decide the fate of Tibet—a different country? Primarily a country's destiny is to be decided by that country. Only because India owed the highest political obligation and duty (in 1950) to defend Tibet against Chinese aggression, the former does not acquire the right to sell Tibetan sovereignty to China. Tibet, not being a party to the India-China agreement of 1954, the agreement is void regarding her. An agreement between the invader and the collaborator, will not bind the victim or martyr.

142) Through the Lhasa Convention (1904) India was acquiring a defacto protectorate over Tibet, though not dejure. Some jurists argue that during the Lhasa Convention, the Tibetan supremo-Dalai Lama had fled Lhasa, and the convention was negotiated and signed only by the so-called National Assembly, and therefore the treaty lacks legitimacy. They argue that as the convention was not personally signed by the Dalai Lama, it remains illegal under international law. It was a time when the British military power was the fear and scare of Asia, and in this respect the Tibetans cannot be an exception. When Dalai Lama ran away to Mongolia fearing the Young Husband military mission, he had left behind a delegated authority, in Lhasa and that authority was the National Assembly and regents representing Tibet. But more important that the Dalai Lama, after his return to Lhasa from the Mongolian exile, never disowned the convention, much less repudiate it. Because of the implicit compliance of the provisions of the convention through long conduct, and usage by parties, the argument of the pro-China jurists stands disproved.

143) Young Husband imposed an indemnity on Tibet, and that was paid. Usually an indemnity is an impost slapped on the defeated by the victorious in war. What more proof is necessary to show that a defacto British protectorate was established on Tibet by the mission in 1904. Certainly Manchu China was alarmed over these developments, and immediately after 1904, a rigorous campaign was launched by her through her official Chao Erh Feng who let loose an armed attack on Tibet in 1909. Fearing the raid, Dalai Lama fled Lhasa once again, but this time to India, and only in 1913 he will return to Lhasa. Chao wanted to unmake the Young Husband treaty, Sinvise Tibet and divide it into different provinces. But the fall of the Manchus in 1911, and the consequent collapse of Manchu authority over Tibet caused this campaign to fizzle out mid-way. Following this debacle the long standing Chinese garrison in Lhasa had to be evacuated. It is in this context, that the Simla Convention becomes historic in many ways. It declared Dalai Lama the master of Outer Tibet (now TAR), it accepted Chinese suzerainty over Eastern and North Eastern Tibet or Inner Tibet, but on condition of the parties accepting all conditions together. During this time, it was true that republican China was internally too busy to push forward with the sovereignty claim. It was the usual Manchu policy for centuries to keep territorial and diplomatic disputes unsettled, by not entering into written and concluded agreements, but at the same time allowing a defacto development (against her authority), to materialise as fait accompli. Peking would postpone many disputes indefinitely.

144) The Simla Convention makes it clear that Chinese suzerainty over Tibet was recognised under the definite condition of limiting it over Eastern Tibet or Inner Tibet. The clauses lay down that there is no power for China to interfere in the affairs of Central Tibet (Outer Tibet) for any reason. In the document what was the definite area coming under Inner Tibet was vaguely defined as the area coming under Chinese influence. What the words "Chinese influence" mean could be ascertained only by going to the spot. Outer Tibet is defined as the territory to the west of a point in the Mekong River bed, and this area has been set out as so much autonomous as independent. After signing the convention, the Tibetans were resentful that they were forced by the British to cede more area to China as Inner Tibet. Because of the vagueness in defining the area (Inner Tibet), fighting broke out between Chinese troops and Tibetans on the one hand, and Chinese troops and local tribals on the other. This fight, starting in 1914 continued until the Chinese invasion of Tibet in 1950, when Red-China will devour all Tibet in a single gulp.

145) One argument raised by Chau En Lai questioning the Simla Convention was that after 1914 the treaty was not ratified later by the Chinese and Tibetan rulers, and the McMahon Line stands unrecognized by China. The Simla Convention, if assumed as unratified by China, is good reason to raise the contrary interpretation repudiating all Chinese claims over Tibet in one stroke. If only the Simla Convention has been accepted, China can stake claim for suzerainty, at least over Inner Tibet. To be stressed that on Outer Tibet, the Chinese writ never ran, until her invasion in 1950. In Simla, what the Tibetans and Dalai Lama were fearing was the military power of the British empire, and in the final stages, the Tibetans were made to succumb to British blandishments, cajoling or coercion, and this state of affairs made more evident in the after-convention response of the Tibetans. After the fall of the Manchus in 1911, China was fast slipping into disorder and disintegration, with many war-lords resurfacing to declare secession from Peking. During this period, Britain, at the high point of her military power and colonial majesty, was facing no threat to her trading interests in China or Tibet. With the signing of the Anglo-Russian Treaty of 1907, the Russian threat over Tibet disappeared. The American opposition to any Euro-Japanese project for colonising China, was not to be ignored by British India also in Simla. The British arguments in Simla were to up hold the claims of China, and the Simla Convention is to be viewed in that background.

146) After Simla, what are the new international developments, enabling China to claim suzerainty over Tibet? Going by Tibetan arguments, after the evacuation of the

Chinese garrison in Lhasa in 1912, there was total absence of any Chinese military power or political power in Tibet, and the new power looming in the horizon was the imperial power of the British. About the terms of the convention, the Tibetans continued to voice protests that they were forced (by British India) to concede more. Does China want to repudiate the Simla Convention wholly? By doing so, she will have to accept the contrary argument that by 1911, Tibet had become wholly independent of the Chinese shadow, and free. Can China question the McMahon Line without questioning the Simla Agreement as a whole? If she renounces the accord, she has to accept the fact that by 1895 and more emphatically by 1904, Tibet has become an absolutely free territory. But Communist China can now contend that after her armed conquest, Tibetan territory is no longer the subject matter of dispute, as her arms have already rode over the law.

147) When the Soviet Union fell in 1989, a number of constituent states wanted to secede, and they seceded. When the Manchu rule collapsed in China, under the ensuing disorder and anarchy, Tibet, was going fully independent of Peking. After the Simla Convention, China can cite no political development, civil agreement or convention to legitimise and legalise her forcible occupation of Tibet. Again to be emphasized that Tibet had never been a part of China, though often dependent on the latter for her security. While the religious bonds between China and Tibet are deep and historic, that bond will not make Dalai Lama a vassal of the feudal lord of Peking and to be treated a colony of China, Lhasa never paid tribute to Peking. On the contrary for a period in the ancient past, the Chinese emperors paid tribute to the powerful Tibetan kings of the old. But present day Tibet is a monastic territory, isolated from the turbulent, fast-moving industrial world, lacking the high technology and large economic resources to build a big standing army, Tibet, after the 16th century, remained too religious and was economically too weak to be garrisoned. She had been a state like Vatican for long, though geographically a huge expanse. Even in 1950, outside military support was her option to resist external aggression, and China was her traditional defender. When the defender himself turned the assassin overnight (in 1950), she could only succumb to the back-stab. At that crisis point, the duty to defend her was mainly on India, but Nehru, then honey-mooning with communist imperialism, decided to abdicate that responsibility, and surrendered Tibet to the dragon with no feeling of guilt. The crimes against humanity China committed on the Tibetans were successfully covered up under the smokescreen of the rhetories of the Marxian revolution swallowing the Chinese subcontinent. Nehru chose to act this unkind way, in spite of the British Viceroy and foreigner—Lord acting the opposite way to protect India through the Tibetan buffer. Was it possible for China to conquer Tibet during the British Raj? Impossible, as the result of such misadventure would have been China locking-horns with the power of the British empire, which in those days the former was least capable of. Regarding the fate of Tibet, this is the difference between the British Raj under and the freedom Raj under Jawaharlal. Communist China found in Nehru "the poor man", as Mary Antoinette mockingly called her husband-Louis XVI, when the latter was allowing the Bourbon House to be overrun by the Parsian revolters during 1789-91.

148) Another curious argument of Red-China against the McMahon Line is that the line had been arbitrarily defined and imposed by British imperialism, when China lay weakened under disorder and anarchy. This argument regarding strong rulers, weak rulers and disorder is to question the basic tradition and propositions of political behaviour and diplomatic history. It challenges the power and validity of diplomatic decisions, treaties and conventions, forming the foundation of international relations. When an aggressor conquers, the conqueror is usually seen as strong, and the defender assumed weak. But the treaty or agreement made between them—the strong and the weak shall endure before man and history. When the Manchus conquered China during the 17th century, they ought to have been strong, but when they abdicated in 1912, they shall be weak. Still the conquest of China by the Manchus, and centuries after their abdication and inauguration of the republic in 1912, are incidents and events of history—accepted by the people of China and the world. If this Chau argument of weak rulers and strong

rulers is countenanced, then world politics will turn upside down. In her border negotiations with Russia also, China raised the same argument. Can India contend that Nehru was a weak ruler (which he really was) and so the 1954 agreement between India and China on Tibet will be repudiated by his successors? In 1914, China was not under occupation by an invader like Japan, and the country was ruled by the war-lord and strong man Abu Shikai. If China wanted to object to the convening of the Simla Conference, she was free to do so by not participating. But she too had her own vested interest to participate, as the convention opened the doors for debating and reviving Chinese suzerainty over Tibet, which had vanished altogether after 1895. The risk a non-attending China shall have encountered was she finally losing all claims over Tibet, and possibly Tibet changing into a protectorate of British India. As a negotiated agreement, the Simla Convention is the final civil accord involving all three parties—China, Tibet and British India. At the same time the default in the 1954 Agreement is that only India and China are the signatories, and Tibet is kept out as the defeated party in the (Chinese) invasion, and therefore irrelevant. When the sovereign power of Tibet is with the Tibetans, what is the authority of India and China—two outsiders, to sign away the fate of Tibet and that is the basic challenge of international law. True, by 1954, the Chinese conquest of Tibet had become a fait accompli, making all opposing arguments irrelevant in the face of the stark reality of armed takeover. If armed conquest is the final argument of China, then India and Tibet need not argue their cases based on the history and conventions of international law and they too may argue their cases through guns. As it is usual in the case of invaders. China too wants her aggression justified through civil as well as civilized pleadings. But only through armed conquest, China argues her case very well.

149) British India was the pioneer in surveying colonial territories scientifically, and therefore the McMahon Line cannot be a crude or imaginary line, as China assails. Until 1959, the conduct and stand of Red-China was accepting and recognising this line as the boundary, and till then this line was never challenged as the impost of British imperialism. But only after 1959, Premier Chau En Lai was making a sudden retreat from the position he had taken earlier. Perhaps, by then, Peking has reviewed and reversed her boundary policy and strategy against India, and was planning to make the line the pretext for war. The McMahon Line was clearly understood by the rulers and local tribes through recognizable, geographical features, though not by erecting boundary stones, survey stones and fences. The line itself covers a width of eight miles affording much give and take. After the invasion of Tibet, it was high strategy that China invaded parts of India also, and this was to focus the attention of the world from Tibet to Aksai Chin. To cover up aggression, Beijing is dashing out strange excuses only to add to the array of insults she passes against India. India's land, though lying unguarded shall be India's land. The basic question remains unanswered. Has China any historic title over the Tibetan territory, where her flag flutters atop the gun barrel.

Chapter 7

1959—The Tibetan Pontiff Flees to India

150) In Sino-Indian relations, the basic factor and reason for bitter rivalry is the Tibetan question and not Aksai Chin and Arunachal Pradesh. During 1949-50, India played a very irresponsible, anti-human rights role over Tibet. The free world had criticized this conduct as dishonest and betraying. The XIV—Dalai Lama, perhaps the last in the divine line to rule Tibet, but still not yet the last in the lineage of holy spirits, is now before the world as the celebrated victim of Chinese imperialism. In the 21st century also Dalai Lama though the venerable guest of India and the world is an exile. In the eyes of the imperial Beijing regime, he is a condemned criminal, jetting across the globe as the agent of the reactionary forces of the world.

151) Tibet has a very long political history dating back to twelth century BC. It was a very powerful, expansive kingdom, and the imperial kings of Tibet ruled not only the vast Tibetan plateau, but a large part of Central Asia and parts of Mongolia and China. One Tibetan king invaded China in the 6th century AD and drove away the Chinese emperor from Xian. The emperor bought peace with the Tibetans by agreeing to pay a tribute of 50000 rolls of silk every year to the latter. During the 17th century, the Manchus made several raids on Tibet, but they failed to subjugate and Tibet remained independent. During the second half of the 19th century, China, till then a closed society, started cultivating friendly relations with the

British empire, and they wanted the latter help them reestablish China suzerainty over Tibet, which remained a vague fiction. It was during the second half of 19th century that Tibetans became more alert and careful not to allow any kind of exercise of Chinese suzerainty over their country. But the 1949 communist capture of power is Peking will change everything by force of arms. The Chinese invasion of Tibet, begining in 1950, was complete by 1957. The free world stood there the indifferent spectator of the rape of this divine land. India was pictured as collaborator to the crime.

152) The 13th Dalai Lama—the predecessor of the present Dalai Lama, was a defiant, powerful ruler and capable administrator. When the Manchus mounted an attack on Tibet in 1909, he fled to India. Fighting broke out between Tibetan troops and Manchu forces, and Dalai Lama appealed for British help, but Britain refused to intervene. The Chinese forces tried to subvert the Tibetan Government under the regent (as the Dalai Lama had already fled to India), but by then the news of the Chinese revolution of 1911 reached Lhasa. Hearing the news, a section of the Chinese troops in Tibet mutineered and attacked the house of the Chinese Amban (resident). In fighting broke out between the Manchu loyalists and the soldiers supporting the revolution. In the fighting, Tibetans also were attacked by the Chinese troops. By this time, the Tibetans have reorganized themselves, and on the orders of Dalai Lama (in India), the Chinese troops in Lhasa and across Tibet were beaten and decimated, and the remaining Chinese were expelled through Nathu La. The military ruler of China-Yuan Shikai tried to send more troops, but at the same time he was attempting to mollify and pacify the Tibetans. He sent orders restoring Dalai Lama with all powers. Shikai recognized Tibet's independence, and declared it too. In January 1913, Dalai Lama returned to Lhasa from his Indian exile, and in the same year, the last Chinese garrison in Lhasa was evacuated, through Calcutta. The same month, a bilateral treaty was signed between Tibet and Mongolia, declaring both countries independent, and effectively ending any kind of Chinese dominion over these countries. Dalai Lama, in March 1913, issued another declaration

asserting the independence of his kingdom. He announced "the Chinese intention of colonizing Tibet under the patron-priest relationship has faded like a rainbow in the sky". Impetuous and assertive, he started the programme for modernizing Tibet. He reorganized the country's international relations, established telegraph and postal services, and started modern transport and communications in the limited way then possible. His passing away in 1933 will again create a void, stagnating, or rather freezing these programmes. The Chinese mission remaining in Lhasa from 1909, was allowed to continue like the missions of India and Nepal. Peace prevailed in the country until the Communist Revolution in 1949, and the Chinese invasion of Tibet 1950.

153) Under the false cover of liberation, China, in September 1949, attacked Eastern Tibet, and captured Chamdo, the capital of the province. On November 11, 1950, the Tibetan Government petitioned the United Nations against the aggression. When Nehru refused to lodge the complaint against China, El Salvador raised the question before the UN General Assembly, but the Assembly decided to post-pone the issue for further enquiry, and that was also under India's initiative. Because of the grave danger suddenly arising due to Chinese invasion, the 14th Dalai Lama, then only 16 years of age, and a minor under law, assumed full powers, both spiritual and temporal, on 17 November 1950. On May 23, 1951, a Tibetan delegation was agreed to be sent to Peking for negotiations, but the delegates were treated as virtual captives. The delegates were threatened and coersed by the Peking mandarins and they were forced to sign a 17 point treaty, agreeing for "Peaceful Liberation of Tibet". If not signing, they were warned of more severe military strikes. Even the Tibetan seal, which, was in Lhasa, was forged and affixed in the document. China began to make Tibet a Chinese colony, violating the conditions agreed to in the 17 point treaty itself and this Chinese fraud was resolutely resisted by the Tibetans. On September 9, 1951, thousands of Chinese troops marched into Lhasa, and began the systematic destruction of monasteries. Freedom was suppressed and thousands were arrested, and many thousands massacred. The nation-wide Tibetan resistance culminated in the violent uprising of March 10, 1959. As usual, China responded with brutal crackdown and tens of thousands of men, women and children across the plateau were massacred by the PLA forces. Monasteries and temples were shelled, and nuns and monks fired at.

154) When Chinese troops marched into various parts of Tibet in 1950 Dalai Lama felt himself fully insecure, and in July 1951, he, along with a select group of officials, evacuated the capital, and set up provisional capital near the Indian border at Yatung. Fearing the adverse reaction of the world, Dalai Lama was persuaded by Chinese officials to return to Lhasa, and he returned. With his return calm returned for some time. By 1954, the strength of PLA troops in Tibet reached 220000, and this was clear sign of what China was planning to do next. In September 1957, 3000-Chinese troops marched into Lhasa, calling themselves 'Liberation' forces. In the meanwhile, China was making some eye washing operations also. In April 1954, China inaugurated the Preparatory Committee in Lhasa, headed by Dalai Lama himself, whose job was to oversee the development work underway, but the real job of the committee was simply to rubber-stamp the imperial acts and crimes of China. Lhasa grew increasingly restive, and a non-violent resistance movement called Mimang Tsongdu was organised by a citizen group. In the beginning the Peking policy was to woo rather than oppress, but in February 1956, revolts broke out in Eastern Tibet, and the Tibetan fighters started inflicting heavy casualties on Chinese troops. The Kham and Amdo guerillas constituted the main force behind the revolt, and China sent more troops to confront the guerillas. Abandoning the policy of passive resistance, the Khampa rebels were becoming more violent, and a massive revolt appeared in the offing. The PLA forces started looting and bombing the monasteries, and arrested and tortured the nobles, monks and guerilla leaders. The PLA publicly executed hundreds to discourage further violence. As the revolt spread across, a large number of refugees streamed into Lhasa from the east, and set up camps on the outskirts of the city. By December 1958, tension began to rise high with a massive uprising on the cards. The PLA threatened to bomb Lhasa, including the Potala palace, unless the revolt was called off and contained at once. About 20000 Tibetan guerillas were then fighting the Chinese troops in the precincts of Lhasa.

155) In the midst of this tumult and violence, the teenaged Dalai Lama was preparing for his master's degree. On 1st March 1959, two Chinese army officers visited Dalai Lama at the Jokhang Cathedral and asked him to give a date for his (Dalai Lama's) visit and tea at the Chinese army headquarters. He agreed to give a date after the ceremonies then underway were over, though this invitation was entirely in breach of protocol and precedents. Usually such ceremonies were held in the palace of Dalai Lama, but now the Chinese army is asking him to attend tea party in the army camp in Lhasa. The practice was that the Dalai Lama goes out under the security of 25 bodyguards escorting him, and when he walks out, the entire people of Lhasa would collect *en route* to salute him. But now there is no ceremony, no bodyguards and the ruler of Tibet is asked to attend the army camp coming alone. Everybody everywhere was smelling danger. On March 7, 1959, the PLA again asked for a date, and March 10 was officially confirmed. March 8, 1959 was the Women's Day, and before a women's rally, a Chinese general gave a lecture threatening to shell and destroy more monasteries if the Khampa rebels fail to surrender immediately. The military situation was such that the Tibetans had to fight the machine guns of China with stones and sticks. On March 9, 1959, the Chinese commander told Dalai Lama's bodyguard that the Tibetan supremo has to come alone, and there shall be no escort when he starts from Norbulinka (The Winter Palace) and no Tibetan bodyguard or soldier will be allowed to accompany him beyond the stone-bridge and wanted to keep the entire proceedings secret. The news of the Tibetan ruler having been asked to visit the army camp alone spread like wild-fire, causing eyebrows to be raised in wild suspicion. The people of Lhasa were anxious and furious.

156) In the morning of March 10, 1959, more than 30000 loyal Tibetans surrounded the Summer Palace and held Dalai Lama the prisoner of their loyalty. The crowd was suspecting a Chinese plan to abduct Dalai Lama to Peking, present him before the National Assembly, and force him to sign on dotted lines, as the 17 point treaty was doctored in 1951. Surrounded by the mass of loyalists, Dalai Lama was forced to turn down the (PLA) invitation for tea. On March 12, 1959, nearly 5000 Tibetan women marched through the streets of Lhasa carrying banners "Tibet for Tibetans", "Tibet independent", and presented an appeal before the Indian Consul for assistance. It was certain that under Jawaharlal Nehru any Indian help would be a far cry, more especially against Communist China. The Tibetan guerilla group, Mimang Tsongdu and their supporters erected barricades in the streets of Lhasa, whereas the Chinese troops took positions on rooftops with machine guns. Three thousand Tibetans have already enrolled to join the rebels, readying to guard the ring of mountains around Lhasa.

157) On March 15, Dalai Lama's bodyguard secretly left Lhasa to take points along the proposed route of escape. Khampa rebels occupied strategic positions, and thousands of Tibetan army men merged with civilians to defend the route as additional guards. By this time, an estimated 50000 Chinese troops, wielding modern weapons and machine guns, were standing deployed around the city. The Tibetans moved their primitive machine guns in place with the help of mules. On March 16, Chinese heavy artillery was deployed targeting the Summer Palace, and more PLA troops were flown in. It was feared that by nightfall the Dalai Lama's palace was going to be shelled. At 4 p.m. on March 17, 1959, Chinese soldiers fired two mortar shells at Norbulinka, but the shells fell in the nearby marsh. This shelling was the last straw to trigger the final resolve of Dalai Lama to leave homeland. When shells were fired by PLA all furore, clamour and conspiracy within the palace were on how to save the life of Dalai Lama, and how to carry out that dangerous duty. Thousands of Tibetans came forward ready to make capital sacrifice. There was still no certainty that he would escape alive, and if he was to escape, what was his safe landing destination, and which country would offer him asylum? In any case he shall escape before the Chinese laid siege to the palace itself, though the news of his escape was certain to invite an orgy of violence, massacre, destruction and plunder by the PLA.

158) At 10 p.m. on March 17, 1959 under the cover of darkness, Dalai Lama stepped out of his home (palace) and set foot on the road. He was under disguise, wearing the uniform of a soldier with a gun slung over his shoulders, and he walked into the darkness, which he hoped was his road to India, to safety and freedom. His family members including his mother and elder sister have already left for the Indian border. In the past, on several occasions many Dalai Lamas had to flee Tibet, fearing enemies and aggression, but only to return after a short interval, but now probably for never. After a very arduous and dangerous trek across the Tibetan plateau and the Himalayan massif, he was going to land in India—the land of freedom.

159) The odds were hopelessly against the unarmed, defenceless Tibetans. On the night of March 19, fighting broke out between the Tibetans and the PLA, and the fight raged for two days. The Chinese started shelling Norbulinka during night, and on the 21st the palace was shelled 800 times. Thousands of men, women and children camping around the palace were slaughtered through shelling and machine-gunning. Almost all the 300 living quarters of government officials in palace precincts' were destroyed, and horrendous that the 200 member personal bodyguard of Dalai Lama were disarmed and publicly shot. Lhasa's major monasteries—Gaden, Seva and Drepung were bombed and the treasures and artifacts looted. Thousands of monks were killed, and many thousands sent to slave labour, and many more deported to the Chinese gulags. Armed people hiding in homes were dragged out into the streets, and shot in the presence of onlookers. It is estimated that during this bloody retaliation and repression, about 86000 Tibetan were massacred by Chinese troops. While the Tibetans were fighting the PLA at home, Dalai Lama and his party were racing towards the Indian border, under top secrecy, often adopting tricky and misguiding flight strategies, but every time fearing ambush by Chinese mercenaries and sleuths. Fortunately for the Tibetans, Dalai Lama, after an agonizing trek through the wilderness of rocks, forests and snow, reached the Indian border at the end of March, and crossed the Khenzimona pass.

160) On 3rd April 1959, Nehru declared in Lok Sabha that the Government of India had decided to grant political asylum to Dalai Lama. Two days after, Dalai Lama and party reached Tawang in the North East Frontier Agency (now Arunachal Pradesh). After taking rest at Tawang for four days, and visiting the beautiful monastery there, he proceeded to Bomdilla where he was received by a representative of the Government of India. On April 18, 1959, Dalai Lama, his mother, sister, brother, and three ministers with about 100 Tibetan officials and escorts, reached Tezpur, and walked into the Indian plains. He was greeted there by Indian officials, and a 200 strong army of press men. The press hailed this escape as "The Story of the Century". At Tezpur, Dalai Lama made the historic declaration repudiating the 17-Point Agreement forged and forced upon the Tibetan delegation by the Beijing mandarins in 1951. For the first time in history, the Tibetan supremo was making a political statement against Beijing. The story goes that in 1951, a Tibetan delegation was sent to Beijing for parleys, but during negotiations, they were forced to sign on dotted lines by the warlords of Peking. It was this 17-Points Agreement—a document of coercion and fraud—that was repudiated by Dalai Lama in Tezpur.

Tibetans Resist

161) Immediately on the communists seizing power 1949, they began asserting the claim that Tibet is integral part of China and the Tibetan people are crying for liberation and reform from the feudal, autocratic regime of Dalai Lama. This blatant lie was followed by they presenting a scheme for "peaceful liberation" of Tibet before the Indian Ambassador. Without waiting for India's response, the PLA forces were marching into Chambo—the capital of the Rham province, which is the head quarters of Tibetan army's Eastern Command. This area was overrun by the PLA, and the Tibetan governor was taken prisoner. PLA then started secretly infiltrating Tibet's north eastern border province—Amdo, but avoided immediate clashes only to avert outrageous international response. Startled and taken aback by the PLA offensive, Dalai Lama evacuated Lhasa and set up temporary capital near the Indian border at Yatung. By this time, thousands of PLA troops landed in Lhasa and from then on the militarization of Tibet was going on in speed. By 1954, Lhasa—the prayer capital was getting politicized, and suddenly there appeared a resistance movement. These underground forces threw stones and dry yakdung on Chinese soldiers, but Beijing directed the soldiers to keep their calm. In February 1956, revolts broke out in several places in Eastern Tibet, and heavy casualties were inflicted on Chinese forces by the Amdo and Kham guerillas. By this time, in Lhasa's perimeter, thousands of refugees were pouring in. In 1958, the most violent revolt was simmering, and in response the Chinese military command was threatening to bomb Lhasa, if the unrest did not stop at once. Red-China was certain that the Tibetans armed with sticks and stones were no match for her machine guns.

162) Fifty-four years after the flight of Dalai Lama, Tibetan autonomy and independence looks remote and far away. After landing in India, he was allowed to set up monastery and capital at Dharmasala in Himachal Pradesh, but his government in exile has not been allowed to play politics within the borders of India. He travels to the capitals of the world, canvassing support for Tibetan liberation and independence. But the dominant free world, including the United States, do not come forward with any meaningful plan and scheme for liberation, and so the Chinese overlords could plant their feet deep on Tibetan soil. At 78, Dalai Lama is a frustrated man, and he fears that his death would make the Tibetan cause headless. His new incarnation is to be discovered only after his death, and the Tibetans fear that China will pollute and manipulate that divine process into a farce and to her political advantage. When China grows into a superpower, the chances are that the world also will find it convenient to forget the Tibetan underdogs, and connive at China's colonization. Tibet is crying for help loudly through the Tibetan diaspora, but the world and the most powerful free world fail to hear her groans. India, from the beginning, has been unkind and unfaithful to the Tibetan cause, and that dishonesty and double speak has forced India to lose the security of the Tibetan buffer between India and China. Post-war America is obsessed with her own body beauty, and so the cause of human rights fails, very abominably in Tibet.

163) Suffering these humiliations and losses, but indomitably carrying on the non-violent fight for Tibetan freedom, Dalai Lama has been awarded the Nobel Peace Prize. The Nobel Peace Committee dedicates the prize for his contribution for world peace, through non-violent war. China's "peaceful liberation" of Tibet turned out a capital crime and a human rights monstrocity. Dalai Lama warns and bemourns that the 2000 year old divine and saintly culture and history of his native land is being decimated by the totalitarian PLA, and the day the divine civilization of monks, monasteries and prayer wheels is extinct may not be far away. When Deng Ziao Ping—the pragmatist and counter-revolutionary came to power in 1978, the Tibetan hopes soared, but once again the numerous negotiations turned out only Peking dramas and China stands where she stood in 1950. They feel Red-China covers up her crimes on Tibet through negotiation farces. Reaching the blind alley of endless impasse, Dalai Lama makes a climb down demanding only autonomy, but China will reject every one of his demands as part of a universal conspiracy against Red-China. His compromise moves reaching nowhere, a desperate Dalai Lama recently shed his temporal powers, and allowed a new prime minister for the Tibetan Government in exile, chosen from the Tibetan diaspora.

164) Independent India, the bastion of human rights, looking at Tibetan agony as mute witness to an unfolding Greek tragedy is not only shameful, but in human. Unfortunately India in the fifties was not only apathetic, and collaborative but volunteering to play the role of a Chinese agent. The main responsibility for the Chinese annexation of Tibet is not on the United States and the west, but on Jawaharlal Nehru. He fawned before the tyrants of Peking instead of swinging his sword. The terrible prospect of an armed takeover of India by the dragon in 1962 alone opened his eyes, but then it was too late. But again to be noted that to respond to a continuing international crime, it is never late or too late. What all frightful consequences India had to face in future because of the loss of the Tibetan buffer. During the Chinese rape of Tibet in 1950, Nehru should have prepared very powerful military schemes to resist and expel China from Tibet, but in dangerous emergences and crises, his usual strategy was to vacillate and them to withdraw. Some will say he was brave enough to welcome Dalai Lama. Giving political asylum has not been considered an act of great gallantry. Or for giving asylum to a harmless Dalai Lama, even China may be thanking India, as the former could escape from the bad name and notoriety of imprisoning or assassinating a divine icon of international eminence. The German legend and statesman Bismarck ended up an exile in London. Einstein was an exile in America from anti-Semitic Germany. Karl Marx—the German Jew and father of communism was the philosopher exile in London. Kerensky-the Russian Prime Minister overthrown by Lenin was for long an exile in France, England and the United States. Former Pakistan President Suhrawardy was an exile in London. During the 19th century, Tsarist Russia's, revolutionaries including the young Lenin flocked to England and London, and Martov, Trotsky and Lenin ran their party magazines from London. For more than two centuries London continues not only the capital of the empire where the sun never set, but the capital of great refugees. Compared to the British act of giving asylum both to the extreme right and the rebellious left, and the London government rubbishing the protests coming from great powers also, Jawaharlal Nehru granting asylum to Dalai Lama, though not an act of courage, was indeed humanitarian. It can be seen that by granting asylum to Dalai Lama in 1959, Nehru appeared more courageous than in 1950.

Chapter 8

America Deserts Kuomintang China

165) Politically, Communist China's finest hour was the Korean War and her greatest ally in the war was the retreatism and isolationism then sweeping the United States. The loss of China to communism continues the biggest setback to American leadership and democracy, and that happening immediately after the full triumph of America in the Second World War was greater national pain. Battered in the war, Britain was no more the global player to play equally with the elephantine United States in the fight against communism. Post-war Britain was preparing to pull out from her overseas theatres of colonial majesty, and go back to the native British Isles. Winston Churchill was sorry that post-war America, her staunchest ally in the war, was championing the cause of decolonization, and so Britain single-handedly becoming unable to save her far-flung empire from break-up and dissolution. After his election defeat in 1945, Churchill came to power for a second time in 1951, but remained there only to see the demand for liberation and decolonization grow more strident. Thereafter, this British imperialist was seen, albeit unwillingly, reconciled to the avalanche of decolonization stampeding his empire. When the French were fighting for their Indo-China colony in 1954, President Eisenhower, one of the weakest Presidents of USA, sent Vice-President Nixon to London to meet Churchill, for enlisting British support for rescuing the French. For the free world, this was another war against communism after their setback in China and Korea. But that master-imperialist felt no hesitation to say 'no' to Nixon, and this reaction was stunningly realistic. "If the British will not fight to keep India for them, I don't think they will fight to keep Indo-China for the French" Churchill told Nixon. This curt reply by the war-leader was in fact un-Churchillean, but it was revealing the art of the possible practised by the British. When China went communist, Britain was one of the Western powers coming forward to recognise the Peoples Republic of China without long wait, and this act ran directly against the policy of the United States.

166) Harry S. Truman, the first nuclear-powered President of the United States, was witnessing the pro-American Nationalists speedily losing ground in the Chinese Civil War, but he refused to heed the alarm bells rung by many pro-Nationalists in America, exhorting for a direct American entry to save the Kuomintang ally. The pro-Chiang faction in America argued that if the Nationalists lose the fight, America will be losing her biggest and most loyal ally in the east. There is no denying the fact that with a reorganized and disciplined strategy, the Kuomintang itself could have won the Civil War. Had the very much indefensible Kuomintang been salvaged by USA, there would have been no Korean War, no annexation of Tibet by China, no India-China War, no Vietnam War, and China and Indo-China would have remained not only pro-west but pro-democracy too. In that case, probable that China could have gone into a full democracy after the world war. But unfortunately, Truman had a faulty vision of the Nationalists and a wrong calculus about the dangerous consequences of a communist victory, then clearly in prospect. True, he was surrounded by moderates and communists apologists like General George C. Marshall, State Secretary Dean Acheson, and a heavily red-infiltrated state department. But it is the president who should take the final decision, and Truman's failure in this respect was thorough. A president gets not only the advisors and lieutenants he deserves but he wants also. In the midst of this American defeatism running high, only General MacArthur Truman's bête noire, could see the writings on the Pacific-sky, and he pleaded feverishly for a major American offensive against Red-China, even as late as during the Korean

War. The president lacked a futuristic vision of the beneficial consequences of an adventurous policy, much less about the domino effect a communist victory in China would produce in the region. Strange that even Stalin was not keenly interested in a communist victory in the Civil War, and he and Molotov were indirectly moving on the side of Chiang. Immediately after the Second World War, Stalin resumed military aid to Chiang Kai Shek. This Russian stand was advantageous to USA, but what the Americans were crazy about was to highlight the chronic corruption eating into body-Kuomintang, and the massive misappropriation and misuses of the war funds and war supplies, America was pouring into the lap of Chiang, even across the hump—(Himalayas), and later through the Burma Road. Many US commissions were sent to China to report on the necessity and feasibility of a direct American entry, but nothing good was done in time, to help the Kuomintang, who were left to fend for themselves at the critical hour.

167) When the world war ended, an uneasy peace prevailed for sometime between the Kuomintang and the Communists, but both sides were preparing for the imminent clash, looking inevitable. It is true that America tried her best to prevent a shooting war between the communists and the Kuomintang, and in 1946 General George C. Marshall—the American chief of staff came to Chunking to arrange the forming of a coalition government of Communists and the Kuomintang, and an agreement was signed. This agreement neither side was eager to observe. Chiang was saying, ever since the Japanese invasion of 1931, that Japan is a disease on the skin, whereas communism is the disease of the heart, and his priority was to fight the communists. Mao too was equally adamant to fight and defeat the Kuomintang by arms, and seize power, when the Japanese threat disappeared forever. After the world war, both sides resumed battle at the earliest, and Chiang had a big superiority in soldiers and weapons, but their first class troops were already lost in the war with Japan and mostly in the Manchurian theatres. In the world war, there was formed in 1937 an uneasy Communist-Kuomintang alliance to fight the Japanese, but the main brunt of the fight was borne by the Kuomintang. Japanese forces captured Manchuria and established their puppet regime there. The Japanese conquerors then turned south, and before 1938, conquered most of the Chinese railway and Manchuria, and they came south up to Nanking and nearly 170 million Chinese came under Japanese rule. In fact in the later stages of the war, particularly after Pearl Harbour, Japan feverishly sought a compromise and peace with China and even attempted to make Chiang Kai Shek their puppet. For governing the vast area they occupied, Japan could not supply the large bureaucracy and police and so they sought a Chinese proxy. But Chiang rejected the Japanese overtures and he remained in the interior fortress city of Chunking. At one stage of the war, the Kuomintang lost nearly eight lakhs soldiers in six months, but Japan got no peace and Chiang got no respite. The communists fought a successful guerilla war against Japan, but escaped heavy losses through regular strategic withdrawals. In the Civil War battlefields the communist soldiers would call the Kuomintang soldiers their arms carriers. Kuomintang soldiers and defectors were selling large quantities of arms to the PLA and collecting money. To supplement it was the large-scale defection of KMT soldiers to PLA with arms, and thus they acting as the main arms supplier of PLA. Inevitable that due to indiscipline, corruption and defections, the Kuomintang were moving towards collapse. For Chiang, the last straw was the Stilwell reorganization plan for the Kuomintang army going hay wire on Chiang's own non-cooperation. This American scheme was to reorganize the Kuomintang forces through special funding and training but Chiang was dead set against the programme. On this question the Stilwell-Chiang differences yawned never to be reconciled. Stilwell wanted some of the best Kuomintang troops guarding the Chinese Soviets called back, and redeployed against the Japanese invader, but Chiang viewed it differently arguing that once he withdrew these forces, the PLA would find a free territory to expand and that area will easily pass into the hands of PLA. The Stilwell plea was that indiscipline, leadership loss and corruption prevailing in the (Kuomintang) army has already reduced the force rickety and disloyal, and therefore reorganization was urgently needed. But

Chiang refused to withdraw and re-deploy them against Japan. At last the Chiang-Stilwell differences grew unbridgeable and the American reorganization plan had to be withdrawn, and FDR was forced to recall the general. The Communist were lucky that the Stilwell plan fell through, and with that the rot in the Kuomintang forces becoming incurable. Whether Chiang was right or Stilwell was right continues the strategic riddle, but most of the pro-Chiang strategists contend that this Kuomintang failure to reorganize played the decisive role in the victory of the communists in 1949.

168) During the world war, the communists will often accuse Chiang as very hard on the communists and soft on Japan and the former never missed an opportunity to accuse Chiang with unpatriotism. Historic that in the Civil War, American openly refused to take the side of Chiang through direct entry and America openly declared it. A good part of the America supplied arms, the Kuomintang defectors and unloyals smuggled to the communists. Anyhow, during the war against Japan Mao Tse Tung was very careful to harbour much of his arms and soldiers in safe reserve, to fight the final war with the Kuomintang and when the Civil War broke out, this stock of arms and soldiers would come handy for the PLA. Critics point out that the fight between the communists and the Kuomintang was really the fight between the wolf and the lamb and the Kuomintang forces, indisciplined, corrupt, demoralised and exhausted was very much reconciled to surrender. The critical flaw in the last stages of the Civil War was the shortage of able commanders in Kuomintang ranks, or if there were a few, suspecting their loyalty Chiang sidelining them.

169) During the world war, president FDR sending General Stilwell to China to reorganise and reconstruct the Kuomintang army into a powerful fighting machine has been referred above. Historians contend that had the Stilwell reorganization went through as planned, Chiang would not have suffered defeat in the Civil War. But, Chiang particularly after his arrest by his own generals, in Xian in 1936, was dead-set against any reorganization, and he will not entrust command to able generals, whose loyalty was suspect. In this respect the Stilwell-Chiang differences became deep and open, and unable to swallow the Chiang defiance, a frustrated Stilwell was recalled by FDR. Another fatal error of Chiang was his failure to order the retreat of his best army from Manchuria, when it was threatened with encirclement by the People's Liberation Army. It is pointed out that that step alone would have avoided defeat, but he will not order withdrawal because, he felt it humiliating. Sad to say that more than a million Kuomintang troops, in the final stages of the Civil War, defected to the communist ranks because of indiscipline, disloyalty and command failure, and viewed in that background, the Kuomintang defeat looks a self-invited one but defeat it was and defeat in black and white. When the communists captured power in October 1949, it became the second biggest setback to world democracy in the 20th century. Why America refused to intervene, when Stalin himself was not very keen about a communist victory? The truth is that Truman had no strategic vision about the future of democracy in Asia, and he allowed communism to devour the Chinese subcontinent in a single swallow. True that the Kuomintang were impossible to be reformed, but was it good reason for America to push China to the communists? A direct entry by America would certainly have added to the morale of the Kuomintang forces to fight with determination and fight for victory. Realising this abominable folly in the Civil War, Truman in 1950 would come ready to commit more than one and a half million troops in Korea, but by then China was lost to communism. A fraction of the troops and arms he poured into Korea was sufficient to rescue the Kuomintang, but Truman has already allowed himself to be guided by the defeatists in the government. Had the communists been defeated, Chiang would have got a China to rule with peace, a peace that he never got from day one of his Nanking coups, through which he seized the mantle of Sun Yat-sen by force.

170) The Kuomintang rule was corrupt and inefficient, but they were hundred per cent pro-American and ideologically pro-democracy. There were signs they will come the democratic way once Japan was defeated and peace returned. To ensure a Kuomintang victory, America could have brandished the atom bomb itself, as Russia then was only in the process of building a nuclear device, and Stalin not being very keen in rescuing Mao Tse Tung at that high cost. The strategic watersheds were many, and one was when Chiang refused to implement the Stilwell suggestions, and their differences becoming irreconcilable. What were the causes for this Chiang opposition to the Stilwell reorganization? One reason was his own generals taking him prisoner in his 1936 Xian visit, which altogether shattered Chiang's entire domestic strategy. Thereafter, never more he wanted capable generals to take important commands, and the much touted reorganization plan came to naught. Stilwell was the commander of the United States army in the region. Chiang refused the demand of Stilwell to deploy 200000 Kuomintang forces in the Burma front and that was on the ground that thereby he will be allowing the communists a free run in the north. Here the Chiang argument appears more realistic, but he refusing the massive and radical Stilwell reorganization of his army was to become fatal in the coming Civil War. It makes interesting reading that it was Chau En Lai, who intervened to negotiate the deal to free Chiang from the point of execution by his rebellious generals in Xian. General Chau En Lai was once Chiang's deputy in the prestigious Wampoa Military Academy, where Chiang was the director. Later he was the communist representative in the Chinese war capital of Chunking. In the negotiations for Chiang release, all parties including the CCP were unanimous that Chiang was the only national leader, indispensable to lead China's fight against Japan. Mao Tse Tung had sent special instructions with Chau En Lai to save the life of Chiang at any cost. This was in 1936, but everything would turn upside down in the 1949. At the end of the Civil War, Chiang avoided his personal surrender to the communists by refusing to make a last-ditch stand in the mainland, and he shifted his government to the Formosa island, just got back from Japan in 1945. Because of the Japanese occupation of the island, the industrial infrastructure had already been well laid there.

171) After the world war, there was the America brokered truce prevailing between the CCP and the Kuomintang, but the

Civil War was ticking to explode any time. After the end of the world war, the United States was feverishly negotiating with the CCP to prevent a breach with the Kuomintang, and for a brief period American military and economic aid also was resumed to the communists. The 1946 ceasefire agreement signed at Chunking between the CCP and the Kuomintang, in the presence of General George C. Marshall and the CCP emissary General Chau En Lai, is not only historic but famous. America cautioned Chiang against provoking a shooting war with the communists, but both sides badly wanted to resume the battle and fight for the final victory. It is the common experience that any ceasefire will work to the advantage of the communists. When the Civil War broke out, the Kuomintang enjoyed clear superiority in arms and men, but the KMT soldiers did not carry on their fight up to the last man. They were disloyal and muddled, and indifferently commanded.

172) It is the knack of history that in all revolutions and reforms, the new comer's propositions and promises are naturally preferred over the cautions and concerns of the incumbent state. When the February Revolution broke out in Russia, the chief cause for the fall of the monarchy was the threatened defection of soldiers and the defeatist generals to the rank of the revolutionists. Again during the October Revolution, the defection and disobedience of the so-called loyal troops was forcing Kerensky to flee to Finland. The Bolshevists, who stormed into the summer palace, were a band of dare devils. In the Chinese Revolution of 1911, it was the defection of the royal commander-in-chief Abu Shikkai to the side of Sun Yat-sen that caused the abrupt fall of the Manchus. This enabled Sun Yat-sen to capture power much early and without bloodshed, but only to hand over power to the authoritarian militarist—Abu Shikkai. After the death Abu Shikkai in 1916, the government was taken over by Sun Yat-sen but his writ did not run over all China. Many provinces seceded and were ruled by warlords. When the Civil War broke out, massive defections among Kuomintang soldiers became the order of the day. These soldiers also were hit by the traditional urge to join the new-comers, abandoning the old masters. Surprisingly, the Kuomintang defectors counted in millions. An American entry, even symbolic, would have prevented these massive defections and kept up the morale of the Kuomintang as a fighting body.

173) If there comes a new revolution in China, possible that the defection from the PLA would be the critical factor, as public discontent and disenchantment with the CCP's authoritarian rule has already reached the boiling point, but the lid tightened every time. True the CCP has made a very thorough job in disciplining, brain washing and decapitating the army, but how long this may go on is the question. Recently, when the Arab Spring flowered and many dictators in the Arab world were overthrown, the country keeping an embarrassing silence over this tempestuous outburst of popular anger is Communist China. Her proxies-North Korea and Cuba also pretend ignorance of the uprising. On the Tibetan Torch Revolt, and the Sinjiang Insurrection, China reacted violently. As the Soviet collapse is ominously before her, the CCP looks at any popular revolt in any part of the world, as a direct threat to the communist government in Beijing. Public discontent ought to be the highest in any totalitarian system and this discontent is forcing the rulers to regularly upgrade oppression. Historic that in every revolution, the security forces of the outgoing regime plays the crucial role. This role was apparent and real in the French Revolution, but was decisive in the February and October Revolutions in Russia. The Chinese Revolution of 1949 was in fact caused by the disloyalty, corruption and the massive defection of Kuomintang forces. This trade behaviour stares at the Chinese authorities, who are wholly distressed of any popular revolt anywhere in the world. In the revolts in the 20th century main beneficiary of the defection of security forces had been the communist parties. History cannot but repeat itself. While commenting on the defections plaguing the Kuomintang during the last stages of the Civil War, it is important to look to the consequences of totalitarian misrule, and the consequent public discontent building up against.

174) From the beginning of the Civil War, the Kuomintang army, even enjoying clear superiority in numbers and weapons, could not produce any impressive record, to justify this superiority and in the last stages their want of effective battlefield leadership was becoming total, as able generals were sidelined or disengaged by Chiang himself for fear of coups and overthrow. In the Civil War front, Chiang committed many strategic blunders. His best troops were engaging the communists in Manchuria and around, and these forces on earlier occasions could drive away the large communist army from their mountain hideouts and camps. But the Kuomintang, by extending the line of fight too wide and long, gradually lost their supply lines, and in later stages they came under unexpected encirclement by communist forces. The communists will make strategic withdrawals, and it was such withdrawals that kept their fighting capacity intact for future. While confronting deadly opposition, they will resort to guerilla tactics which would keep their forces undamaged and undestroyed. On the other hand, Chiang will not allow the Northern Army to make any tactical withdrawal when they were about to fall prey to the enemy's pincer movement. This blunt heroism of Chiang was another fatal flaw, contributing to the final collapse. When a proposal was made by his advisers to stop the Yangtse crossing of the communists by appointing some able generals in the theatre, Chiang again refused, and his weak but loyal nominees went there only to fail. As it often happens, some accidental decisions change the course of history. If the northern army had been withdrawn into the south for some time, military strategist say Chiang would have won the Civil War. At the end of the world war in 1945, a large number of Japanese troops, who surrendered in Manchuria and in other places, according to their proximity, joined the Kuomintang army or the Peoples Liberation Army (PLA), and fought in the Civil War, on opposite sides. In the last stages of the Civil War also, the Kuomintang forces were larger and better-equipped, but they lacked discipline and motive, and having no able command, were set for the final rout. In the confusion of the last stages, also there occurred massive defections from Kuomintang to the PLA. Now the history of the Czarist army defecting to the ranks of revolters in Russia in February 1917 was repeating itself. At one stage, Chiang himself was heard to wail that his troops have decayed into disobedience, disloyalty and corruption and his commands go unheeded. When the PLA entered Peking, there was still about 2,50,000 Kuomintang troops stationed in the capital, but their general entered into a conspiracy with the CCP and the PLA, and without firing a shot, the entire garrison went over to the PLA, and in no time Peking was in communist hands. This defector-general was later appointed minister for cultural affairs in the revolutionary government of Mao Tse Tung. Commentators say that in the last stages, the fight between the numerically superior and better-armed Kuomintang, and the less numerous and badly equipped PLA, degenerated into a fight between disorder and discipline, and for the Kuomintang, it was reverses all around. Chiang Kai Shek did not make a last-ditch stand against the PLA in the mainland, and months before the final collapse, he resigned as President of China. Before resigning he exhorted the free world to rescue China from the jaws of Communism a real and prophetic call but the world stood before him dumb founded and uncommitted. When America turned her face away, he decided to resign and go to the island of Formosa. Before he resigned, he nominally handed over power to his Vice-President Zongren. Mao Tse Tung himself was surprised at the speed of the fall of the Kuomintang, considering the latter's superiority in arms and numbers. Again it took more than eight months for the communists to cross the Yangtse and reach the eastern sea-board. The mighty question again and again asked by the world is who is really responsible, or rather who is the real culprit for the loss of China to communism. Was it Chiang Kai Shek or Truman or the Japanese warlords? There is no doubt about the wrong policy followed by Chiang in military strategy, leading to its tragic finale. But from the day he assumed the leadership of China, he never got the peace to consolidate power, and establish his firm authority over the length and breadth of the Middle Kingdom. In this respect Japan was the real villain. America alone had the means and instruments to defeat the PLA, but the former lacked the will and resolve to do it.

The Sun Yat-sen Heritage and Revolution

175) Again a look back into history. After the fall of China's last emperor, it was hey-day for the secessionists and warlords, and the disintegration of the empire itself was around and threatening. In the last phase of the Sun revolution, the emperor's commander in chief Yuan Shikkai defected to the rank of the Sun revolutionists. In a secret deal with Sun Yat-sen, Shikai betrayed his loyalty to the royal throne, abandoned the emperor and joined the rebels to seize power through military conspiracy. The royal house of Peking was appalled and the many millennia-old empire came crashing down. Based on the secret deal Sun Yat-sen after a brief stint, handed over the presidency to the warlord Yuan Shikai. Again as warlord he ruled China from 1911 to 1916 as dictator. He could not take effective steps to consolidate the country by suppressing the other warlords and rebels. The sudden disappearance of monarchy created a power vacuum, and so anarchy and disintegration, were threatening the new republic. Abu Shikkai died in 1916 and Sun Yat-sen got back the presidency he had surrendered in 1912 (after being China's first President only for ten weeks), Sun, though the national hero and icon, was an idealist spearheading international revolution. He proved a bad administrator also as most idealists are, and his political illusions forced him go to many idealistic and unpragmatic schemes. Establishing his capital in Nanking, Sun could administer only a part of China, though he had already risen up as the only leader establishing sway over the entire Chinese subcontinent. His weak side was that he was liberal minded and irresolute, and in the face of criticism he would elect out of power. In 1920, in a fit of anger, he sailed to Japan, where he had his early political training, but came back after sometime. In 1922, he sailed again to Shanghai—the commercial capital of China, and returned after a while. Because of his waverings and idealism, once again the warlords in different regions went active and separatist, and they were moving to secede.

176) The Chinese Communist Party (CCP) was founded in Shanghai in 1921. It was two scholars in the Peking University who are the founders. They were Liu Dhazhavo the librarian, and Chen Duxiu—the dean of the faculty of letters in the university. Liu was entranced by the Russian Revolution of 1917 and he delivered lectures in many educational centres. Many students in Peking University itself became his followers, who rose to prominence in the party in later years. An impoverished clerk in the university library was Mao Tse Tung whom Liu had employed. The Chinese Communist Party (CCP) was born the product of the May Fourth Movement, which was the violent Chinese response against the decision of the Versailles powers to entrust the German colony (concession) of Shandong to Japanese Mandate. It was a violent agitation sweeping China, and students in universities and academia went into turmoil. This explosion of nationalist anger was giving rise to many political movements in the country. The force behind the founding of the CCP was the Bolshevik message that China needs a revolution to check Western imperialism and reestablish her power at home. In March 1920, the Soviet Union, through it Karakhan Manifesto informed China that Russia was prepared to return the Chinese Eastern Railway in Manchuria, and this declaration was at once taken by the people of China as the new generosity of Bolshevik Russia towards their country. This Soviet decision stood in contrast to the Tsarist policy of exploiting the weakness of the declining Manchus. The result was a spurt in pro-Soviet and pro-communist feelings in China. But unfortunate that Russia later renounced this promise, but the favourable impression already created would enable to found the Chinese Communist Party (CCP) in Shanghai in 1921. In 1920, the Comintern despatched Gregory N. Votinsky to China to advise and guide the founding of the CCP. Votinsky met Li Dhazhao and Chen Duxiu and advised them to form the Youth League. They started recruiting and training young students and activists. Mao Tse Tung has already become a protégé of Li Dhazhao, and the former formed his cell in Changsha. The CCP held its first Congress in Shanghai in July 1921, with only 13 delegates. The Dutch communist Maring came as advisor, who later became the head of the Comintern in China. Chen Duxiu was chosen the leader of the CCP in the Shanghai Congress which Mao Tse Tung attended as the delegate from Yunan. The party attacked the imperialism of the west and the militarism of China. The CCP organized railway workers and formed factory unions and by 1923 the CCP had a membership of 300. In 1923, the CCP held its Third Congress in Guangzhou, under the guardianship and care of Sun Yat-sen. Maring wanted the CCP to join the Kuomintang and several leader including Li Dhazhao and Chen Dixiu joined the KMT accordingly. Joining the other parties as a step in political strategy, the CCP was determined to maintain its ideological identity, and its control on labour unions. By 1923, Soviet financial help was offered to the party. The Russian Bolshevik Borodin was sent to China as principal advisor to Sun Yat-sen, and Maring was replaced by Votinsky as advisor to CCP, Soviet Russia (Comintern) appointed three representatives to China-Karakhan in Beijing, Borodin in Guangzhou and Votinsky in Shanghai. The Soviet aim was to bring Communist revolution in China and take her into the anti-imperialist camp, and thereby weaken the hold of Britain, USA and Japan on China who were set on a course to establish a new order in China. The Washington Conference (1921-22) was a watershed in this respect. China emphasized in the conference her sovereignty and independence. The Washington Treaty was signed as the Nine Power Pact. At the same time, China and Japan reached a new agreement in which Japan agreed to return the Mandated Holdings (German before 1918) in Shanghai back to China, though allowing some privileges for Japan in the province. Britain, USA and Japan decided to take a more favourable view on the question of political stabilisation of China. But war-lordism, separatism and anarchy would lead the country into uglier turmoil.

177) This was time for the Nationalist Party make its presence more national and powerful. The KMT party Congress was held in Guangzhou in January 1924. Under Borodins advice, Sun Yat-sen reorganised to Kuomintang Party on Soviet lines, with power centered in a small committee elected from above, with the regimented discipline of the lower cadres controlled from above. Sun's decision to admit the communists into the KMP was accepted, but the conservatives in the KMT pleaded emphatically that the communists will hijack the KMT itself in due course. A small number of communists including Li Dazhao were elected to the KMT executive committee. Initially Sun and followers succeeded in raising in the image of KMT as a national

party and made Guangzhou (Canton) their main base. They set up the Wampoa Military Academy in an island near Canton, where the KMT cadets were trained. Sun was collaborating with Zhang Zaolin against the warlords of Beijing, Caokun and Wu Peifu, who held sway over Beijing. While Sun was reaching Beijing to negotiate a settlement with the warlords, he suddenly fell ill due to cancer and died on March 25, 1925.

178) By this time the KMT could recruit more than 200000 members while the CCP membership reached 10000. The policy of the communists was to split the KMT. The pro-Soviet Liao Zhonkai was assassinated. In retaliation Chiang Kaishek Wang Ching-wei and Borodin have decided to deport many conservatives. Some KMT veterans in the North wanted to expel Borodin and the communists, and they established a new KMT headquarters in Shanghai. This was the time when Chiang would catch the national attention.

179) Chiang was born in a farmer family in the coastal province of Zhejiang. From 1909 to 1911, he served in the Japanese army. As a man of energy he was attracted into political adventures. Many Chinese compatriots were then in Tokyo planning to overthrow of the Qings, and their companionship and interaction would turn Chiang into a revolutionary. Hearing about the Sun revolution in China in 1911, Chiang returned home to organise the fight to protect the new republic. He participated in the fight against the warlords and the new emperor Yuan Shikai, and then came a short period of political lull. When Sun Yat-sen began to reorganize the KMT on Soviet lines, Chiang was sent on a visit to the Soviet Union. On his return to China, Chiang became the head of the Wampoa Military Academy, whose military backing proved critical in his political rise. Chiang became the commander of the Nationalist Revolutionary Army (NRA) and he tried to place curbs on the communists. He sent away some Soviet advisers who, he thought, were plotting against him, and the communists were banned from high offices in the KMT headquarters, but at the same time demanding communist help for the Northern military expedition he was planning. He showed consummate skill in managing the power equations in the party and the military.

180) The communists were forming labour unions and organising revolt in northern China. For some time the warlords have resurfaced and they came in control of many provinces in the North. The foreign governments in Beijing and in many trading areas cooperated with Chiang and helped him with money and resources for defeating many warlords or winning many over to his side through military threat. Through the successful Northern Expedition Chiang emerged the central political figure in China and people looked at him for restoration of normalcy, and the return of effective governance. By 1928, the Kuomintang Party was able to establish the central authority of the country and the KMT Government established its capital in Nanking. As the capital of China, Nanking underwent speedy reconstruction and renovation and the city turned into a charming metropolis with its beautiful Opera House also. But peace will not last long as the Japanese militarists would invade Manchuria in 1931. Militant trade unions organized by the CCP were raising its head in northern industrial cities, creating unrest and disorder. After the death of Sun Yat-sen in 1925, General Chiang, through his political and military master strokes seized the leadership of the Kuomintang Party and he became the effective ruler of China and very much as successor to the father of the nation. Chiang headed the Kuomintang Party until his death (in Taiwan) in 1975. Sun and Chiang had married sisters, and though a militarist himself, Chiang was mouthing the preachings of Sun Yat-sen emphatically and repeatedly to his political advantage. Sun's teachings were so vague and unreal that any pretender can assume the role of his disciple and commentator without committing evident contradictions. Though becoming a militarist, Chiang represented Marxian thinking in his formative years, and while in Japan he turned a revolutionary. He accepted Soviet aid and advice, and this was his mainstay in the beginning stages. Because of the loose and idealistic policy of Sun, the warlords usurped power in many parts of China, and for sometime it appeared that the empire was facing immediate disintegration. Chiang decided that his first task is to crush the warlords or to win them over, and prevent the break-up of the empire, and in this attempt he

succeeded in a large measure during 1925-26. All along he could enjoy the patronage and blessings of Moscow, and was receiving regular aid from Lenin and Stalin. Always a representative of the Comintern was stationed in China. Stalin had only a love-hate relationship with the CCP, though the CCP working had been supervised by the twenty-eight Bolshevists—largely a nominated body of the Comintern. Though professing himself a Marxist, Chiang was convinced that the suppression of trade unions was vital for the economic reconstruction and well-being of the country. In his Northern Expedition of 1925-26, he slaughtered tens of thousands of communists in Shanghai and in other northern cities and under the same campaign, he fought and defeated many warlords. It was through the Northern Expedition, he re-established the central authority in China once more, but the job could never be completed, mainly because of Japanese invasion and the war against communists. In fact the Japanese attack on Manchuria in 1931, took the wind out of his sail, and this fight was to go unabated until the end of the Second World War. His misfortune was that he had to fight the warlords, the communists and the Japanese conquerors at the same time. Often he fought the Japanese joining hands with the communists. To escape the Japanese marauders, who occupied a large part of coastal China parts of Peking and Nanking also he moved his capital first to Wuhan and then to the interior city of Chunking, walled and surrounded by mountains and from 1936 to 1945, Chunking housed his capital. In 1927, there was a temporary reproachment between the Kuomintang and the Communists, and Mao Tse Tung himself was inducted a member of the Kuomintang Central Committee. But before long they parted company, but strangely the Chiang-Stalin comradeship continued, irrespective of these domestic breaches and conflicts. This conflicting politics was creating a very strange situation for the CCP. Even after the slaughter of thousands of communists in Shanghai in 1926, Mao Tse Tung remained in the communist faction pleading not to break with the Kuomintang. Perhaps Mao too was of the view that the first part of the proletarian revolution shall be mounted only by the petit bourgeoisie, and the bourgeoisie, and by none else.

181) The Leninist theory, although opportunistic, says that the first stage of a proletarian revolution has to be carried out by the bourgeois parties, like the February Revolutionists in Russia. He argues that the first part of the revolution is possible only in cooperation with the bourgeoisie, and the second part alone will be the real proletarian revolution. Stalin and Molotov had pleaded in the Comintern that Chiang has been carrying out the first part, and so they urged the Chinese Communists to follow Chiang in any case. Whatever may be the merit of this argument by examining the general history of many communist victories it is seen that this policy was coming to fruition ultimately. Only with the American entry in the Pacific war during the Second World War, was coming the lucky times for the Kuomintang. But the Soviet entry in the Pacific war, though belated, can be seen as basically harming Kuomintang interests in the final analysis. It is history that it was Russia who helped the Kuomintang with substantial financial and arms aid until the war clouds of the Second World War began to gather over the Pacific sky. Stalin, in his directives asked the CCP not to break with Chiang as a united China alone can fight Japan whose threat Stalin feared very much. But after the war, Stalin's moves were not only not friendly but exploitative. Even the CCP will not exonerate Russia of the crime of the vandalistic loot of industrial equipment from the Manchurian industrial plants, immediately after the Japanese surrender in 1945. The massive thrust made by Russia into Manchuria at the fag end of the war even after the Hiroshima and Nagasaki bombings, resulted in her capture and occupation of industrial Manchuria in lightening speed. The conventional war in the Pacific was expected to last much longer, but the Russian campaign became unnecessary with America dropping atom bombs over Hiroshima and Nagasaki. In the post-war settlement, Chiang got back all the lands she had lost in the long war with Japan, right from 1895 to the end of the war in 1945. But the home situation in turmoil, there was no domestic peace inside China. In the above background, a direct American entry in the Civil War alone would have rescued the Kuomintang, but America was not ready to make it, as she thought it a job too heavy

and risky at that time. The American attempts to improve the discipline and organisation of the sick and corrupt Kuomintang military machine was an impractical and impossible dream to realize in the confusion of war torn China. While the world war was raging, was it possible for America to wait till the day the Kuomintang government would reorganize itself into a disciplined fighting force, and re-establish its battling credentials? For example, the French government had gone fundamentally aimless, leaderless and directionless, before the start of the Second World War (in Europe), but the Allies decided to rescue the French from the German terror. If America had decided to reorganize and retrieve the French army from that diffident general Gamelin and the German-dummy Marshall Petain, and wanted to build its fighting prowess, what would have been the fate of the war in Europe? In spite of Chiang Kai Shek's policy blunders in the past, still he deserved to be rescued only to prevent the loss of China to communism. The question is it possible for America to rescue the Kuomintang through direct military intervention, and this is once again history's blunt interrogatory to the Truman administration. Was not America possessing the military might to carry out that onerous job? Truly it had, but America wanted to shirk that duty, and that was the blundering folly of Truman and his kitchen cabinet. At that time, the decision to intervene would have been a decision momentous and dangerous to Washington, but then a dangerous decision alone would have been the proper decision.

182) Retrospective examination of past reasons cannot undo the past, as it is part of recorded history, but the future has not only the right but the duty also to reflect on its logics. Regarding the loss of China, conflicting opinions and assessments are still agitating the thoughts of the people of the United States and the free world, and unlikely that that controversy would die down in American political debates in the near future. The 20th century American democracy's obsession and fetish is that she will not strike when the iron is hot. Many post-war American presidents were only captains of irresolution, and courtiers of dilemma. All American efforts during the Chinese Civil War were to reform Chiang and his disloyal and corrupt military establishment. If the Chiang strategy was competent and capable and his troops loyal and disciplined, there would have been no necessity for him to seek American help to fight the communists. Only because Chiang was a bad strategist, that the services of the disciplined and powerful American forces had been summoned, as the factor able to rescue the battered ally. A direct US entry in the Civil War alone was the remedy, but that role America refused to play. Had America at least stationed a contingent of troops in China even as reserve, that step alone would have boosted the morale or the Kuomintang forces and prevented the massive defection from its ranks. But all American attempts were to reform the unreformable, and if the Kuomintang will not reform themselves, let them go to the hell, was the American policy and resolve. During the Civil War the United States was sending commission after commission to China to study the Civil War situation and to suggest ways to prevent a Kuomintang collapse. When Truman was unready to intervene, what was the purpose of sending such commissions except only as eyewashes to cover up the retreat policy already decided upon. Truman failed to foresee the multiple disasters awaiting Asia, and consequently America too when a communist takeover of continental China was set to become a reality. Again to stress that it was in the midst of the Chinese Civil War that the 1948 Truman-Dewey contest for presidency was taking place. The Civil War was to end only in October 1949. If the president election in America came immediately after the communist victory in China, a humiliated and shocked America would not have voted Truman back to power. At the same time a Dewey victory was promising America's direct entry in the Chinese Civil War, and this was the prominent Republican platform also in the campaign. The Democratic platform was non-intervention. The Republican platform for immediate intervention was supported by a large section of the media and it did not look unpopular. The pollsters predicted a Dewey win, but it was Truman who made it. The Chinese Communists were euphoric to witness the upset victory of Truman, supporting the defeatists and the pro-communists then staying in the White House and in state department.

183) The general look back shows that there was no effective, anti-communist American strategy in the Chinese Civil War. It was all apathy, indecision, hopelessness and fault-findings around, but always missing the real point. Any change was possible only with change in the presidential policy. Truman, who from the course of the Civil War, could easily anticipate the fast approaching fall of the Kuomintang, was probably apprehensive that an American direct intervention was too large a project for the war-weary United States to undertake and that too so immediately after the Armageddon. At the same time, the Chinese Communists, who were ill-equipped, ill-fed and war-weary as long as from 1931 onwards, were ready to fight even with the scanty resources and rickety instruments at hand, and that is the difference between the democratic America and communist China. In the 1948 president election, the initial trends were showing Tom Dewey—the Republican hawk, slated to win. Dewey, the young and dynamic governor of New York was considered a strong man, openly advocating American entry in the Chinese Civil War. The prominent and powerful Pro-Kuomintang faction in the United States was hoping that with very active support and demand from the Congress, it was possible for Truman to support Chiang with troops and arms. Madams Chiang was given rousing receptions wherever she went in the United States including New York. Even very prominent Americans like Wendell Wilki were persuaded by the charming Madame Chiang, but Truman wanted to ignore her brashly, which went against the popular pro-China sentiment in the United States. Pro-Kuomintang America believed that a Dewey victory is clear and present and that victory would turn the tables against the communists. But a Truman victory was rather the surprise verdict of America, and the fate of the Kuomintang was sealed.

184) The strong American war policy during the Second World War, and her weak policy during post-war years stand in clear contrast, but the weak policy becoming the deadly factor deciding the fate of China forcing her go communist. If incompetence, corruption and lethargy will disqualify an ally from getting American military help, the first country that ought to have gone down the drain during the Second World War was France. The French people wanted to fight Germany to the finish, but the leaders were back-tracking, and the army was headed by thorough misfits like Gamelin. The British Governments of Baldwin and Neville Chamberlain too were abominably guilty of encouraging German rearmament to go at furious pace. If President Roosevelt also thought the Truman way, the former could have told the world that these complacent, sleepy governments of France and England do not deserve help, and the German attack on Europe being a self-invited one, America had no moral duty to intervene. The final question to be asked is whether America was capable of defending the Kuomintang and defeat the communists through her armed power. She certainly had the military might and the unlimited resources to carry out that job, but she, becoming irresolute and motiveless, resiled back. The task of reforming the Kuomintang, battered beyond repair by Japan, was not a duty to be undertaken when the enemy is at the gate. The first priority ought to have been the defeat of the enemy, and only after that the reform question ought to be addressed. Let the free world count the future tragedies and dangers thrown up against Asia through the American indecisions and vacillations in the 1946-49 Civil War? The communist victory in China is the basic cause making the most deadly challenge to the free world in post-war years. Nuclear-powered Communist China is now so confident to take on the nuclear armed America by its horns, and with impunity. In all post-war military contests waged in the Far East, East Asia and South Asia, Communist China and her protégés and clients have come out the winners. As John Mc Cain says, America is often getting only spineless leadership in Washington. In post-war American elections, it is the defeatist and demagogic rhetorics that ride rough-shod over the words of courage and adventure, and this populist debility is disabling democracies, including the America superman.

185) General MacArthur—the hero of the Second World War in the Pacific was continuing the American Commander in the Pacific, when the Chinese Civil War was raging. But General George C. Marshall—the American Chief-of-staff was directly dealing with the civil war, and in the civil war theatre, MacArthur was given no role. Marshall was particular that in any event, there shall be no direct American military intervention in China. He himself came down to China many times to negotiate a compromise with the CCP, and at one stage, in order to compel Chiang to behave, America imposed an arms-embargo also on the Kuomintang lasting about one year, and this step was taken when the communists were on ropes. This act of aid was doing serious damage to the Kuomintang. In the immediate aftermath of the Second World War, when Russian troops withdrew from Manchuria, America had dispatched a contingent of marines to guard these areas on behalf of the Kuomintang, and the presence of these marines was proving devastatingly effective in keeping status quo in the area. In the case of an American direct entry, perhaps MacArthur would have been put in charge of the operation, but the green signal never came from Washington. The White House and the state department were engaged in the futile game of reforming the unreformable, and finally they lost both the reform and the war.

186) Ideologically the communists cannot think of truces and peace, so long as any part of the globe is under non-communist rule. China hit the soft-target of Tibet in 1950, and surprising that she escaped that ghastly crime with flying colours. While China was raping Tibet, the Chinese-proxy-North Korea, suddenly attacked the non-communist South without provocation, and in the beginning the former could make an easy walkover. America, standing wounded and shocked of the loss of China, became furious, and that anger forced President Truman to act promptly in the new battlefield. The American troops, entering under UN auspices, pushed back the North Korean invaders to the Chinese border, and this counter attack had upset all Chinese calculations. The North Korean supremo Kim Ill Sung had promised Stalin to complete the conquest within ten days. As the North was committing aggression on the South, there was no obvious reason for China to feel aggrieved of the American entry, unless she was deeply committed in the enterprise through a pre-war agreement or conspiracy with the invader. A large Chinese army at once marched into North Korea, and the war escalated into a full-scale conflict between China and the United States. The fight continued for three years, but no decisive step was taken by America to execute a strategy for a wholesale win. Again America was staggering and irresolute. At the height of the war, MacArthur, now commander of the Korean operations, pleaded with Washington to extend the war to China proper, bomb the major cities of Peking and Shanghai, and unleash Chiang Kai Shek over the mainland. The general reiterated that the Korean War was the second opportunity, and perhaps the golden opportunity for America to correct her fatal error in the Chinese Civil War. But the American defeatists accused him of contemplating the use of atom bomb, in case conventional arms fail. As the Soviet Union was not an open combatant in the Korean War, atom bomb was a possible option for America. But Truman was taking this MacArthur advisory an affront to his presidential authority. Declaring that the general was exceeding his brief by speaking so dangerously, he dismissed MacArthur from Korean command and appointed Gen: Ridgeway in his place. The fall of MacArthur the hero of the Second World War in the Pacific was shocking news for America—who thought the president was defiling and dishonouring the great winner of the Second World War in the east. Truman won a victory over his defiant general, but he was losing the war on communism. American defeatism that brought success to the communists in the Chinese Civil War has already sunk its deeper roots in the halls of power in Washington, and then inescapable that many more pro-democracy and pro-American governments in Asia and elsewhere will again fall before the communist juggernaut.

187) In the Chinese Civil War, General Marshall was very particular to give the message to the CCP that in any contingency, there will be no direct American entry, and this assurance was the most important signal bolstering the confidence of the communists, but frustrating and demoralizing the Kuomintang. Again the question was asked why the Kuomintang were not assisted in the Civil War, if America had the means to rescue her strategic ally in Asia? The President was ambivalent throughout, and it is believed that Truman had practically written off China much before Chiang had decided to flee to Formosa. Who could

then comprehend the domino effect of this very dangerous American climb down, and the chain of tragic events this might produce for Asian democracy in future? Only later Truman would be puzzled to see how dangerous was his apathy in the Chinese Civil War. The problems and perils that American and Asian democracies would face due to the loss of China, ought to be mountainous. If a fraction of the arms and troops poured into the Korean and Vietnam theaters had been sent to Chiang during 1946-49, the Kuomintang would have easily defeated the communists. True, the Kuomintang rot had gone to dangerous, desperate ways and days. But what mattered was that in the hour of need, America wavered under a strategic amnesia and such Washington dilemmas are usual in the post-war behaviour of the American superman. After 1950, America entered many Asian wars as democracy's defender, but she will desert the client midway, and thus the superpower has been coming down as the most undependable ally of her allies and protégés, and this American drift and demoralization leaving the world democracy itself unsafe. When the enemy is fighting at his highest capacity as every combatant ought to be, that war the opponent cannot win unless he too expends his highest power in the battlefield.

Democracy—Always Defensive

188) The post-war democratic world is duty bound to examine why in the battlefield, democracy alone makes complaints about the pains and privations of war, and why the people under dictators and authoritarians air no grievance about their war agonies which are often deeper and more traumatic. War, certainly is a period of agony and anxiety both for the aggressor and the victim. Even while a war is in progress, the people in a democracy questions the very relevance and necessity of an ongoing war. When the soldier is fighting with his life, the comfort-seeking, fearful democrat at home is questioning the propriety and justifiability of the capital sacrifices committed in the battlefield and the massive economic lossess suffered in combat. These critics will question the very wisdom of going to war, and unashamedly they try to explain the lesser pains and the cheaper costs of defeat, as if war is a trading operation.

It now appears that the consumerist society of the freeman, which is the other name for a cowardly society, has become so unnationalistic, unpatriotic and shameless that they cannot stand the risk, misery and sacrifice needed to fight and win a patriotic war. Why do man go to war? War is to protect freedom, and to protect the people from subjugation, and consequent enslavement. It is to defend the national territory and defend its culture and honour but still the democrat neglects the war, and why? It shows the decline in the political morals of democratic patriotism, and national honour. Also this shows the appalling erosion of human values based on the ungallant preferences of the modern democrat for idle pleasures. At present, democracy sharpens its swords diligently only to wrest out the petty rights, but defiantly refusing to defend the fortress of freedom, and this has become the inbuilt self-contradiction of post-war democracy. In this decline of political values, surprising that America—the world policeman, shows the way for other democrats.

189) Democracy is bound to live a high-balanced life because of its moral accountability to the people. Under the dictatorship of the proletariat, the people are abruptly robbed of their rights, and forced to lie exhausted through the staggering physical and mental tortures unloaded on them by the state, and that done only to prove a wrong ideology right. At the same time democracy imposes upon the citizen the responsibility and duty to construct and maintain a state-machine, upholding his right to enjoy the fundamental human rights. A democrat, simultaneously has to defend his rights against state power, and defend the democratic state against the foreign and domestic enemies. Democracy, being a system under checks and balances, is expected to succeed easily because of no blockading walls standing between the state and citizen. The British have succeeded, America and Canada have succeeded, India is assumed to proceed towards success, and post-war Japan, Germany and Western Europe also are on their way to success. In this respect, Africa and Latin America tell a different story, or a mixed story. In these two continents democracy has sudden rises and comic falls, and again its irregular or incomplete resurrections. Except South Africa, many democratically born African states are in the hands of dictators, autocrats, semi-democrats, secessionists and civil-warriors, but presently the situation showing signs of improvement. Democracy's inherent strength is it being basically driven by the laws of nature and the laws of natural persuasions. When an artificially and coercively built up political system falls, the spontaneous preference of political events is towards democracy. As said already, democracy's rulers are restrained and restricted by the checks and balances of a constitution and the rule of law. The dominant element in checks and balances is separation of powers. That the real ruler, even under the law of separation, is the executive is the self-evident truth, and this fact the critics of state power shall always remember, while commenting on the turf-wars fought over the theory of separation of powers. The powers of the legislature and the judiciary reached the present stage as the designer and corrector, and these powers have taken shape by drawing it out from the original stock of executive power. This separation, codification and consolidation of legislative and judicial power came through innumerable installments, and this division of power will become more defined through the growth of democracy. A democracy, under parliamentary or presidential method, elects an executive as prime minister or president as the real power-holder. Usual and possible that the same ruler will be tempted to look at the unrestrained, unlimited authority of another dictator or despot, and may wish such power for himself too. Once placed in power, the democrat also will dream of arbitrary power. Many democrats, employing the police power in hand, had turned into dictators, and these dictators last in power for months, years or for life, and some does not hesitate to found their ruling dynasties. Hitler and Mussolini came to power using the instruments and techniques of democracy, but violating its basic commands, they overthrew the same democracy that enabled them to reach power. Such topplings and repudiations presently take place in many newly decolonised democracies in Africa and Asia. Latin American dictators and semi-dictators are a common legacy of the continent, ever since their days of liberation in the 19th century, but they, except perhaps Fidel Castro, were not long-enduring. Many were democratically elected, and many deposed by other dictators. In Argentina, Juan Peron came the unelected President in 1945, but he, through his political and ideological romances, threw up a lot of political fireworks and myths, ending up destroying the country's economy. Brazil, Argentina and Chile are today on fast track to build their economy and democracy. South American freedom is not yet getting a clear and smooth ride into full democracy in any country including the big brothers—Brazil, Mexico and Argentina. True, Brazil, Argentina, Chile and Mexico are changing fast, to stabilize democracy. Chile—the state that under-went a Marxian revolution under Allende, and thereafter taken over by the military junta of Pinochet, is now a political showpiece of democracy, bristling with high economic growth. A stable democracy in Latin America is Costa Rica, but too tiny to make an impact on the big neighbours.

190) Why a superpower like American democracy, who masterminded and led the free-world win the two world wars, and set herself up as democracy's power house in post-war years, is utterly failing to defend democracy in recent times is the question perplexing and haunting the 21st century democrat. During the world wars, America's national press, which then constituted the main-frame media in the country, stood by the president, enabling him to battle at any cost and sacrifice. The only national motive was the defeat of the conqueror. Morals of war demand that a warrior has to fight up to his highest capacity to win, and any cost in blood and matter is worth it. But the war-psychology and patriotism of the free world in post-war years, dominated by Cold War and its chilling aftermath, is going unashamedly apologetic. In a democracy, like the United States, populist cowardice and trepidation has risen up as a kind of neo-nationalism, and this decline is the root-cause of America's failure in post-war battles. Take the cases of the Chinese Civil War, Korean War, Vietnam War, Cuban Missile Crisis and other battle-fronts where she failed to succeed. This surrender-happy American majority was the real agent encouraging Truman to allow the annexation of Tibet by Communist China in 1950 and China doing it more cleverly under the cover of the Korean War. As the ward of India and the free world, the large territory of

Tibet ought to have been as much important to them as South Korea, or more important. When during the Second World War, Chiang Kai Shek made the move to encroach into Tibet and Sinjiang, the warnings of America and Britain made him turn back. History tells that the millennia-old Chinese desire and design to annex and incorporate Tibet into China had been consistently resisted, fought and foiled by the warring Tibetans. In 1903, the Russian move on Tibet was preventively resisted by Lord , but in 1950 Britain had left India and China found Nehru the poor man, Communist China took the adventurous step of seizing Tibet by force, and surprisingly the Indian response to this high crime turned out not only cooperative but collaborationist. While the American response was mute and weak, they were willing to accept the lead of India in this respect, let it be war or peace. But a China-friendly, pro-Communist Nehru appeared eager to surrender Tibet to the Chinese warlord as his personal trophy. Surprising that he was executing this surrender deceptively, euphemising this monstrous crimes China unloaded on the monastic, defenceless Tibetans. Nehru was hiding the severity of the Tibetan tragedy from the know of the Indians and the free world as long as much as he could. To give the cover up, and then gloss and shine to the sins and terrors of Red-imperialists on Tibet, there stood the International Communist brigade in the frontline, openly speaking treason and working as China's spy-ring across the world. As the chief and chosen defender of human rights, and possessing the military might to perform the job, an assertive, unfearing America alone will guarantee the free society on earth. Britain was the model and guide of world democracy and often its imperial defender, but in the 20th century that role passed on to the United States, who for some time fitted into the job satisfactorily. It is especial that the economic and military power and the technological lead of the United States was enduring unusually long, even in the exploding age of science, where the birth of a single new technology like the atom bomb will overturn the world's balance of power. Democracy's unmilitary rise and expansion has been truly terrific during the post-war era, as the spontaneous first preference of the liberated and liberal society. Democratic philosophy threatens other political systems not through her military arsenal, but through its rights-friendliness, and equality. Democracy's economic dominance is the other factor. So it becomes inevitable that the democratic system throws its ideological challenge to all non-democracies and non-democrats. Common man judges power by its power to destroy. Even in the discourses of political philosophers in the Hellenic era, all great arguments were in favour of democracy. The same democracy is now made to live under the spell and threat of the military power of the modern state. As Bertrand Russell said, the power of the modern state is the power of the gunpowder. Civil supremacy and military power are (now atomic power) permanently fighting and conflicting agents, and that conflict continues the basic threat to modern civil society. Once the military power is abolished, the state will cease to exist. The armed power of the state acts simultaneously as the guarantor of (democratic) civilian power as well as its enemy. The faculty that checks military power from going on rampage is its commitment to professional discipline to keep the civilian power dominant. In many democracies like the United States, Britain, Australia, Japan, Germany, Canada, India, France and the like, because of system stabilization, a military threat to the (democratic) state looks remote or absent. But in a country like Pakistan, after long spells of military rule and military shadow, democracy is again inching forward on come-back trail, but again retreating. The military threat to civil rule from President Musharaff was over with his resignation in August 2008, and after that a democratic government is in saddle, but again shadowed by the undemocratic combination comprising terrorists, the military and fundamentalists. The threat to world democracy from communism and red-terror is fast on the decline after the fall of Soviet Union and Eastern Europe. Red-China appears to have put a brake on her reckless imperial adventures of the fifties and sixties, though her aggressive chauvinism towards India, Tibet, Sinjiang and the South China Sea continues unabated. Communist influence is waning in Africa also, but many African and Latin American dictators jump on to wear the socialist robe, only as political armour to prolong their anti-people rule. By reviewing the post-war political behaviour of man and state, can political pundits assert that democracy will be the ultimate winner? This question may look as puzzling as asking whether power wins or ideology wins in the ultimate field-test of politics.

191) The problems of power are numerous and infinite. Power is a deceptive-person having no human face, and for any ruler power will look intoxicatingly delightful. At present, democracy is the preferred popular route to reach power, but admittedly a very difficult route. A leader reaching power through the democratic process is bound by a bundle of promises he made to the people, often as his election platform, and these promises he is bound to perform. This includes the promise how methodically and softly he will exercise power, and how harmless and modest his power dimensions will be. Will he keep this promise and will he keep it in letter and spirit, are the concerns of the voter, never getting a satisfying answer. Some will, and some will not, and that is an endless puzzle. Every age has its political preferences, and even in the liberal world of human rights, there are people who hate the uncertainty and instability produced by periodic elections, and therefore in heart, preferring a benevolent despot or monarch for stability's sake. This preference becomes stronger when democratic freedom degenerates into indiscipline, disorder and anarchy, and the harassed people crying for peace but this wish for political stability and order, through undemocratic means, finds rare support in the electoral arena. Once the democratic discipline is found enduring, it is unlikely that the people will go for another system.

192) All non-democratic systems have their birth and continuance through the suppression of peoples' opinion by illegally employing the police power of the state. Such threats come from a ruler getting possession of the armed power of the state. But the frightening side is that this armed power of the modern state is too strong for any political protester or agitator to challenge and confront. The world is yet to contemplate an unarmed state. When Bertrand Russell says that the power of the modern state is the power of the gunpowder, that is a statement of fact utterly harsh. When the American Constitution was being debated in Philadelphia, the plea by a large section of the delegates was that the new republic shall not keep a standing army. The contenders feared that the new president (yet to be defined in the Constitution), by looking at the power of the British monarch, may declare himself the new king of the New World, by arbitrarily brandishing the fire-power of the standing army. After long arguments, the contending delegates reached the consensus that America can have a standing army, but its number shall be constitutionally limited to five thousand troops. Then the soft-spoken, rather reticent George Washington (the President of the Convention) stood up to say that there is no harm in limiting the troop-level at five thousand, but the Constitution shall contain one more clause ordering all (enemy) countries in the world not to attack the United States with more than five thousand troops. Then alone the delegates could see the futility and ridiculousness of their troop-limit argument, when it comes to the security of the country. The democrat talks too much, and in the tumult of noisy dialogue, he misses the vitals in the working of the state machine. He will jump up to tussle with the dialectics and logic of pure theories, but when a catastrophe descends suddenly, these arguments come in the way as political imponderables, standing against practical solution.

World War II—How it Benefitted the Communists

193) During the Second World War, the Tokyo Express (Japanese navy) was riding the Pacific waves high and mighty, and for some time it looked that in no time the whole of Asia will fall to Japan. A very large part of Asia has fallen already. The struggle was bitter, deadly and enormously costly both for the aggressor and the defenders. Which democrat then thought that this war ultimately would pave the way for the communist takeover of China, an event the pre-war free world would have prevented at any cost. If there was no Pearl Harbour and no Japan-America war, the American response to the communist programme for takeover of China from the Kuomintang would have been massive retaliation. But by 1945, America, who led the free world to victory in the 6-year long war, and presided over the post-war division of states and the final territorial redistribution of Europe, Asia and parts of Africa also, was declining into a fatigued, motiveless war leader. In checking communism, post-war presidents including Truman went irresponsible and aimless causing the retreat of democracy in many parts of the world, and more particularly in Eastern Europe. America, victorious in the war, but having no long-term strategic view of post-war political currents and undercurrents, had to battle simultaneously on two fronts. On the one side, she had to prosecute the Cold War and on the other, fight the ideological war against communism in the home front, where the media and leftist populism had been rebelling against the dangers of war, already troubling the human race. Unfortunately, this media-Congress joint rebellion was strengthening the new American political platform of liberal defeatism, whose other name was surrender to communism. In her post-war armed battles against the communists, America became generous enough to fail. The sins of Hiroshima and Nagasaki, and its curses and groans ought to have been already deafening the American ears. Truman, reelected and continuing as president till 1953, had the misfortune to preside over three wars continuously—the Second world war, the Chinese Civil War and the Korean War. Except the World War, the conclusion of the other two wars went bad not only for American democracy but for world democracies as well. The American delegation to the Yalta Conference—the conference where FDR surrendered Eastern Europe, Outer Mongolia and many parts in the Far East to Stalin, was found to contain a large number of communist spies including the notorious Alger Hiss, who held an important position in the US state department. After surrendering Eastern Europe to Russia, the second most dangerous decision of America was to demilitarize Japan. War veterans in Japan were wholly turned away from the post-war power structure as war criminals. It was the Japanese militarists, who in 1941, took the country to the disastrous path of confrontation with the United States—then too the economic and military powerhouse of the world. Truman's post-war Secretary of State, Dean Acheson was defeatism incarnate, whose surrender-mania was found to border on a treasonable worship of communist invincibility. In crisis situation matters of state are to be decided by the president, and not by his deputies and mandarins. The President wanted only defeatists to implement his uncertain, wobbly policies against Chinese imperialists. If advisers decide the policy and programme, why Truman refused heed to the advice of General MacArthur to overthrow the communist regime is Beijing by escalating the US war machine. Truman had advisers pleading for strong policy as well as weak policy, but he accepted the weak one which shows that he was on retreat from the Chinese Civil War. While Truman wavered too long, that was finest interval for Mao and comrades to drive Chiang and his battered Kuomintang army out of the mainland. The loss of China to communism is a policy failure still haunting America as her biggest setback in the twentieth century. This failure exposes in full relief the face of democracy's empty and populist rhetorics, always pulling her back from dangerous decisions, when dangerous decisions alone are safe decisions. A review of the events of the 20th century will show that had there been prompt and diligent risk-taking by world democrats, there would have been no communist state in existence after the collapse of Soviet Union and satellites in 1991, though communism surviving as the philosophy of murderous class warriors, who want the most beastly alone to survive as the fittest. Totalitarians bank on the irresistible power of human envy, running amuck through bloody violence.

194) The fatal weakness of modern democracy is that it seldom dares for a preventive armed strike to defend itself and defend human rights. Democracy's response in the defence of man's rights, usually come very late, when the defeasible enemy has become overgrown, and indefeasible. The Khemer Rouge in Cambodia butchered a million and a half people in merciless delight in an open demonstration of totalitarian human engineering. These bloodhounds were leaping into massive slaughter of political innocents, and the terror-struck people are now fearfully moving back from the barbarous killing fields of Pol Pot. They now embrace the liberal route of market economy and (guided) democracy as the new political profession. Important to see that these ideological failures and collapses could not be barricaded and hid within the bamboo or iron curtains for long. Again to be emphasized that the biggest post-war strategic folly of America is the demilitarization of Japan, binding down that warring race to peace and a Peace Constitution. Today's Japan, by constitutional oath and political profession, is a pacific territory renouncing war as the instrument of resolution of disputes. How long can a country keep herself afloat under unarmed peace, when her neighbours stand against overarmed and roaring? That from 1946 to the present, Japan is wholly keeping her word for 'peace' is surprising, when we read into her militant past. Though the Japanese Self Defence Force constitutes a powerful military arm in the Far East, she is yet to flex her muscles internationally. Once Japan has been forced down under peace, the communists battled victoriously in China, Korea, Tibet, India, Indo-China and Vietnam. Red-China conquered her poor neighbours—Tibet and Sinjiang like knife cutting butter. Recently, when the Chinese troops were cracking down on the protesting Buddhist monks in Tibet and China's Tibetan regions, a Japan sitting silent witness to these high crimes (on Tibet), was really an unusual sight, particularly in the midst of China's madding arms race. Immediately after the Second World War, the gallant Japanese battle power had been taken hostage by the United States, and never after released from US custody. Why the country is still held under American control and captivity, in the face of the appalling military reverses suffered by America and her protégés and clients, in the region? The suppression of human rights in China, North Korea and Cuba are the rising international crimes. When China entered the Korean war, if the Japanese had been called in to battle the invader, Red-China would have been beaten by the Japanese armed with American guns. America's political vision and war prejudices against Japan have become obsolete long ago, but the former continues blinded by the latter's shocking war crimes during the Second World War. In Korea and Vietnam, the infirm, lackadaisical American generals and soldiers, led by the fawning retreatism of the political leadership in Washington, mismanaged and mishandled the war to a pre-planned surrender. The only warring people China fears are the Japanese, but Japan never allowed to fight a post-war battle with her pre-war underdog-

China. Post-war Japan's military actions are confined to some police duties at home, and, at times, certain UN peace-keeping missions abroad.

195) Post-war developments in Asia declare in uncertain terms that the disarming of Japan and binding her down to a Peace-Constitution are the continuing America foreign-policy blunders, and more so after the sixties of the last century. In a world defended by arms, there can be no permanent national formula on how to negotiate and reach peace with a future enemy, who is presently unknown. Let me recall the strange policy advocated by the American State Department official—Morgenthau to decimate German militarism by dismantling all German industrial structures wholesale, and turn the German territory into an agricultural pasture. That strange suggestion was finally vetoed by the Allied top brass, allowing Germany to reindustrialize, and that too on fast track. She is today Europe's strongest economy, and the bulwark of European democracy and defence, though not going nuclear. In the case of economic reconstruction alone, a benevolent policy was taken by America towards war-ravaged Japan. The Japanese were allowed to rebuild their economy, and within ten years after the war and defeat, she rebuilt herself again into the industrial powerhouse of Asia. All Asian countries in the forties and fifties were simply agricultural economies, with India alone producing a motor car before the war. Free India and Red-China, until the eighties and nineties of the last century, were wrestling and struggling with ideological illusions—India with socialism and China with collectivism. These two sleeping giants could break out of their ideological shells only in the seventies and nineties respectively, and in this respect Communist China is leading the race. Deng Ziao Ping inaugurated China's age of economic liberalism in 1978, when India, toying with her socialist obsessions, and prejudices was suffering economic comma and stagnation. In 1991, Narasimha Rao, sensing the dangers awaiting a bleak and standstill economy, and perhaps taking a leaf from the Deng theory itself, suddenly executed an about-turn in India's economic thinking, and rather clandestinely pulled India into the superhighway of market economy. This Rao shift was

surprising and it shall be frightening the Indian Socialists, the Congress Socialists and the Marxian-left also. But unminding the objections and political war cry, the Rao locomotive moved forward, though with disabling hick-ups in the beginning stages. Today the world looks at China and India as two giants in scramble for seizing the top economic slot in Asia, and undoubtedly China is in the lead. The forces of economic recession in America starting in 2008 and later in Europe has cast its shadow over India and China also, but both countries once again came back to the recovery regime. The economic liberalism pursued by Japan and Germany in the fifties and sixties with a six per cent plus growth rate was hailed as the economic miracle of the century, empowering these economies to double their GDP every six years. Post-war European economic resurgence was led by Germany (the miracle economy of Europe till 1989 was West Germany) which still is the biggest economy in the continent, and the fourth largest in the world (overtaken by China when this is written). A powerful economy builds a powerful military machine, capable of defending the state against the enemy wearing modern arms, and this plea is especially relevant in the case of democracies. Today the big strategic question facing Asia is why Japan is not allowed to build her own military power to check the rising imperialism of China, hurrying to swallow up whatever soft territory she sights around. The imperial march of China has been naked and strident, since the founding of the communist state in Beijing. Because of the mute and cowardly policy pursued by free India against Chinese imperialism, not much international opposition happened to be voiced, when China invaded Tibet, annexed it and colonised it. In fact the invasion of Tibet was the glorious imperial inaugural of Communist China. The democratic world remembers that China made all these conquests when her internal economic condition was as bad as famished and starving. But in the totalitarian march, the question whether the people were starving and suffering because of the ravages and shortages of war, is the absolute un-concern of the collectivist state. For Mao, the people were merely cannon-fodder for revolution. The Peking rulers started territorial expansion first by striking at defenceless, monastic Tibet. The next Chinese jump was upon South Korea. Though mauled and tasting blood, she was unpunished there and so she threw herself headlong into the Vietnams. The amount of human toll these wars took inside North Korea, North Vietnam and China was so staggering as running into hundreds of thousands. But under a communist system, there is no public opinion and mournings, and so the tragedies of war, state-terror and the consequent genocides are all lost in the eerie dungeons of state secrecy. The enquiring world has to guesstimate what actually was the dastardliness and death unleashed by these wars. Assume such man-made tragedies consuming millions of souls in a democracy like India or the United States or Britain. Certainly, there would break out popular protests and uprisings to end the war and the war agonies, even by ending it midway through a dishonourable, humiliating surrender. In the pre-world war years, such talks and acts constituted the offence of treason. Whether such withdrawal is to end in defeat and abdication of vital national interests and honour is the unconcern of democracy's modern protesters. In the Korean War and the Vietnam War America suffered a human loss, far smaller than the enemy, but American democracy's public opinion was clamouring for accepting defeat, and this clamour was to save the life of the remaining soldiers. The media screamed for the recall of soldiers, and to bring them back uninjured from the bullets whizzing past the battlefield but they damn caring if America wins or surrenders in the battlefield. Most post-war defeats of America and the free world can be traced to the calls, clamours and pressures of democracy's public opinion, often manipulated manufactured and mounted through T.V. channels, campus revolts, pro-red demonstrations, media assaults, and in the case of USA, through the thoughtless surrender calls issued by congressional resolutions. The world later would discover American public opinion being manipulated and distorted by the ungallant, fickle and leftist die hards and spies and intellectuals in the country. The most recent default of American democracy is that the Congress is institutionally and habitually at war with the president, and in the course of this reckless turf war, the former is eagerly seeking the defeat of the president, even at the cost of national loss and honour. In democratic politics, the most humiliating debacle a president or prime minister suffers is losing a war. Of late, in order to accomplish this presidential defeat, the Congress is placing legislative barricades around the war power of the president. The War Power Resolution of the US Congress is a naked, unprecedented assault on presidential power, and the house is committing such unconstitutional, anti-American acts during and after the Vietnam War. While the congressmen fight to win their war against the president, the country is losing against the enemy. Latterly, in congressional debates and media dialogues, patriotism and national honour take the back seat. This fall shows the decline in American political morals, and this is a post-war development. Look back to the FDR days during the Second World War. Another president would have had all clear and convincing excuses for not going to war against the Axis. By giving some last-minute concessions to Japan in raw material and oil embargo, the Pearl Harbour strike could have been averted. On the other hand, for FDR, the Pearl Harbour strike came as the bolt from the blue, supplying the long awaited pretext and provocation to declare war on Japan, and then on the Axis itself. Was not Pearl Harbour intentionally invited by the Secretary of State-Cordell Hull by snubbing the Japanese premier Prince Konoye, through rejecting the latter's final appeal for a personal meeting with FDR? But in the war against Japan and the Axis, the Congress and the media stood solidly behind the president, and the war-efforts went apace in full steam to total mobilization. Within no time of declaring war, America was converted into a military-industrial complex functioning as the in-exhaustible armoury of the Allies, including totalitarian Russia. In the above background, it remains a puzzle why the more powerful, nuclear-armed America failed in China, Korea and Vietnam. The growing diffidence of American populism, the weak and irresolute presidents, the defeatist and anti-war media dominated by the American left, and an adversary Congress fighting all out turf wars against the president, all joined hands to ensure the victory of communist imperialism in these theatres. America—the winner of the two world wars, suddenly undergoing a monastic conversion, was running away from the final battle. At the final stage of any post-war battle, she unashamedly throws her protégés and patrons to the communist wolves, and go home in sinful regret. South Vietnam's last President General Thieu's farewell address to the nation, before leaving his homeland on the eve of American surrender, gives eloquent testimony to the sweeping defeatism and moral collapse, paralyzing the American political psyche.

196) When America, fearing adventures, was readying herself to abdicate her national honour for the sake of conspicuous consumption, the different but more important question is why she failed, and again fails to utilize the Japanese power for battling and stopping the communist juggernaut in Asia. Post-war America never asked Japan to join the war against Chinese imperialism, and this Japanese exclusion was a shot in the arm of China to invade Tibet, Korea and Indo-China. At the same time, America was giving demilitarised Japan the protection of her nuclear umbrella, under whose spell the Japanese could go into their dynamic economic business and undynamic military sleep. Even today, China, fears the battling power and strike power of Japan. Japanese discipline, battle-courage, strategy, tactics and gallantry, as demonstrated during the pre-world war and world war years, are notorious and legendary. But that erstwhile militarist today is a committed democrat, more committed to peace. Why should her peace-commitment prohibit her from those battles and wars, which in effect, were battles to defend Asia and Asian democracy? In democracy, the people have their freedom and human rights to be lost in war, and therefore they are expected to fight with all powers to defend the country to defend freedom. But in practice what happens is the reverse. In a dictatorship or tyranny, the people, through losing a war, have nothing to lose but their chains, but still they fight a war up to the last man, this is to defend their serfdom and slavery. In truth, their victory in war is to defend their own enslavement, and make it more enduring. Considering how much important it is to defend human liberty and democracy, it would have been eminent strategy and high moral for the free world to rearm Japan and call her to fight communist aggression in Korea and

Vietnam. As usual democracy talk too much and act too little to defend her ideals. Ideological fulminations and moral arguments have never won battles and wars because battles are to be fought by blood and arms. They are to be fought to the bitter-end, as limited wars are never to reach victory but to make a dishonest escape from the battlefield.

Who Wins—Ideology or Arms

197) Interesting that though political ideologies have never won wars, when victory comes, the politician is hell-bent to superimpose his ideology upon the sweat and blood already spilt in the battlefield and then he sells out this victory as triumph of ideology to the ideology-sauvy. Innumerable popular uprisings had been mounted in history, and most of these revolts were defeated and decimated by state power. Some alone reach success. Later, a naked victory of arms will be held aloft by the ideologue as victory of the ideology, he champions. Not surprising that the people readily endorse this ideology impost, while no argument stands furthest from the truth. Mao Tse Tung and Chiang Kai Shek fought each other before, and during the Civil War, and in the final contest, Mao won and Chiang lost, and this Mao victory was the victory of military strategy and arms. But Mao and comrades would call it a communist revolution, masterminded by the theory of Marx and Engels. After the military victory, Mao fashioned the party ideology and structured the government machinery in such absolutist terms that he himself will continue the ruler and party supremo until his death, as Lenin did in Russia. It may be true that in this strategy of seeking a life tenure, the leaders need not always be successful, but Mao succeeded, very much like Lenin, and he perpetuated himself at the top of the power pyramid till his death in 1976. During his reign, whenever there came a challenge within the party to his personal power, sooner he would engineer political purges, bogus named 'Let Hundred Flowers Bloom', 'Cultural Revolution' and so on, but all programmes were aiming to eliminate his political opponents, up to the last man. When the Great Leap Forward foundered, causing a famine that killed at least 45 million souls, the unrepentant Mao launched the 'Cultural Revolution', which brutally continued for the decade from 1966 to 1976. In 1976 when Mao died the project came to a grinding halt. The hot period of the Cultural Revolution was two years, and thereafter the Red Guards were restrained, but already thousands were killed and millions persecuted and uprooted from settled life and tens of thousands of party leaders and workers were sent to farms as slave labour. After 1968, this programme continued, less brutally till 1976. Through these orchestrated ideological manoevres, Mao eliminated his political adversaries in the power hierarchy almost to the last rebel. His massacres in dissent elimination during his reign is put at several million, but compared to Stalin, this is counted a lesser proportion of the population, though recent reports say it was higher than Stalin's. State-induced famines precipitated by Mao, consumed more than thirty million souls, even by party count, but recent reports say it was above 60 million. Emperors and dictators in history felt no need to kill so massively in order to confirm themselves in the throne of power. The master guide of Mao in this respect must be Lenin, who invented the terror state and state-terror as the devastating instrument for power capture, power endurance and power exercise. When, quite accidentally and incautiously the Supreme Assembly of Soviet Dictatorship comprising the Socialists, Bolsheviks, Mensheviks, Compromisers conferred power on Lenin, he, at once, to the utter shock end amazement of his electors themselves, converted that power into authoritarian power to rule with guns. By misusing this power, he crushed the majority, who unsuspectingly elected him, knowing not a bit about the murderous state machine he had been contemplating in his Swiss exile. Hitler, who came to power through popular election, betrayed that trust in order to destroy the Weimar Republic, democracy and political opposition. Anyhow his political victims do not count even a fraction of the tens of millions killed by Stalin and Mao Tse Tung. Of course Hitler's final solution to the Jewish problem would run into six million during the war years. Mussolini came to power through a popular assault, and getting power in the half-democratic way, he, without wait, proclaimed himself dictator of Italy, but in theory, he ruling under King Victor Immanuel II. Leading the violent march of thousands of Brown Shirts to the gates of Rome, he was able to cover up his dictatorial intentions, and under the colour of revolution, he launched his new political dogma-Fascism. Lenin, Stalin, Mao, Hitler and Mussolini—all will die in office, as revolts and revolutions simply fizzled out under their genocidal crackdowns. In committing mass murders, persecutions and suppression of human rights, there are no tyrants in history to match Stalin, and he was faithfully followed by Mao, Kim Ill Sung, Pol Pot and others. Historic that no popular uprising erupted against these genocidal demons, or if erupted it was brutally and secretly crushed. Still the popular myth survives that a revolution mounts itself up spontaneously against bad rulers and brutal regimes. This high-sounding proposition, the totalitarians of the 20th century would rubbish down as a hollow myth. Revolutions succeed only against weak-rulers, and popular revolts are irrelevant movements against the heavily-armed, modern state. If bad rulers invite revolutions, there ought to have come revolutions very early against Lenin, Stalin, Mao Tse Tung, Pol Pot and Fidel Castro, but no popular revolt could be even whispered, much less conspired against them. The prospect of murderous crackdowns by these tyrants was looking deadly. State-terror and the scale of genocides by communist regimes are so huge and thorough, that all revolters are forced to go underground or before the firing squads. Tzar Nicholas-II was a very weak-ruler, and in spite of a fast growing economy, the revolutionists could overthrow him because he did not know how to use his huge armed power to his advantage. Louis the XVI was presiding over the French Revolution to its success, he too being among the weakest rulers in history. Even his affectionate wife Mary Antoinette, called him "the poor man". It is a different thing that historic research recently discovers that in order to strengthen the charge sheet against the French monarch and queen Mary Antoinette, a mischievous revolutionary invented the story of the queen insulting the popular demand for bread declaring "if they don't eat bread let them eat cake". The new story goes that the queen never uttered these words, but it was framed to incite mass hysteria against the royalty. Strategists point out that more than one hundred options were open to the French monarch to suppress the revolters storming the Bastille, but he simply ran into dilemma, and sat there watching the revolutionaries seize his citadel by force. In Cuba, it was rather a skirmish between the Batista forces and the Castro forces that brought Fidel Castro to power in 1959. Batista, a weak ruler then riding on a prosperous economy, failed to fight, and lost to the small band of Castro-partisans. In fact, Batista once wanted to enroll Castro into his army, but the latter evaded, saying that there exists a generation gap between them. Cuba, a country of eleven million people, is holding a permanent contingent of political detenus numbering one hundred and twenty thousand. Even with a collapsed economy pushing the citizens' living standards to an un-American low, there is no sign of any popular revolt, even after 50 years of Castrovian tyranny. Now this Caribbean island is a police state, completely purged of the rights of expression, assembly and human rights. The fall of Soviet Union was not due to any armed uprising, but was the inevitable end of a bankrupt economy, destabilising and demolishing the foundations of the Soviet state. When the decadent state machine collapsed as if in a violent earth quake, the long built up popular anger was exploding like a dam-burst. The armed power of the modern state is so huge, that by employing that power any column of revolutionary marchers can be mowed down or decimated. In the pre-atomic era, often the firearms of the revolter defeated the state, but now what is the way open to the revolter to fight the nuclear powered state? Emotive political fulminations continue to contend that popular revolutions will inexorably move on to trample over arbitrary power, but now this is mere illusion, as the armed power of the modern state threatens the destruction of rebels enmasse. This power of the modern state challenges the very notion of popular revolutions. The nuclear-armed state is in fact an added threat to popular power and civil power.

198) The ideological risks and political disadvantages China faces to keep the party-dictatorship going against popular will are discussed in another place. It is the logic of history that but for the Soviet collapse, no human thought would have been exercised over the possibility of a Chinese collapse due to totalitarian terror. Communist propaganda ran the story that the Soviet society has been purged of all dissent and discontent, and the Marxian state is secure at least for a thousand years. Hitler too hoped that his Third Reich was perfectly constructed to last a millennia. But the Iron Curtain was hiding it from the open world the irreversible political, economic and cultural rot, corroding the Soviet system, and these forces compelling the impending collapse. Still the international bluffs and blusters of the totalitarian state brain-washed the world to believe that the Soviet state was in complete control, implying that the Soviet people will never be freed, and never needs to be freed from Marxian tyranny. Any way the final crisis precipitated and exploded all on a sudden. The Soviet ruler Michail Gorbachev, himself a liberal, was convinced that no more he can preside over the abysmal economic tragedy, and he allowed the mythical, all powerful behemoth to fall like a castle of cards. Strangely this counter revolution succeeded without spilling blood. The difference between the present day world and the world of 1917, is that with the phenomenal rise and reach of the modern means of human communication, it has become impossible to keep state-secrets secret, and prevent the tunnelled secrets of totalitarian terrors leaking out. What plagues Red-China is whether she has learnt any lesson from the Soviet tragedy. Even after 1989 and the Tiananmen bloodbath (which, strangely is now attempted to be denied officially), there is no freedom of expression and there is no democracy in China, and this accusation Peking does not care to deny.

199) Can the CCP hold on to power indefinitely without addressing the popular, thunderous question of human rights? Today, the Chinese Communist Party is believed to contain more liberals than conservatives. Former Prime Minister Wen Jiabo was said to be in the liberal faction, and his recent speech in Hong Kong (Oct. 2010) and in other places suggests a strong political undercurrent running down the party hierarchy seeking political liberalisation. Reports say he has been instantly silenced by the party conservatives, and about this Wen Jiabao plea, nothing has been heard afterwards. In November 2012, the new rulers have taken over and the new President Zhi Jinping, though he, his father and family suffered serious humiliations during the Cultural Revolution, does not appear to support any move for political liberalization. The CCP wants to be the exclusive political authority for China and even after the 2012 transfer of power, every party move is to protect the dictatorial authority of the party. The party once more sends the clear message that any reform process is possible only under the political dictatorship of the party. Political reform means the CCP loosening and then losing its hold on power. President Hu Jintao had been a hardliner, not knowing even to smile. He qualified himself for promotion to the top slot through his bloody record of suppression when he was in charge of the Tibetan region. Recently, while addressing a naval meet, he exhorted the sailors to get ready for war, and this declaration makes new strategic dimensions in the background of rising tension in the South China Sea. In November 2012, the National Peoples Congress met in Peking for the power handover ceremony. The reformists contend that the Hu Jintao rule did not liberate any political right, but only tightened the lid, and therefore his rule had been a repetition of Mao's dark age. The CCP argues that political stability alone will guarantee growth, and any relaxation of the CCP hold on power will lead to an abrupt economic decline. The Chinese growing rich will be politically more 'rights aggressive' and the current political protests are put at 180000 during 2011, but observers say the real number is more than its double. Presently the CCP is well entrenched in power with princelings and heirapparents, and a communist dynasty is already in place who very much fear loss of power, and therefore reluctant to change. Some political think-tanks in China and outside hope that the Xi Jinping team may carry out political reforms and open a new era in political rights. Still Communist China continues the biggest security state in the world and state security alone consumes a hefty 110 billion dollars which is almost equal to China's defence outlay. As in 1979, any political reform depends on who wins the power-struggle. Chinese Communists—the realists they are, may not hope that they can hang on to the totalitarian system indefinitely against the rights of the people. Peoples' laws, like natural laws, operate similarly and irrevocably in all political societies, and no political system, much less a Marxian steel frame can stand against the born impulses of man. At the same time, critics have to take note that 21st century China is not a totalitarian state under the hardline Leninist-Stalinist proposition. The economy, though partly dependent on state enterprise and state controlled labour, is liberal, market controlled and market oriented. The state adopts the capitalist laws of economic motion without let or hindrance, and this radical spin away from Marxian dogmatism, has assuaged the Marxian economic discontent and desperation to a large extent. Historically this change-over, is the vital stabilizing factor in Chinese politics, and therefore the Chinese Iron Curtain is now only half-high. Still, the most vital political freedom being denied to the people continues the flash point for a Russia-type counter revolution and necessarily the CCP is in big dilemma what to do next, and whether it is fundamental to grant political freedom and human rights. Will the new rulers opt for a liberal democratic regime, and undergo a self-conversion, inviting danger to the authoritarian power the party now wields? Is China on her way to discover a Chinese Gorbachev? Deng Ziao Ping certainly played the half-Gorbachev, but not a bit he relented to ease the strangle hold of the CCP on political power. That the Russian repudiation of totalitarian economics and politics in 1989 has been wholly total, is the Damocles' Sword hanging above Red-China.

CHAPTER 9

Economic Freedom vs Political Freedom

200) About the impact of economic freedom on political rights and human rights, the behaviour of man in democracy sets the precedent. Economic freedom, and especially economic prosperity, usually acts as the launching pad for political freedom and political rights. The socialist experiments undertaken by radicals, and sometimes by democrats also, failed to produce the necessary goods and services to meet the rising public demand for consumer goods, its varieties and variations. The human rights responses in democracies like America, Britain, France, India, Japan, Australia, Canada and Germany serve as examples, especially with the coming of economic liberalism sweeping through. Once economic freedom has become the reality the peoples' concern focuss on political rights, and now China faces this new danger. Political rights, once granted to the people or self-granted by themselves, are regularly under self-evaluation by the people themselves and they take to the streets for any miss-step or violation by the state and the state forced to be on guard. In most post-war democracies and their constitutions, more particularly in the Constitutions of the Russian Federation, Eastern Europe and the White-Russian states of Latvia, Lithuania and Estonia, they have established independent court systems to oversee the functioning of the state (the executive). In these new democracies, any violation of human rights can be complained to the court. The rights and its observance serve as safety-valve

for democracy's survival. But in a communist system, where the people had been deprived of economic rights, a market economy and economic freedom will act, as the temporary safety-valve for the survival of the (totalitarian) system for some more time, but that will not be the end of the political road. Once economic freedom has been got back, the people, without wait, ask for political rights, and once limited rights are granted, they ask for more rights, and the demand accelerates in course of time. The state may opt to accommodate or compromise with, or reject it, and this negotiability settles down as the behavioural pattern of popular governments. The communist state, according to ideology and practice, does not admit that there exists any political right for the citizen (if at all there is a citizen in the system) to be denied, because communism's political business is assumed to be infallible. Once freedom of expression, free and fair elections and cultural rights are conceded to the people, the communists are set to vanish from the ideological scene. The Chinese Communist Party (CCP), like any other communist party, is not a popularly elected body, and it cannot and does not want to be popular and majoritarian. Asking for political rights in China is like asking for the overthrow of the state; or for the voluntary abdication by the ruling class. Demanding a Bill of Rights in Communist China is asking for the moon. When no human rights are granted, political discontent builds up, and finding no safety-valve to let off steam even in installments, the situation takes to an explosion of the kind that led to the thunderous overthrow of the Soviet state. At the same time, it is true that economic liberalization has averted the immediate danger to the communist state in China, but being a state under party-dictatorship, the people are forced into indefinite and impatient wait for political-rights.

201) The grant of economic rights in a democracy is not the grant of any right, as economic right is not a peoples' right even in a tyranny or dictatorship. Economic rights are related to the physical and physiological needs of the human body, whereas political rights are to feed the intellectual and emotional wants of man. Physical wants are the same for all people in all systems as it is for all living bodies. All systems of government, except communism, begin from the basic foundation of economic freedom granted to the people to work and earn, and it is on that foundation that any political society is built up. The universal behaviour of the state had been to allow people the unfettered, un-interfered economic freedom to work, produce and earn, and the state apparatus to exist on the tax paid by the citizens and subjects. No state will exist without tax. Emily, the sister of Napoleon Bonaparte, was once asked "Is there anything more certain than death" and he quick repartee was. "Yes, it is tax". The communist state, on the other hand, has wholly taken over the ownership of all property whose management places so huge, complex, and unbearable a burden on the state and bureaucracy that no state can carry on with the burden, without causing utter distress, wholesale confusion and destabilisation of settled human life. It can be ironically said that the totalitarian state owns and works, and pays tax to the people. It was because of the mountainous burden placed on the state that the Soviet state collapsed in 1989. In the usual course, this collapse, ought to have persuaded China to accelerate the economic reforms launched already, and speed it to the take-off stage. The people of China, following a capitalist, liberal economy, no doubt, enjoy a large amount of un-communist (economic) freedom and prosperity. The agent of Soviet collapse was the total failure of the state to provide the minimum amount of goods and services to the people, which the free economies were delivering so freely and smoothly. The public distribution system in Soviet Russia had been a system of permanent shortages and queues, and notorious that the lions-share of the people's living-time had been wasted in bureaucratic waits and queues. There were no quality goods, and there was utter scarcity of goods. When the people of the non-communist world were getting better goods, more goods, quality goods and services in limitless choices, the Soviet customer will look on with desperation and envy, he not having even the right to complain. There was the tale of Indian tourists to Moscow that he can carry 2 pair of shoes in his baggage and by selling it there, he could cover his airfare. The doyan of Indian industry G.D. Birla on his return from touring Russia opined that the Russian living condition are not better than India's. This miserable life in want and scarcity has been compounded by the terrors of the secret police, spying on the citizen day and night. What followed after 72 years of political terror and economic want and misery, was the overthrow of the Soviet tower of horrors with no tears shed by any. The new Russia is limping into democracy, with the hick-ups and coughs of a violent transition from terror and collectivism to half-democracy.

202) Because of economic liberalization, present day China is a half-liberated, half totalitarian society, and by Marxian concept a half-renegade. A state liberated only economically is not a democratic state either. Economic freedom is not one of the rights of man under the ideology of human liberation, as expounded and established through history's violent movements for political liberation. All through human civilization, the economics of man had never been wholly state-owned, and much less state-managed, except that all property has been taxed by the state. In history, innumerable popular protests and revolts were mounted against the rate of tax and burdens of tax. For a democrat, Communist China is neither free nor half-free, but wholly unfree regarding the political rights of the citizen. Economic right assumes the character of a right, only after the advent of communism, professing state-ownership of everything. Compared to the totalitarian Soviet state, communist China is half-free, and the Chinese state is becoming the half way house between democracy and communism. Based on democracy's basic principles, China is a country with people, enjoying no political rights. The disturbing question confronting Beijing is how long state-terror can hold down the citizen under the trauma of non-rights?

203) The Soviet state viewed the economic freedom of the citizen as the agent supplying the critical, economic might to the threatening revolter to rebel against. Any kind of political insurrection, revolt or rebellion need the economic wherewithal to do the programme, and in non-communist systems it is private property and private riches that supplies the means and raw material for rebels and revolters. Even Karl Marx had his rich patron in Engels—a German industrial magnate in

Lancashire. The Chinese communists had many wealthy patrons and rich warlords like Chu Teh, and others. A pragmatic Mao was willing to accommodate rich patrons like landlords and warlords in the party, primarily for economic support for the fledgelling party machine. Chau En Lai came to the CCP during the founding days of the party itself, and he established the first foreign branch of the CCP in Paris. Deng Ziao Ping was Chau's mimograph operator there. Mao was an utter realist, and in the formative years of the movement, only to please the middle class, he even stopped the distribution of the landlords' lands in communist controlled soviets, and this soft approach continued until he captured absolute power in 1949. It was the only policy then pragmatic, and thus he won the confidence of the middle class and rich peasants, in the process of building the party. He will show his true colour only after he lands on absolute power in 1949, and thereafter so abruptly he will turn merciless on the same landlords. Millions of landlords, who opposed land reform, were brought under commune trial and executed. Lenin and Mao can be seen diluting the content of Marxism for the sake of early seizure of power. Lenin himself was the scion of a wealthy family possessing extensive land holdings. After the October Revolution, for the long interval the impoverished, property-less and means-less Soviet subjects found it impossible to raise the material means to mount an insurrection against Stalin. Revolts and insurrections are capital-intensive projects. This Soviet approach, the Chinese rulers gave up by granting economic freedom. Raising funds for a counter-revolution in China is now easy and possible as the citizens have the money to fund a rebellious movement. But the new question is whether any amount of private funds will be enough to challenge the nuclear powered state? Within the iron curtain, arms purchase and import are exclusive state business, and in China there is no open shop, selling arms. The revolter has always been shadowed by the all powerful secret police, against whom there is no legal remedy at all.

204) If China wants to continue a communist state, it is pertinent to ask whether it is safe for the party to liberalise the economy and open it to the world at large. Invariably coming

with economic liberalism are the dialogues and crosscurrents of foreign trade, foreign investment and the accelerating intercourse with the free world. Opening the economic gates of China to the outer world is followed by the flow of liberal economic and political ideas, abounding the free society outside. Communism survives on the uncompromising proposition that political dissent has to be eliminated, in spite of the power of the revolt, and the ghastliness of repression needed to put it down. They believe that only in this way the communist state can resist the permanent threat to its tension-packed existence. That the suppression has to be through massive manhunt and manslaughter, the totalitarian ideologues are never bothered of. Rulers in history went for massive killings only in wars, but genocides were not their method to suppress internal political dissent, but communist states want to eliminate up to the last dissenter. The dissidents are picked up in hordes, and after a show trial they are sent to gulags or gallows, and this bloody business is euphemistically traded off to party loyalists as political 'purge'. These purges are not only to crush, but to eliminate political opposition within the party also. Often the tragedy is that this game against a threatened political conspiracy turns out imaginary, resulting in the martyrdom of thousands of innocents, but the party will not take any risk in this respect, as communism will not harbour a rebel inside. Dictators and tyrants had attempted the suppression of rebels and revolters, but the difference is that these state crimes take place in the open, and therefore when the world comes to look at these high crimes and sins, invariably the ruler is forced to go into the defensive. But these purges and suppressions practised by dictators and despots were of a far lesser scale than the terrors and genocides executed by Stalin and Mao. Through a different explanation these ghastly murders are sought to be justified as ideology clean up. The most infamous scheme in this political strategy is that they black out all news in state-terror by building the Iron Curtain. Even in open China, the onlookers and foreigners are turned away from trouble spots by redirection, misinformation and conducted-tours. The world knows much about the Tiananmen massacre, as it was committed in the capital city of

China, but the same world knew only hazily about the massive anti-government demonstrations then ripping through the bosom of the country, and the general unrest gripping the nation following the 1989-91 counter-revolution, pulling down Soviet Russia and Eastern Europe. It was obsoletely late when the news of countrywide protests percolated through the Iron Curtain. Through maintaining a secret society rigorously guarded and spied upon by the secret police, the communists were highly successful in shielding and hiding their crimes against humanity from the free people abroad. But this terror-regime was all set to founder, because of the abhorrent internal decay corroding the tower of horrors and surprise that the one-party state survived in China for more than six decades. The question is how long the regime can endure denying political rights to the people, and how longer they can defy history's logic. The rulers of China do not answer these questions, again hoping that the ghastly completeness of state-terror can write new history, defying the long-standing political logic that suppression of human rights cannot last long.

205) Again a look back into the political past of modern China and India. The people of modern China inherit a more violent political background, compared to other Asian countries. A mass-struggle in India's freedom campaign was that misnamed 'Sepoy Mutiny' of 1857, which in political reality was the First War of Independence consuming half-a-million armed mutineers. The second mass-struggle in the freedom movement was the Indian National Army (INA) of Ras Behari Bose and later of Subhash Chandra Bose. The INA battle for Indian freedom was fought mostly outside Indian territory and it was a war fought by Indians on foreign soil for emancipating mother India. In the long fight for India's freedom, there occurred violent uprisings in several parts of the country with bombings, shootings and assassinations. These gallant deeds were involving a smaller number of fighters and collaborators, compared to the 1857-revolt and the battles fought by the INA. Indian uprisings in the 20th century were less-bloody and more reformed, compared to the insurrections and rebellions rocking China in the 19th and 20th centuries. It may be true that India's freedom struggle would have gone violent and turbulent, but for the entry of Mahatma Gandhi and his hard pursuit of non-violence, as the ultimate weapon of liberation. It is true that in spite of this massive sweep of non-violence over the people, often there erupted incidents of arson, destruction, uprisings and encounters, breaking the Gandhian code of conduct. But Gandhiji could restrain them and bring them back into the mainstream of non-violence once again. Muslims and Hindus jointly fought the British under Congress leadership, but after the Indian Union Muslim League came under the captaincy M.A. Jinnah, the League fight turned into a mixed war, seeking both freedom and partition but more emphatically calling for the new state of Pakistan. Once the Muslims started their exodus from the Indian National Congress, the League response to British power was becoming more complacent than violent. But the partition-violence and killings were opening a new chapter more horrible than the political violences rocking China during the declining days of the Manchus. The partition of India and the ensuing mass-killings and mass-migration of more than twenty million people to and fro remains the most violent Indian cataclysm, in living memory. That India and Pakistan could manage and survive that deluge of violence and turmoil, and hold together the respective territories is historic, showing the political resilience of Indians, who now live in the divided parts of the (erstwhile) undivided India. During the Chinese Civil War, in the last stages, there existed the possibility of dividing the country between the Kuomintang and the Communists, but the American decision for non-intervention sabotaged that possibility also for the Kuomintang. Symbolically, China too now stands divided without dividing the mainland, the breakaway part being the small Taiwan state, ruled by the Nationalists.

206) The political struggles in modern China were bloody, massive and radical. After the British conquest of India and the establishment of the Raj, India did not face a foreign invasion by another imperial power. But in the 19th and 20th centuries, China suffered repeated foreign incursions and invasions, but substantially the empire could be held together by the monarchy. During the declining phase of the Manchus, there broke out many political insurrections and revolts in China, like the Taiping and Shays Rebellions in which millions of revolters perished, Taiping revolt was the largest manslaughter happening due to civil unrest in the 19th century. The Boxer Rebellion was a war against foreign powers and in that state aided, state-induced rebellion also, tens of thousands laid down their lives. Due to the new policy of the emperor to educate his subjects in science, arts and political philosophy, thousands of Chinese youth were sent to America and Europe for studies. Consequently, from the second half of 19th century onwards, liberal ideas were storming into China, and the liberation zeal was everywhere in ferment. Political secret societies sprouted and mushroomed everywhere. The writings of Kant and Hegel were making its impact in politics and academy. Universities and their faculties were turning into storm-centres of political debates and enlightenment. Socialists and Anarchists started to establish cells far and wide. At the same time, the European powers and Japan were foraying into China, each one vying to establish trading posts and colonies like Canton, Shandong, Hong Kong, Macao and Peking. Japan started the China raids from 1894 onwards, and in 1931, Japan embarked on the naked conquest of Manchuria in a big way and occupied Manchuria and many coastal and interior regions and parts of Peking. After the war and the pact of 1895, China was forced to cede Formosa (Taiwan) to Japan. When the Versailles Conference decided against China and allotted the Shandong province (German controlled) to Japan under League mandate, that decision set fire to the violent May Fourth Movement. Massive demonstration broke out across the country with students taking the lead. The monarchy was already overthrown in 1911. The first meeting of the Chinese Communist Party (CCP) was convened in Shanghai in 1921. Mao Tse Tung came from Yunnan as a delegate to the founding assembly, but playing no major role. Soviet Russia and Lenin were serious in empowering the Chinese Communist Party and they were keenly watching its progress.

207) The new political awareness hitting China at the end of the 19th century was ultimately helping the Sun Yat-sen movement to force the last emperor to abdicate. With this

abdication, the sudden triumph of the Sun Revolution became reality. The secret societies and the freedom movement led to the meteoric rise of Sun Yat-sen to the leadership of the nation. After many unsuccessful attempts, finally the Kuomintang movement and the defection of the emperor's forces under their new commander-in-chief Abu Shikai to the side of the revolutionaries, led to the abrupt abdication of the last emperor. During the second half of the 19th century, the country had to face frequent raids from foreign powers like Britain, Germany, Japan and the United States. But these powers could not subjugate and colonise China, as the British could do in India, the United States and Philippines. These powers, by threat of military action, acquired trading rights, Treaty Ports and colonial pockets in many parts of China, but till 1911, the effective ruler of China was the emperor. The political ban imposed on Western ideas, education and military system was abandoned, by the court itself and it was in that background thousands of youth were sent abroad for studies, making possible the flow of Western ideas and liberalism in high speed. Even in the Peking court, the reform impulses were strong. The empress Dowager Cixie's nephew Tongshi and new emperor discovered and installed by the dowager herself in power turned out a reformist, and he was advised and assisted by liberalist administrators. In 1898, the new emperor adopted revolutionary steps for reforms, but his administration lasted only 100 days. Dowager Cixie, by organising a palace conspiracy, toppled him and took over the administration and once more ran her autocratic rule. Critics point out that had the 100 days reform went ahead, the empire would have survived longer, and in fact it was Dowager Cixie who cut short the life of the empire. Dowager Cixie, entering the court as a concubine of the emperor, seized power through a court conspiracy. She ruled China as regent since the emperor's death in 1865. When her minor son also died, she because of her strength of character and administrative acumen, could control the court for long. In the Opium War, she collaborated with the revolters. She died in 1908, naming the three year old Puyi as the new emperor. Cixie's death caused a power vacuum which could not be filled and thereafter the empire's collapse was speeding on. Revolutionary Secret Societies were mushrooming across, particularly in the eastern seaboard, and universities became the breeding centre for revolutionary activity. During the second half of the 19th century, the empire was on decline and the country's political stalwarts were suddenly waking up to the reality that, the Western powers, if they so desired, could have divided China and taken it over in shares. Then it was America who stood against and dissuaded the other powers including Japan from that naked imperial endeavour. It was also true that China was too large a subcontinent for a smooth and easy takeover. Long time back, Britain could conquer and takeover America and India—two very large subcontinents. But it was the rivalry between Western powers and Japan and the dissociation of America from the imperial programme that saved China from foreign takeover and wholesale colonisation. To be reiterated in the context that for many centuries, there stood the royal ban on contact with foreign countries, and thus China lived isolated and estranged from the outside world for many centuries. Even the modernization of her armed forces was banned, and finally that ban itself was to become the major factor causing the fall of the Manchus. The monarchy, because of system decay and aversion to modernization, was crumbling under internal rebellions, secret societies, and foreign occupation of several beach heads on the eastern seaboard. The large part of the capital city of Peking came under the rule of foreign powers until Chiang Kai Shek could persuade the European powers to leave, before the Second World War.

208) After the fall of the emperor in 1911, democracy could not make a triumph in China as the world had hoped. Following the revolution, Sun Yat-sen had to concede the presidency to the warlord—Yuan Shikkai, and that done under a dubious political deal. Yuan Shikkai ruled the republic of China practically a dictator and then he proclaimed himself the emperor of China. He died in office in 1916. Sun, an idealist wrestling with political illusions, could not provide the effective central leadership necessary for the newly liberated society. After the death of Yuan Shikkai, and the assumption of power by Sun himself as President, it was feared for some time that China may go

into immediate disintegration. Warlords re-emerged powerful in different parts, and once again many provinces were coming under their control. Sun was not an effective administrator and his liberal ideology, remained vague. He was an internationalist in revolutionary rhetorics, and he would drag himself into ideological confusions while in power.

209) During the 19th century there was looming the threatened invasion of Tibet by the Russian Tzars, but that plan was foiled in the 20th century by the adventurous steps taken by the Indian Viceroy . After the Russo-Japanese war of 1905, and the defeat of Russia in the war, Japan emerged the new imperial power in the east, and thereafter, China was facing her most dangerous threat from Japan, who occupied Formosa in 1895 and colonized it. Thereafter the Japanese moves were to harass, intimidate and destabilize China, and this harassment continued until the final confrontation in the Second World War. After conducting continuous raids on China's east coast at short intervals Japan in 1931, invaded Manchuria on the refrain that the growing Japanese population was in urgent need of more living space. Through armed invasion, she occupied and semi-colonized Manchuria and set up the puppet regime there under the last emperor of China-Puyi. History would recall that Japan was unsuccessfully invaded by the Chinese emperor Kublai Khan in the 13th century, and having failed in the first attempt he repeated the campaign three times more but to fail. The frustrated Kublai then turned south and redirected his wrath by conquering Vietnam. That 13th century victim—Japan is returning to retaliate in the 20th century. But the Japanese occupation of Manchuria produced a positive result in the economic front. Under Japan that colony was fast growing into the industrial hub of China, following the fast pace industrialization then storming through Japan. By this time, the Chinese republic was entering its tumultuous phase of power-struggle following the death of Sun Yat-sen in 1925. Chiang Kai Shek, the young general serving Sun Yat-sen, successfully fought his way to the leadership of the Kuomintang. By this time, the Chinese Communist Party (CCP) was born in Shanghai in 1921, and they were organizing units in the east coast and later in interior countrysides. The

CCP organised militant trade unions in the northern cities like Wuhan, Beijing and Shanghai. In areas under their control, the communists started organizing peasants into soviets, and started political unrest. In his march to consolidate power, Chiang proved an able and ruthless ruler, with a vision for unifying the country. When the emperor was deposed in 1912, Sun Yat-sen was obliged to hand over the presidency to Abu Shikai, who then was the chief commander of the emperor. But Shikai failed to keep the promise to uphold democracy and liberty, and he ruled China for five years a dictator. Only after his death 1916, Sun Yat-sen could again assume power as president. The idealist he was, Sun turned out a weak ruler, though he alone could claim the high position of national leader and political icon. He established his government in Nanjing. It is important to note that after the fall of the emperor, the central authority weekend suddenly, and the subservient, low-lying warlords in different regions resurfaced powerful, and many parts of northern China came under their spell. Paradoxically, Chu Teh, later the top CCP commander and leader, was once such very rich warlord keeping many mistresses. Chiang the military commander-after a brief training and sojourn in Russia—returned as director of the prestigious Wampoo Military Academy. That by this time the Kuomintang party was reorganized under Russian advisors on the same lines of the Bolshevik Party is historic, and this political structure would later prove too robust to be manipulated and sabotaged from below, and thereby helping the Chiang leadership emerge stronger. This Kuomintang reorganisation was carried out under the supervision of Sun himself in 1924.On reaching power, Chiang's first attempt was to suppress the warlords and trade unions. The northern expedition of 1926 was a big gamble for Chiang, but it was big success and the warlords could either be won-over or suppressed, and Chiang reestablished the central authority in the country. Interestingly, he was patronized by Moscow often over the head of the CCP, and this behaviour was another Comintern paradox. What Chiang immediately did was to crackdown on the communists in Shanghai and the north, and the latter, driven away from the north, went migrating into countrysides and mountains. High controversy it was that Chiang, the so-called ally of Moscow, was butchering communists, and Moscow still looking favourably that he was a Leninist. Chiang maintained intimate contact with the powercenters in Moscow, though the communists were regularly complaining to the Comintern and Moscow that Chiang was a cheat, truly on collision course with the red-brigade, and attempting to eliminate the CCP from the north. In the notorious crackdown in the northern cities, about two hundred thousand communists were shot down by Chiang's militia. There followed a series of battles, and the communist pockets in the east coast were crushed and the red-corps were driven to the Yunnan mountains from where they in 1934 would start the historic Long March the most commented political episode in the struggle of the Chinese Communist Party. But in spite of all these military triumphs, Chiang never got the peace-interval to consolidate the large country, and bring it under total peace and order, and the main reason was Japan. The Japanese invasion of Manchuria in 1931 and the Chinese resistance and the continuing military attacks by the former on many Chinese cities, ports and towns, and the beastly Japanese cruelties slapped on the Chinese population and prisoners of war were the real destabilising factors. In 1936, in the Japanese rape of Nanking, nearly two hundred thousand Chinese perished, and this crime remains the most notorious chapter of Japanese occupation. Chiang, before 1931, restored the central authority in the country, and he emerged the national icon without a rival but because of Japan's marauding and raids, Chiang had to shift his capital to the interior city of Chunging in 1936, and he continued there till the end of the world war. The war against Japan sapped the power of Nationalist China to utter exhaustion, and the inevitable result was political debility and uncertainty. But with the defeat of Japan in the Second World War, everything was turning upside down in favour of China and Chiang Kai Shek. Overnight, Chiang regained all territories lost to the Japanese conqueror during the course of six decades. Korea was liberated from Japanese rule and divided into the Communist North and capitalist South. All Japan-occupied areas in China including Manchuria were restored back and the island colonies of Formosa (Taiwan) and Hainan also returned. Thus at the end of the war, Chiang was standing triumphant as one among the big five. In the Cairo Conference of the Allies in November 1943 he participated along with Roosevelt and Churchill. Because of the Neutrality Pact then existing between Russia and Japan, Stalin refused to come to Cairo to directly confer with Chiang Kai Shek, and so, immediately after the Cairo meet, Roosevelt and Churchill flew to Tehran to see Stalin, leaving Chiang behind.

210) In 1946, a joint body of the Nationalists and Communists was formed to write a new democratic Constitution for China on the American model. The Constitution was to provide five branches of government with separation of powers, and this document was jointly adopted in 1947. But this constitutional partnership did not last long, as civil war revived in its brutality and fury in 1946 itself, and in 1949 the nationalists were defeated, and forced to shift their seat of government to the island of Formosa (Taiwan), leaving the mainland to the Communists. Chiang fled the mainland with the vow to return sooner. Shocking to the free world that mainland China, rescued by America in the world war at very heavy cost in blood and arms, was so suddenly passing into communist hands under Mao Ze Dong, and the war-hero-of Nationalist China driven out of the Chinese mainland and forced to live like an exile in the Formosa island. But to the surprise of the world, the Formosa Island thereafter achieved miraculous economic growth, astonishing the mainland. But the Chiang dream of recapturing the mainland failed to materialise, as this programme again and again failed to get the American military support. In 1975, Chiang Kai Shek died failing in his grand dream of returning home. In 1976, his opponent Mao Tse Tung, the founder of PRC also died, leaving the large political space wanted by Deng Ziao Ping, to manoevre and launch the much needed, but least expected, economic reform and liberalization. Today that adventurist-policy launched by Deng is taking the PRC to new heights, and the country is on its way to capture the new status as the economic and military superpower. Economic liberalization means anti-communist counter-revolution, but the new generation communists in China, anxious to build a wealthy economy, appear least concerned of this ideological breach. Communism or no communism, they want to rise into a superpower and super-economy and in the process, what the world witness is the aggressive nationalism of China in high profile. In the Soviet Union of the nineteen fifties and sixties, the call of the state was to produce more and beat the United States. The former did not produce more, and did not beat the United States. Communist China dreams a different but larger dream, and now, she being half-free and half-communist, stands upbeat.

211) A comparison between the modern political history of India and China has been adverted to in order to explain that India, during this period, was going through times of peace, revolts and struggles as a British colony, whereas China was coming through innumerable political tumults, storms and human tragedies caused by rebellions, wars, conquests, political confrontations, and more critically by Japanese occupation and persecution. This Japanese beating was to lead China to communism in the year 1949, and the attempted destruction of the many millennia old civilization by communist warlords. China, though liberated in 1911, had to pass through revolts and bloody confrontations especially through rebellions and revolts. Chiang Kai Shek, never got the peace to consolidate the country under a single political authority; but still he did a splendid job in reestablishing the central authority, and prevent the country's imminent disintegration, then very much on the cards. The merit of the ommunists, who came to power in 1949, is that they could consolidate power through systematic slaughter and suppression—a terror-operation which Chiang failed to practice on the same scale during his reign lasting a quarter century. Chiang was a military dictator, but not a murderous totalitarian psychopath like Stalin and Mao Tse Tung, and in no sense a military genius particularly during the last stage of his reign. He was claiming himself a democrat, and as the self-appointed successor of Sun, was loudly repeating the vague and undefined Sun-dogmas time and again. The difference between Mao and Chiang was that after 1949, Red-China was able to change into an imperial conqueror from the position of a harassed, battered, persecuted victim of Japanese imperialism. Economically, pre-war and post-war China was a country chronically hit by famines and food-riots, but the scale and ghastliness of starvation deaths caused by the human-mischiefs and economic blunders of Mao's collectivization, were set to run into tens of millions, and these state-induced tragedies looking incomparably horrible and massive. Massacres caused by collectivization, communes, the Great Leap Forward and the Cultural Revolution are guestimated at tens of millions. The collectivization-cum-commune slaughter is officially put at 14 million, but the latest research discovery will put it at a whopping 60 million. This is what the revolution and its violent transformation delivered to the people as the immediate present. But as these massive crimes go unreported to the world audience, it failed to invite the worldwide condemnations and mournings the Tiananmen tragedy would invite later.

212) While looking back to the subdued Indian response against the imperial misdemeanours of China, it is often doubted whether free India's will to make violent responses even against foreign invaders has been seriously impaired by her political profession of non-violence. Was the failure of India to fight China resolutely in the 1962 war, was the result of this monastisation of the Indian psyche, by misinterpreting and misconceiving the content of non-violence. Gandhi said "if you practise non-violence due to fear, I will advise you to go violent". In practicing non-violence, do India follow the real message of the father of the nation? As explained above, compared to China, India experienced a less violent political life during the 19th and 20th centuries, mainly because India was a colony and the British empire was the ruler. Before 1949, the capacity of the people of China to react to breaches of human rights and human honour had been prompt and gallant. Having viewed this Chinese conduct in the last two centuries, the world can assume that the Chinese people will not quietly suffer the suppression of political rights without a fight. But after 1949, this popular capacity and will to express is seen handcuffed by state terror. In spite of the massive suppression of human rights through massacres and genocidal purges carried out after the communist revolution, if the students and the people have risen to revolt against state-terror, as they did at Tiananmen and by staging hundreds of violent demonstrations across the country, that is evidence that the people, fuming and fretting, are impatient to get their political rights back. The rights they enjoyed even during the monarchic days of the Shang, Qin, Han, Sui, Tang, Song, Mongol, Ming, and the Qing (Manchu) dynasties, and after the overthrow of the empire, under the Kuomintang also, have been decimated by communist oligarchs. During the days of the empire, the people had the freedoms of property, religion, education, art, culture, and social and family living, and the only freedom they were denied was the right to question the emperor's political authority. Kuomintang government was not a free democracy even under Sun Yat-sen, but under them the people enjoyed all the rights they enjoyed under the emperor, added with many democratic rights, though these rights were not wholly-justiciable. The people elected the National Assembly and the provincial Assemblies though the democratic content of these election were often in question. After the Second World War, a general election was conducted and Chiang was elected president with a massive majority. It can be said that but for the communist threat, there existed a good chance for Chin, to proceed to full democracy speedily. After the war the communist, preparing for the Civil War, refused to attend the National Assembly meeting in Nanking. Anyway under the Kuomintang many democratic rights were there for the people, and the people lived much under democratic shadow. Without the continuous Japanese attacks and marauding, perhaps the nationalists would have got the peacetime to consolidate power, and go ahead with their experiments in full democracy. But Japan happened to be the real villain. The Japanese did not allow the Kuomintang to have a peace-interval to consolidate the administration and restore order. A state of emergency was in force almost permanently during the Kuomintang rule. Still Chiang, by reestablishing the national authority across China, could fight the two enemies simultaneously—Japan and the home communists. In that emergency, it was big credit for him that he could achieve a large measure of territorial consolidation. In the pre-war days of Kuomintang rule, besieged and battered by the Japanese marauders, the country was forced to live the sick man of Asia. The Japanese drubbing and beating had weakened her body politic so badly that ultimately it led to the triumph of the communists. Mao himself would later confess before a visiting Japanese delegation that but for the Japanese invasion battering the Kuomintang, there would have been no communist revolution in China.

Collectivism—Abandoned

213) The democratic experiment in China from 1911 to 1949 was far from complete but that experiment gave the people the idea of what democracy can be, and what are the rights of the people in a free society. The Tiananmen revolt of 1989 was the aftershock of the violent overthrow of communist regimes in Russia and Eastern Europe, and it would be political blindness for Chinese communists to assume that the peoples' movement for democracy and fundamental rights stands wholly controlled and checked by the police power of the state. In the 21st century, communism is a fast-shrinking political institution, and a recoiling ideology, and the remainder of the totalitarian system now existing, are under the vigil and scrutiny of the human-rights-watchers of the free world. Today, to represent, spearhead and defend the world communist movement, the only powerful state and springboard is China, as others are only namesakes like Cuba and North Korea. The latter are territorially and economically small and fragile, with the Iron Curtain alone shielding their Socialist Utopia. North Korea—the client as well as the prodigal protege of China, still refuses to adopt China's economic liberalization programme. True, some past leaders and dictators in Latin America like Allende of Chile and President Hugo-Chavez of Venezuela had been loud Marxian mouth pieces, but their political religion was rooted in demagogic anti-Americanism. Under socialist pretensions, they reserve a pseudo-revolutionary constituency to cover up their administrative failings and anti-people crimes. But when national and international realities attempt to pass judgment on a political ideology, it is the peoples' rights which count. In their pursuit of temporal happiness, people ask for more goods and services, once the bluster, gusto and harangues of revolutionary rhetorics reach its vanishing point. China, of late North Korea and Cuba are the enclaves where the Marxian creed is in action. Until the Soviet collapse in 1989, the world democracy saw its powerful rival in the communist block, in all her political and military struggles. But today that wide and powerful Marxian landscape has shrunk into the Chinese state—the only country where too the Marxist ideology is not ruling, but held in captivity, never more to be freed and worshipped. Communist China is a capitalist economic society embracing the rules and tendencies of laissez-faire very fast. Then how do the Marxian theorists in China justify the portraits of Marx, Engels, Lenin, Stalin and Mao smile behind the leaders in conferences, ceremonies and military parades is a question adding to the ideology's increasing self-effacing contradictions. Conservative Marxians call it ideology sabotage. And more recently, Chinese Marxism is pulling out all ideological stops to pick up the latest maxims of corporate capitalism. Departing from Cold War years, China's anti-Americanism is now less than one-half, though the communist parties in the world are stuck with that ideological motif. By throwing collectivism and state-ownership overboard, China since 1978, and more especially since 1983, is rapidly freeing herself from stranglehold of statism, and in this relentless march into economic stardom, she is on the winning spree. From her economy, she has dropped the Marxian formulae altogether while wholly embracing the same political formula to hold and monopolise political power in party hands. Communism is not meant to be constructed and maintained under popular mandate, and Karl Marx condemns popular democracy as the instrument of bourgeois rule aiming the perpetual enslavement of the proletarian class. Philosophers including Plato have propounded theories designing different types of popular governments, and each one putting forward his own theory as the most ideal. But no system, even Plato's Philosopher King, contends that once the ideal state has been established, the voice of the citizen shall be muffled and stifled forever. Historic that dictators keep vested interest in total power. As the Soviet Communist Party once did, the Chinese Communists also contend that the political right to rule the country is and shall be wholly vested in a Communist Party, because Communism is human perfection embodied, and so they will not allow any other political ideology to compete with that totalitarian infallibility. The CCP will be frighteningly aware of the political storms that threw away the collectivist state ruthlessly built up by Lenin and Stalin under the spell of state-terror. In Communist history, it is a watershed that through liberalization, economic freedom has been granted to the Chinese citizen, and based on this pragmatic grant, the citizen is prospering economically, and along with him the state. The reorganization of the communist state into liberal economics, undoubtedly takes away the danger of economic bankruptcy, that rattled the totalitarian structures before 1989. But there is the dangerous side to this change over. It was when Czarist Russia was forging ahead in industrialization and territorial expansion as the world's most expansive empire and the fourth industrial power, that the February Revolution overthrew the Czar in 1917. A booming economy, in real life, is the agent urging the people to think more easily, leisurely, and forcefully about political rights. Under economic paralysis and want, the people, being famished and exhausted, are forced to think less about political rights and more about physical wants, as it has been in totalitarian countries. Democracies, producing economic miracles like Germany and Japan, also do not hesitate to dethrone rulers, who acted as the makers and keepers of miracles. In popular elections, an economic miracle is no safe guarantee that the political party presiding over the miracle, will perpetually be garnering a majority vote in a future ballot. National democratic parties are in constant competition to win elections, and for this they bank on economic programmes. These changes of rulers, based on popular verdict, in fact removes the danger of overthrow (of governments) through revolution and rebellion. Periodic elections in democracy work as the safety-valve, sustaining and securing the system. The Chinese leadership cannot rest contented that through economic reform they have got rid of all political risks causing a Soviet-type counter-revolution. It is common knowledge that in Russia, the critical agent of the 1989 counter-revolution was the whopping economic misery unloaded on the people, through the failure of the state to produce the minimum of goods and services to meet their demand. Economic liberalism opens the gates of China wide for foreign technology, capital and enterprise to march in, and this massive inflow of foreign personnel and 'free-world-ideas' cannot but include liberal political ideas. As pointed out already China before 1949 remained the hot bed of liberalism in Asia. The American revolutionists of 1776 admits that for the War of Independence, their philosophy, and scheme came across the Atlantic, and surprisingly more from Britain herself, who was the mother country as well as the colonial master, they were planning and battling to overthrow. Communist China's interaction with foreign countries is mostly with liberal democracies like USA, France, Britain, Germany, Japan, Indonesia, Australia and of late India also. These democracies, whatever the clashes and confrontations inhereing domestic politics, and the uncertainties, paradoxes and frailties they confront during crisis situations like war and national calamities, stand up united in one case—upholding human rights. The people of China does not miss to see the behaviour of world democracies, and the democratic spectacles, in spite of the Iron Curtain blocking the peoples' view? Under the pervasive eye of the information superhighway, and its prodigious progenies like the Internet, the Blog, the Twitter, now state secrets are impossible to be hid.

China—The Hotbed of Liberalism

214) The historic fact the Chinese communists have to contend with is that modern China, especially after the second half of the 19th century and till 1949, had been the hotbed of liberalism and democratic upheavals. After the overthrow of the emperor in 1912, the country was endeavouring to practise democracy under Sun Yat-sen, and theoretically under the Kuomintang also, but without a system of rule of law and justiciable human rights firmly established. For the nationalist agitator and for the liberated China of 1911-12, the American and German democrats and democracies were role models. The Versailles Treaty, discriminating against China, led to the political explosion called the May Fourth Movement, setting fire to nationalist zeal. Universities including the Peking University turned into hotbeds of nationalistic and revolutionary activity and political literature, and it is from the precincts of the Peking University that the communist movement itself was launched in 1921. Well-known that for some time Mao Tse Tung was a library clerk in Peking University under the legendary CCP founders Liu Dhazhao and.... Hundreds of secret societies, as part of the freedom movement, mushroomed in the east coast, and China was reentering her violent days of political agitations in the 19th century. Had Sun Yat-sen had been a visionary in real politic, he had all opportunity to establish a firm democratic structure in the country. But his vague ideologies coupled with his reluctance to go for full democracy at one leap led to the failure of the democratic state. To confound matters, was that he was a poor administrator. From the beginning of the 19th century, the flow of Western ideas into China was continuous and stormy, giving new impetus to liberal thought, democracy and nationalism. In the latter part of the 19th century, Chinese students going to USA and Europe in hordes were to lay hand on the teachings Locke, Hobbes, Rousseau, Kant, Hegel, Schoppenhoeur and Karl Marx, and these ideologies were spreading like wild fire among the intelligientia and the academia. The call for political rights was reaching down to the common man, and his response became intense and irresistible. During the empire, the campaign for democratic rights resulted in the establishment of Provincial Assemblies, and after sometime for the founding of the National Assembly also, but under the veto power of the monarch. The National Assembly was less powerful compared to the Provincial Assemblies. These assemblies were growing popular and powerful even with the majority of members being nominated by the monarch. As already said, compared to India, the democratic movement in China was more impetuous and violent, finally resulting in the overthrow of the Last Emperor, though this overthrow, finally came in the shape of a military coup and palace revolution.

During the monarchy, franchise was limited to the gentry and the tax-paying class, but this new step itself was giving momentum for the Chinese people to invest faith in democracy without reservation, and they felt that with periodic elections, their fear of an arbitratory state can be kept at bay more often than not. A free and fair election to elect the ruler, more than anything else, supplies fresh air for humans. But there are democrats who, after winning popular vote and power, would later refuse to quit office, but established democracies like USA and Britain, and post-war democracies like Germany, Japan, Italy, India, and Australia did not produce an elected dictator, though amongst them India suffered a 19-month emergency and anti-constitutional dictatorship during 1975-77. While comparing China's communist system with a democracy, that comparison shall be with an established democracy, and not with the fractured, irregular and mangled democracies of Asia, Africa and Latin America. Many new Afro-Asian democracies have been fragile enough to be overthrown by the military, or by an attempting dictator, but still democracies continue the only system able to spread it wings without the help of an artificial ideology or godfather. The strength of democracy depends on the strength of the political rights the people enjoy.

215) Communist China is charged with the crime of keeping the largest number of political prisoners under illegal detention without trial and without the process of rule of law. She is again charged with the high crime of executing the largest number of political dissidents in the world. For the outside world, China is touted as the tourist paradise containing the Great Wall, the Forbidden City, the Peking Palaces, the Summer Palace, the Ming Tombs, soaring skyscrapers, snow-clad mountains, endless deserts, pagodas, monasteries, superhighways and superfast trains. But the same China is home to the largest mass of unfree people on earth, mocking at the brilliance of her economic castles towering over the skyline. For this Marxian terror-state to survive, the Stalinist bulldozer has to perpetually move on with unquenching bloodthirst. When the winds of democracy and its roaring calls batter the gates of China's power-centres, how long state-terror can keep the people hostage to brute power, is the anxiety and dilemma, rocking the high mandarins in the Beijing court.

216) After economic liberalization, the next but immediate question is how Communist China will find a safety-valve for the increasing democratic demands for political rights. This demand is now open and emphatic. Communism's core theory rests on economic equality and state ownership of property. But Deng Ziao Ping mustered courage to jettison this theory and enter the capitalist road without let or hindrance. The hard-core Chinese Marxians were aghast that the Deng programme was nothing but the total denunciation of the codes of Marx and Lenin. Still the odds are that economic liberalisation is not followed by political liberation and as follow up and the CCP fails to add even an iota of democratic liberalism to the rights of the citizen. Beijing fears that this grant will be as bad as political suicide. The rulers' reaction to the criticisms of world bodies like Human Rights Watch, Amnesty International, the International Commission of Jurists and the banned underground rights bodies and the rights activists within China itself has been emphatic denials and remonstrations supplemented by crude condemnations and denunciations. In spite of the surge of liberalism across China, the political mood of the ruling class is unlikely to grant any of these rights. When the economic philosophy governing the Marxian doctrine has been given the go bye, what remains is the political structure harbouring a permanent ruling class on whose creation and coronation, the people have no role. That the 1350 million Chinese people have no role to play in the governance of the country appears mind-boggling, battering the freedom conscience of the world and inviting the biting criticism in international human rights meets and dialogues.

217) The Peking response to the Tibetan revolts and the recent revolt of the muslim Uyghurs of Sinkiang—a muslim majority province, serve deterrent warning to the future revolters for human rights. The bloody, merciless state response to these agitations with dastardly crackdowns comes to the know of the people of China only through hearsay and whisper, and rarely through the internet and the electronic waves in the absence of an independent fourth estate in the country. Lately, the state has to fight the new hurdle that a technology-sauvy world makes secrecy, privacy and even high-secrecy truly impossible. With the penetrating eye of the Internet, and its progeny the web, the Blog, the Facebook, Twitter, etc. and the spy-satellites and the living spies, how long can China keep her stories of state-terror secret and going? The free world is holding a vigilant enquiry on human rights in China. A liberal Chinese economy will find itself hard put to co-exist with a despotic political order, especially in the midst of the accelerating democratization taking place in the economic field. But the Chinese Communist Party, who rules the country for the past six decades with absolute unaccountability to popular opinion, will only refuse to surrender political power to a liberal regime, and submit the fate of the ruling class (CCP), to the uncertain, speculative game of popular ballots. On political rights, the attitude of the Chinese authorities will again be the obstinacy of power hunger, an obstinacy springing from the vested interest of the CCP to cling on to power without public criticism and scrutiny.

How the Monarchs and Dictators Survived?

218) In a frantic comparison, the communists ask how monarchies and empires lasted not only centuries but millennia with no democratic rights allowed to the subjects. China had been ruled by many imperial dynasties and emperors for more than two millennia in continuum, and during this long period of power and struggle for power, how did the emperors survive? A discussion of the basic reasons facilitating such survival has been made in another place. Under monarchs and tyrants, the people do not suffer the totalitarian suffocating controls a communist state downs on man's daily bread, butter and breath. Except their right to govern, the kings and emperors allowed the subjects all other rights to pursue all happiness, available under the sun. They allow the people to have all rights to property, religion, education, profession, art, culture and literature, and the right to learn from anywhere, anybody and any discipline, the right to choose one's spouse, the racial, tribal and conventional rights, the right to travel and leisure, the right to communicate with others, and then what not? Under the monarchs and tyrants a citizen is not spied upon, and the ruler allowing the whole environment free, except the political rights expounded and declared by the French Revolution. The only thing denied to the subject is his right to question the—power of the king or the despot. It is important to remember in the context that before the French Revolution, the theory held sway that the monarch is the representative of God on earth, and he rules by divine right. In those days, kingdoms and empires perished only because of internal decay or war, and any victorious conqueror was supposed to enjoy the blessings of the Almighty. Only after the French Revolution, there germinated the popular awakening that a ruler can come to power only subject to peoples' will, and he continues in power under their continuing scrutiny and endorsement. All revolutions, including the Russian Revolution of February 1917, can be seen as inspired and idealised by the pioneering spirit of the French Revolution. It was the French revolt that launched the first challenge of the common man to have his voice heard in the practice of state power. Paris, in 1789, was suddenly overturning the basic philosophy of state power, and that overturn thereafter leading the world campaign for democratization. Historically viewed, democracy is much older than the French Revolution, as it is at least as old as the Greek civilisation. But ever since 1789, the speed and momentum of democratization of world politics has been accelerating, and more importantly in the post-war years of the 20th century. Still to say that the course of democracy had never been smooth. Following the footsteps of the French revolters, there entered ideological cheats and frauds also calling for reform and revolution, and in this respect the biggest betrayal on peoples' rights has been committed by the Russian Bolsheviks. It is true that Socialism, Syndicalism, Fascism, Nazism, Anarchism and their hundreds of off-shoots sprouted around the theory of democracy, and more particularly since 1789. Afterwards giving to themselves the role of self-appointed high priests of ideologies, many despots and tyrants would grab power is another story of the 20th century. Once grabbing power they, under the cover of the fantastic, and romantic attributes they impose on the ideology, unleash a reign of terror to perpetuate themselves in power. It is history's paradox that a military dictator like Napoleon got power as the child of the French Revolution. Napoleon was not a revolutionary; neither he was party to the French Revolution. He was a military genius, and the French people stood dazzled at his military exploits more particularly what he achieved in foreign lands. Though he was launched into power as the child of the revolution clamouring for the establishment of peoples' government everywhere, never he made the pretence that being the (accidental) progeny of a popular revolution, he was bound to uphold the ideology of the revolt. As it often happens, dictators come to power paying obsequious court to human freedom, but treacherously they end up enemies of human rights. Lenin seized power in the name of the proletariat, but what followed was the founding of the most savage terror-state in history, where man was made to live (or die) exclusively for the sake of an ideology, whose preachings never stood the test of peoples' will and history's rationales in political pragmatism. The Leninist steam-roller was suddenly converted into the—most barbarous killing machine, and Bolshevism was reducing the citizen as the entity in absolute political irrelevance. To reach that nightmarish point, they invented the magic slogan 'class-war' and pitted one economic unequal against another unequal. While exercising power, the Bolshevists were well-aware that economic equality is a tantalising phantom always to be chased, but never to be got or caught. Still they mercilessly batter this doctrine to brainwash the unequals, and thereby inflame human envy, which works as the sharpest psychological spearhead of class war. Once reaching power, they declare, they are the masters of a political ideology eternally infallible, and therefore entitled to rule unchallenged. With this infallibility-spectre held aloft, they sit in power suppressing opposing political opinions enmasse. The Soviet terror-state survived for 72 years, and then it suddenly came crashing down. In human affairs, war continues the maker and unmaker of rulers, dynasties, political systems and civilisations. Soviet Union successfully fought the Second World War and she emerged triumphant in company with the democrats, but forty-four years after the war, a counter-revolution toppled the behemoth. More important that all political parties contemplated and born after the French Revolution are bound to propound a system of government, proposing to make peoples' life freer and happier than all their predecessors. Some promise something they know well they cannot fulfill, some promise the possible which they can accomplish partly but never fully; and some, while in power, refuse to redeem any promise, and behave deceitfully, as if they tricked the people into an electoral farce or fraud. Most of the political parties play partial fraud, and some play violent fraud. But in this respect, the communist breach of promise and betrayal has been frighteningly thorough. Hijacking man's freedom through misinformation and lies, they ruthlessly proceed to sabotage popular will. In the place of the Socialist democracy established in Russia through the February Revolution, the Bolshevists through the October Coup constructed a terror-state, which they perfected to the highest efficiency through banditry, savagery, genocide and the omnipresent secret police. Thus the final and colossal fall of the Soviet state as a castle of cards would surprise only the communists, and none else. Historic that the reformist Chinese communists, being live witnesses to an impending Soviet tragedy, could mount a mighty damage control operation in advance, by suddenly and radically liberalizing the economy, and today China is the halfway house between economic liberalism and totalitarian absolutism. In the immediate past, when India and China lay undeveloped, poverty-haunted lands, the world's concern was in what manner these two lethargic Asian hippos be pulled out of the morass of stupor and in activity and make them move forward. Ameliorating the misery of 40 per cent of humanity inhabiting these two subcontinents, then looked an impossible task. Deng broke his Leninist and Maoist chains and entered the (anti-Marxian) capitalist route, as the only feasible route to break new ground for economic reconstruction and wealth-making. Through a single-blow, he bade farewell to wholesale state ownership. By welcoming economic capitalism, long condemned by communists as the exclusive legacy of the imperial bourgeois, China began to surge ahead by producing enough goods and services for her billion-plus consumers, and this was wake-up call for other socialists including the ultras and the pseudos. Free India, whose Nehruvian commitment to socialism and socialist-pattern was a near-total, suffered economic paralysis for four and half decades, and the socialist politicians of India were fooling the people by feeding them with empty slogans. Narasimha Rao, the loyalist of the Nehru dynasty, possibly taking his cue from Deng, and also from the Soviet crash (two years earlier), decided to pick up the gauntlet in 1991 and pulled India into the highway of market economy. Strangely, this repudiation of socialist pattern he carried out through an almost clandestine political operation, whereas an open challenge to socialism and its patterns was unthinkable for an Indian politician in those days, when the people lay there brainwashed to believe that socialism was panacea for all economic ills. But through this seemingly dubious political act, Rao was launching India into the age of economic liberation and take off. The Rao programme was to cause the radical, and systemic overhaul of economic reconstruction. The world's anxiety, as to how to end the poverty of these two Asian giants from doomsday privations, Deng and Rao put to rest. That worldly sympathy is now giving way to their dangerous anxiety about this economic rivalry producing a deadly arms race between these Asian Titans again they fear that the danger caused by these two countries is not only against each other but against all Asia, upsetting the world's balance of power. Such fear-some reactions from the Asian neighbours, are lately becoming louder. Economic analysts argue that if India and China can pool their economic powers in joint partnership, as the European Community could do, they can challenge the world economic order itself. On the other hand, if they opt to confront each other with their growing military muscle, that would be new disaster of Asia. In the state of bitter rivalry due to the border dispute and the increasing imperial shadow Beijing casts around there is only remote chance for the first option. But the more probability is for the second one, which is madding arms race, moving towards another head-on collision between the two Asian giants. These conclusions are based on the optimism of the two economies galloping in high momentum, and that affluence funding a deadly arms race. A madding arms race can go reckless and run amuck anytime, and that is the fear of Asia.

219) Being a free democratic society, there is chance that the Indian economy can be slowed down or sabotaged by a political leadership inept, inefficient, romantic unpragmatic or ultra revolutionary. Except these negative possibilities coming through the electoral uncertainties of populism, there is no risk-factor shadowing India's future economic growth. Politically, any threat to India's economic development is likely to come from the left, and more so through any Marxist participation in governance. A Marxian partnership will put brakes on economic acceleration, as India has already experienced during the Left-UPA coalition of 2004-08. Under the present electoral calculus, there is little chance for the Indian Marxists to gain a party majority (of their own) in parliament, and so much so the growth momentum of Indian economy is ensured. On this question, the new development is China herself coming under market economy. The state-structure in China is unchangeable through popular beatings. The Chinese Communist Party is having a permanent economic policy, and there will be no political shackles and populist hick-up in the system forcing the state into ideological slowdowns and upsets. Communist China's economy now grows according to the pure theory of market-forces and laisse-faire, and to guarantee this momentum there is the political construct, firmer, stronger and more thorough than in a dictatorship. The principal agent of economic growth is political stability and continuity. About the stability of their economic policy, there is no uncertainty in China, as the chance for a radical shift in policy derailing high growth is most improbable there. But the dangerous question is how long the people of China will remain compliant to a party-dictatorship, permitting no role for popular voice in administration? This is not a new danger, but the permanent danger haunting China's ruling class. Even the post-war economic miracles of Germany and Japan could not persuade their people to permit the authors of these miracles to sit in power for long. And how thanklessly and rudely was that great miracle-builder of West Germany-

Ludwig Erhard has been trounced in a popular-vote afterwards! In these places, either the ruling party was replaced or its policy asked to be changed according to changing popular calls, even when these populist calls failed to stand merited scrutiny. The response of the Beijing Government towards popular uprisings and revolts has been crackdowns and suppressions, and no middle-road found by the rulers. It was in the Tibetan Torch revolt of April-May 2008 that the CCP, for the first time since 1949, was agreeing to talk with the representatives of Dalai Lama, but that too on international compulsion, but later events showing that this was a ploy to project the fair name and glamour of the Beijing Olympics, going to be held immediately. Beijing Olympics 2008 was an event that China wanted to showcase to the world as the symbol of her rising economic and political status. She wanted the new status to be acknowledged by the wide, wide world. The talks with the Tibetans was merely a Beijing eyewash to save face until the Olympic Games was over, as later events would confirm. When the reformist Deng Zio Ping came to power in Beijing, the Tibetan hopes for more political rights soared for reaching a compromise, and talks began on a positive note. Several rounds of talks proved fruitless, as China was unwilling to relent on her Tibetan policy, much less give Tibet its lesser demand for autonomy and Dalai Lama's return to Lhasa. China, being a vast territory comprising too many cultures, races and minorities has to continuously address the racial, tribal, religious and cultural questions which are conflicting as well as violently contradicting. The Tiananmen crackdown sends clear message to dissidents that even six decades after the revolution, the CCP lives hypersensitive, uncompromising and mercilessly punitive on the question of freedom of expression and political dissent. The rulers believe, often rightly too, that any concession to political dissent in a communist system is too dangerous a grant, inviting a chain-reaction, which after a stage, will be impossible to contain even through massive manhunt. The communist doctrine and the Soviet practices under Lenin and Stalin provide no precedent of tolerating any political opposition. These practices say that through continuous, genocidal purges, any kind of popular revolt can be controlled and contained, and its cast of characters eliminated forever. The essential faculty of the party-leadership confronting a revolt will be not to get unnerved and shocked by witnessing the terrible bloodbath needed to suppress it. As some kind-hearted dictators are prone to be any dithering and diffidence in crushing the mutiny would finally result in surrender to the rebels. Lenin and Stalin were able to stand the sight of the horrendous bloodbaths committed in the mass purges. The CCP must be aware that the power-monopoly of the party is inextricably bound up with the theory of party-dictatorship. At present it is seen that the domino effect of the collapse of totalitarian systems in Russia and Europe could be temporarily halted in China by liberalizing the economy and making people the immediate beneficiaries of an economic boom, thoroughly unknown in communist states. After the French Revolution, the denial of political freedom and the denial of space for popular will to express itself, invite permanent threats to any government. Considering the destructive power of the modern state, now entrenched in the atomic-arsenal, there is little chance for popular revolts or armed uprising to succeed in China. For the Chinese citizen hoping to put his voice in governance, the alternative is counter-revolution or a coup-de-grace or as in the Soviet Russia, the fall of the terror-state due to economic bankruptcy and political decay. It was strategic desertions from the ruling class and internal sabotage that caused the fall of the soviet state. It can be argued that regarding China, the political circumstances are not similar, and therefore the critic cannot draw it in direct analogy with the Soviet collapse. Compared to the Soviet economic pauperism, the people of China are enjoying good respite from economic want and privation, and this change is really celebration time for totalitarian society. People of China got economic freedom as the unusual, unprecedented state gift. But how long the uneasy peace will prevail between state-terror and peoples' rights? Dissidents and revolters are aware that popular power today is no match for the armed power of the state, and therefore the latter shall live robbed of all chances to wrest out democratic rights through armed revolts and rebellions. When the state remains insensitive to the sins of keeping power through persecution and genocide, the prospect for a "rights regime" looks depressive. Communist China carries out the largest number of political executions in the world, but the 'free world media' especially the left-dominated media, maintains a dishonest silence on these totalitarian crimes. The modern suicide-bomber can kill a large number of innocents by pulling a lever, but he is unable to threaten the modern state, much less threaten the terror-power of the state. Human rights is the aggressive, spontaneous human force in the world, and the history of human behaviour says that the forces of human rights can be challenged only for sometime. Commenting on the terminal political illness that killed the Soviet state, materialists argue that the economic liberation of the Chinese citizen has taken the thunder out of the gathering storm in China. But historically, it is inevitable that the storm will regather and regroup to rage more furiously later. The present hope of the people of China for political freedom, is dependent on the internal political decay corrodding the all powerful state-machine. Seeing people not as sovereign, but as the enemy of the state, the Chinese authorities maintain high-alert that any small concession will set off a chain reaction, which assuming demoniac shape, will soon engulf the state itself. This perception makes communist rulers sit sleeplessly on the watch. The Soviet fall says that peoples' power is set to march to irrevocable triumph. The monopoly political power the CCP is enjoying so long, supplies a power-blindness, preventing rulers from conceding even a small amount of political liberty to the citizen.

Chapter 10

Chinese Imperialism on the March

220) Should two different political systems existing in two large countries make one the enemy of the other? China is an one-party totalitarian dictatorship; and India a multi-party parliamentary democracy. Indian democracy allows people to choose their rulers through free-ballot, whereas Communist China denies all political rights including adult franchise and free-elections. The question repeatedly asked is why China is targeting India as her Asian enemy from day one of the 1949 Revolution? What overtook China in 1949 was no popular revolution like the Taiping Rebellion or Shays Rebellion or Boxer Revolt or the other uprisings that rocked the Middle Kingdom during the last two centuries. The 1949 revolution was the product of communist military victory over the Kuomintang in the 1946-49 Civil War. It has to be pointed out that even in 1949 the Chinese Communist Party was nowhere near to the Kuomintang in popularity and the communists never claimed or believed that they can win a popular vote. In 1948, Chiang Kaishek was elected President of China in the general election but the communists ignoring it went to continue the armed fight against the Kuomintang. Japan, the enemy of China and her oppressor for long, and later the inseparable companion of America in the post-war and the Cold War years, was suddenly forced into military sleep in 1945 on American advisory and compulsion. (That inveterate enemy of China is now China's

biggest trading partner.) Under her Peace Constitution of 1946, and under her post-war good conduct, Japan's commitment to peace remains total both in word and practice. From a half-military dictatorship, Japan was abruptly changing into a manufacturing hub, a consumer's paradise and the world's supermarket. As the workshop of Asia, within a short time after 1945, she built herself up as the second largest economy in the world. If she so chooses, she is capable of building a large military machine, but she is abstaining from massive rearmament. Ignoring the mighty and dangerous Japan, why China is picking up India as her main Asian rival, and why this target change? For thousands of years, India and China remained the homes of the world's two great civilizations and they lived companion civilizations. They were never political rivals. But abruptly, everything was turning upside down in 1949. No Indian emperor attempted to invade China, and no Chinese emperor threw aggressive stares against India. True, in the long past, the high Himalayas stood there the geographical barrier, separating India and Tibet, but this mountain massif never erecting a cultural barrier or causing political rivalry in between. Kuomintang China's rulers, including Sun Yat-sen and his successor Chiang Kai Shek were great friends of India. Chiang's fraternal endeavours in the international arena to secure early freedom for India is well-known. In the Sino-Japanese wars of the last century, though India was then a British colony, all Indian sentiment and sympathy was with China, and India never absolving Japan of the war crimes she committed on the Chinese. Buddhism was born in India, and from India's Buddha Gaya, the great religion and the philosophy travelled to China to convert that country also into the Buddhist creed of Ahimsa. From China and Cylon Buddhism migrated to the East Asian countries including Japan. It needs mention that non-communist China always acted deeply conscious of her cultural bonds with India, especially as the birth place of Buddhism. How these historic factors in cultural and religious bonds and political brotherhood were ignored by China with the coming of communists in power? At this juncture, it is bad memory that, in spite of India's deep obligation towards Chiang Kai Shek and Nationalist

China, free India was one of the few countries, somersaulting into the communist camp, and award recognition to Red-China over the heads of others. Pandit Nehru (the Indian Prime Minister) was striving hard even uninvited, unsolicited and unhonoured to plead the case of Red-China before the world fora, and that too after Mao had unequivocally declared and demonstrated his hatred and contempt for India and the Indian leaders including Nehru. He called Nehru the lackey of Western imperialism and colonial agent. In 1949 itself, Beijing openly demonstrated that she harbours imperial ambitions against her neighbours including Tibet and India. As usual, in the beginning stages, the invader will be in search of soft targets, and in the process she did not ponder whether the soft target is a friend or enemy or ideological fellow traveller. Any territory soft was China's target. While proceeding with mass-executions and mass purges in the domestic front to eliminate the opposition and to consolidate his deadly-grip on the CCP, Mao and company were losing no time to embark on a programme of imperial expansion through naked conquest of the weak, unprotected, friendless, neighbours. As a test case China invaded Tibet, and to her surprise she found the Indian Prime Minister Nehru a willing conniver in the brutal subjugation of the defenceless monastic land. Gradually Nehru—the great democrat—was becoming a blind and squeamish admirer and accomplice of communist imperialism anywhere, and consequently the free world started to look at him as the chief communist spokesperson in Asia. Exploiting this suicidal Nehru obsession for communist company Mao and his clever Prime Minister Chau En Lai successfully accomplished the programme of conquering that large Asian plateau called Tibet, without causing much tumult and uproar in world capitals. As the ruler of the country directly and imminently jolted and threatened by China's annexation of Tibet, Nehru—the human-rights-activist and decoloniser, who was duty-bound to alert and awaken the world about the new dangers thrown up by imperial China, appallingly failed even to make an open and strong protest. The alarmed free world, especially Western democracies, were puzzled and disappointed of this abject Nehru surrender before the new Asian imperialist.

India's unconditional surrender of Tibet to the dragon restrained and shackled the world democracies also from voicing powerful protests much less give arms aid to the Tibetan freedom fighters. A puzzled and surprised free world saw Nehru—stooping down as the apologist of Chinese imperialism, and this stand tarnishing his image as double-faced and dishonest. For Communist China, Tibet was to test the Indian mettle to challenge her, and after this Nehru capitulation, India herself coming as the next target of China was only natural. The persistent anti-American and the anti-western harangues of Nehru and his sycophants among the Indian left, even after India becoming free, gave a good cover up to the Chinese rape of Tibet. When Tibet is so easily in her hands, as the great Indian trophy presented to her by the credulous Jawaharlal China was growing more confident of her imperial designs against India. Now she can cross the Himalayas in high confidence. With Tibet so easily in hands, the enemy became certain that Nehru is a romantic demagogue, and he being viscerally anti-west also, can be cajoled and flattered into submission, and if not, threatened and panicked into surrender. Later events would prove this Mao assessment a very realistic reading of the Indian ruler. China was certain that Nehru's India was not only friendless, but absolutely isolated, she being not a member of any military pact. While ceding Tibet to China as the autonomous region within the Chinese subcontinent, Nehru did not think of committing China to the McMahon Line, as according to him the line remained non-controversial from 1914 to 1959. Nehru did not know that China has already drawn up plans to make claims on Indian territory, and the publishing of wrongs maps was the initial shot. Thereafter, without raising an open claim over the land, China forcibly occupied Aksai Chin (in Kashmir), and secretly built the Aksai Chin Road and the Karakoram Highway. The Karakoram Highway is cutting through Pakistan Occupied Kashmir to the rebellious Sinjiang province. Pakistan, in a display of blind malice towards India, was assuming that one day the Pakistan Occupied Kashmir (POK) is likely to be wrested back by India, and therefore it was safer to cede a portion of POK to China (as if to a more powerful tenant) of about 5150 sq. kms. of territory. Through this gift of landed property, Pakistan wanted to punish India, though the strategy would be self-defeating in the long run. Even after Aksai Chin was occupied, and India's top military generals pressing Nehru to make urgent military preparations to meet the PLA, Nehru's love of the enemy was changing into fear, and surprisingly this fear, preventing him from making the necessary policy review. From the Indian public, he even suppressed the news of China's occupation of Aksai Chin, as long as it was possible. Many opposition leaders fore-warned him repeatedly about the aggressive designs of China, but all these pleas fell on his deaf ears. Seeing the Chinese maps, General Cariappa, the first Indian C-I-C of the Indian army had warned Nehru of Chinese intentions as early as in 1949. When general Thimmayya, another distinguished soldier and C-I-C, reported to the prime minister about the invasionary preparations of China, Nehru brashly snubbed him. Nehru was prepared to ignore the report of a very distinguished and patriotic army chief about the impending Chinese threat. Steam rolling over realities, he wanted to live in his world of illusions and dreams. India's defence minister and the principle foreign policy architect in the Nehru court during the period of confrontation and capitulation was V.K. Krishna Menon. He was the diabolitical friend and defender of the Indian-left and world communism, appearing in Congress clothes. Menon played the critical role in alienating the west especially the United States, through his vitriolic diatribes, pouring out his visceral spleen on Uncle Sam. When Nehru surrounded by pro-China spies and communist partisans, was willingly walking into the deadly jaws of the dragon, the west was practically demoralized and neutralized on the Tibetan question. They were really puzzled and taken aback on the Nehru bear hug. It was the anti-west tirades of Menon in the United Nations that provided the diplomatic and political cover up and also the red-herring for the Chinese partisans in-filtrating India's defence apparatus, whose hidden agenda was to sabotage the impending war against China. Things would not stop there. China was certain that the infiltration of the Indian left into the ruling party had been complete, and she can be more defiant on the Himalayan borders, even if that will lead into a shooting war. A war under Menon and Nehru cannot but end in disaster, as one was a dreamer and the other the friend of the enemy. Krishna Menon, as defence minister, has already manipulated his power for the forced demoralization and disarming of the Indian defence forces into a toothless, motiveless, non-fighting, infighting apparatus. It still remains a mystery how Menon and his collaborators, sabotaging India's war-efforts, could escape the arm of the country's security laws. A weak parallel to this sabotage of the Indian military machine can be seen in the Hitlerite bribing of the leading newspaper editors in Paris, who spoke vehemently against any active French plan to resist Germany, especially during the German re-occupation of Rhineland. The Fuhrer, through the defeatist preachings of the Parisian press, could demoralize the French political leadership from making a preventive strike against Germany—a strike that would have stopped Hitler at the starting point itself. India lost the 1962 war by not fighting it, but she could realise the gravity of that tragedy only when that idol of world peace—Nehru honoured the world over, lay there in smithereens.

221) Why China picked up India as her main rival in Asia is a complex issue which can be variously answered. Communist China, from her founding days, was making her imperial drive in different directions. In that reckless chase to found her ever expanding totalitarian empire the conqueror did not pause to distinguish between friend, brother, ideological ally or political opponent. Conquerors, usually select the most convenient victim, and under that policy China found her easy prey in Tibet lying before her almost a no man's land. In the beginning, the Chinese leaders were highly skeptical and apprehensive about the free world's response to this outrage. But Nehru—the demagogue was lying low like collaborator and spokesman of red imperialism. With Nehru already in her camp, silenced and dithery China was able to mount her least risky expedition against the land of the lamas. Hugely successful in Tibet the next Chinese jump was into Korea which though very costly was not a full success neither it was defeat for the marauding dragon. Korea gave China and the Soviet Block the real taste of things to come if confronted with the west and the mighty United States, in real combat. There is no doubt that China was fearful of the destructive power of the military machine of the United States in Korea, but post-war America was making a climb down from the high-role as the world policeman and defender of democracy. In the Korean theatre, the communists could test and conclude that even if a red-assault fails, they will not be punished in the rigorous way Japan and Germany were done at the end of the world war. They assumed from real experience that the most they have to forgo in defeat will be the victory trophy and nothing else. Totalitarian countries produce no public opinion to restrain rulers from jumping into adventures and conquests. When war comes inevitable that it will unload its mammoth miseries and agonies on the people but anti-war protests and fears are the specialty of democracy alone. No protests are there to restrain communist rulers because they allow no protests. A recent development is that in democracies, public opinion is largely manufactured by the media, which institutionally and behaviourally is anti-west, anti-war and pro-left and they restrain and obstruct the democratic state from full mobilisation for war. Latterly, it is no secret that public opinion continuously resist, discourage and even destroy democracy's war making power. The war for Afro-Asian decolonization was another important diversionary factor, helping the communists to camaflouge their imperial march across Asia. Contemporaneously was going on the Afro-Asian fight against Western colonialism, and during the fifties and sixties, this war of liberation was raging in all the unliberated Western colonies in Africa and Asia. By vociferously joining this de-colonization campaigns against the west, the communists were able to throw a perfect cover over their own imperial projects in Asia. In 1950, while Tibet was being conquered and over run by Red-China, the latter was holding out as the spearhead of world revolution and colonial liberation. Consequently Asia and Africa were inclined to look to her for lead and aid to fight Western imperialism, then very much on the decline and retreat. Under the cover of that call and its ideological cutting edge, imperial China could pose as the champion of Afro-Asian liberation movements, though her underlying agenda was the establishment of communist rule in the colonies to be liberated. But to their dismay after decolonization, the verdicts in most of the (liberated) colonies went against the communists in popular elections, and the reds, being a minority, could not seize power by force in any of these countries. The most they could do was to abet and incite civil wars as in Angola but failing to seize power.

222) When democratic or half-democratic governments came in South Korea and South Vietnam, the Communist Norths unleashed open invasions against the southern halves. In South Vietnam, the North started a guerilla war, and these guerillas were armed, paid, trained and patronised by communist powers. It was high political strategy that these naked conquests were code-named by the aggressors themselves as 'wars of liberation' which meant liberating the 'liberated', which ultimately would end up in 'deliberation' or recolonisation. When America entered to resist the conquerors of South Korea and South Vietnam, these communist conquests were again code-named 'patriotic wars' against foreign imperialism, and this false propaganda was surprisingly well-received by Asian democracies. These two colonies were already liberated from foreign rule, and America came to Korea and Vietnam only to prevent the free people of these territories from succumbing to totalitarian conquest. Through false propaganda and ideological offensives China was able to gain huge political advantage against America in her imperial wars and mainly this became possible only through the pro-China policy followed by non-communist Asia. Russia too though not much love lost in between after the sixties helped China as the child revolutionary challenging her Cold War enemy—the United States. At the same time the new democracies and the pro-left media would flatter Nehru's capitulative China policy.

Change Focus from Tibet to Indian Border

223) Once Tibet succumbed to China without the latter firing a single shot against India or Russia, the next Chinese attempt was to acquire legitimacy for this naked conquest. This was thoughtfully and cleverly done by making claims on Indian territory lying adjacent to Tibet. Against the Chinese invasion

of Tibet, the Indian opinion went furious, which, China feared would be permanent threat to her assumed suzerainty over the plateau. Strategic think tanks in Peking were certain that by making claims on Indian territory the spotlight will shift from Tibet to the Indian border, and thus India forced to ignore Tibet, and concentrate on her border and the McMahon Line. With her claims on Indian territory going more and more militant, the Chinese leaders concluded that their claim on Tibet is a fait accompli, and later the Chinese strategists became thoroughly satisfied of this assumption. The fatal lapse of India was that all strategic moves were allowed to be initiated and decided by China herself and New Delhi was picking up the bulletins of Peking foreign office, reading it and filing it. This apathy and irresolution of the Indian leadership on Tibet was recklessly and cheatingly exploited by China, and gradually the latter became certain that she can make any claim over any part of India, and so the pre-emptive way to confirm her title over Tibet was to make fresh claims on Indian Territory without break. Peking thought that by calling a blatant conquest a "border-dispute" will euphemise and camouflougue her aggression and annexation of Indian territory will be high strategy and she enjoyed the plan.

Russian Support—Not Sought

224) Another fundamental Indian default was her omission to canvass the help of the Soviet Union on Tibet. For many centuries the Russian Romanovs were setting aggressive sights on Tibet, and this attempt continued all along and the Tzar attacked Tibet at the end of the 19th century, but it did not succeed. Till the beginning of the 20th century, such attempts continued when the Indian Victory Lord openly resisted the move. In 1950, when China conquered Tibet, the most aggrieved party ought to be Soviet Union—but, may be communism stood in the way of that country making open opposition to Peking. If Nehru had objected and protested against the invasion, Stalin would have been willing to support him. But Nehru did not know anything about the undercurrents of Chinese imperialism or Stalinist intentions. Neither he wanted to know it and

purposefully supported the imperial projects of Red-China acting as China's political spokesman. If Nehru had moved to resist China's Tibetan expedition, Stalin would not have moved his little finger against India. In fact Kremlin was furious about China occupying Tibet but the Cold War equations and the most affected India's collusion and apathy would prevent Stalin also from openly coming against China. Instead of China if Tibet had been annexed by Russia (in 1904) then after 1989 that country would have got the option to secede from Russia as a separate state like Turkmenstan or Uzbekistan. All these options are now hostage to history only because of Nehru's suicidal China policy.

China Itching for Show Down

225) After 1959 China was deliberately moving towards war with India and the dangerous turn came in 1962 when India driven to the wall decided to return fire. This was a war for which India was not only partly but fully unprepared. It was during the war the world was fully told about the story of the forced flight of Dalai Lama from his homeland, and the ruthless repression and mass killings unleashed on Tibetans by the warlords of Peking. In the 1962-war, China occupied a part of the then Assam state, but suddenly she executed a unilateral withdrawal from the area, now called Arunachal Pradesh, but holding on to Aksai Chin. After Aksai Chin was silently occupied in the fifties, China constructed the strategic highway across the land, connecting Tibet with Sinkiang. Today, the 10,000 km. long mountain railway built between Quinghai and Lhasa at a height of more than 10,000 feet above sea level is an engineering marvel. Strategists say that China has built more than 55000 km. roads and a network of railways in Tibet, connecting important strategic points in the plateau. There are, at least five operational airfields near the Indian border. For India, as in the past, these are wake-up calls once again. Unfortunate that these are the inevitable consequences of a defeatist leadership reigning in Delhi during the fifties and sixties. Is there is any serious rethink even today to review the disastrous China policy of Nehru? India makes requests and appeals for talks, but China scorning at these embarrassing entreaties.

226) China tested the Indian mettle for war in Tibet, as she tested the American mailed fist in Korea. Taking a militant stand, if India had protested and challenged the Chinese invasion of the plateau, not only Tibetan autonomy and the rule of Dalai Lama would have been protected, but that territory would have remained the security buffer between the two Asian adversaries, as it stood through thousands of years. According to political geography, there is no common border between India and China, as India had a common border only with Tibet, which is the kingdom of Dalai Lama. Mao and Chau En Lai, the great statesmen they were, could learn through hard experience that Nehruvian India is (permanently) the soft target for a rough ride. This is not because the people of India are soft, but because free India's leader and ultimate ruler-Nehru was a dreamer and an apologist of world communism. Nehru loved the enemies, and the bitter enemies of India were his personal friends. Before the end of the Nehru era, China could accomplish what she wanted, and now after Nehru, these conquests look a fait accompli, difficult to unmake. The enemy could invade and occupy Tibet and Aksai Chin and these booties were safely in her kitty before India woke up to see the dragon sitting atop the Himalayas breathing fire. While China exploited the American dilemma and her world war-fatigue in Korea this (partial) Korean triumph encouraged her to foment guerilla expeditions in Indo-China after 1950, and particularly to South Vietnam in the 1960s. For communism these Sino-Soviet expeditions unlike in Korea turned out wholesale triumphs. To camaflouge red-imperialism the all encompassing Chinese strategy was mendacious propaganda through Goebellean lambasts, lies and misinformation campaigns. A good part of Chinese imperialism could thus be traded off as 'war against Western imperialism and colonialism'. It was under the cover of these harangues against Western imperialism that China successfully covered up her new imperialism. Strange that all these Chinese and Soviet posturings happened after China has established her new colonies in Tibet and Sinjiang and Soviet Union founding her satellite colonies in Eastern Europe. The leftist world media would black out these colonies from the news world. Political

critics believe that Mao selected India as China's potential Asian opponent during the days of the revolution itself, and never it was an afterthought after 1949. China's targeting of India goes on by encirclement, diplomatic offensives, fifth columns and naked encroachments. But the fact that revolutionary China selected only soft targets, needs to be emphasised. She invaded Tibet as Hitler invaded the unguilty, poorly defended Austria in 1938. When the Indian reaction to the conquest of Tibet was mute and apologetic, China concluded that the Indian leadership, viscerally anti-colonial and anti-west, and standing isolated from the militarily powerful west, can be the next and easy target. China went on with this programme very conveniently as India remained anti-west and pro-communist. If Sardar Patel had become India's first Prime Minister, as the Congress party had wished, and he lived longer, there would have been no Chinese-occupation of Tibet, and the Kashmir question would have been resolved in India's favour in 1948 itself. But on the advent of freedom, Gandhiji threw his lot with Nehru—the idealist, the pacifist and the dreamer. Nehru, in turn threw his political lot with the treacherous left the communist world as particularly with the biggest butches in history—Joseph Stalin. This association caused his own undoing as well as the undoing of India's security and economy. Gandhiji and Patel left the scene very early, leaving Nehru the unbridled political horse running amuck on India's large political space. And unfortunate, that the reward for his services to world communism was armed attack, rout and humiliation. China targets India not because India threatens her Asian ambitions, but because free India is a country of pacifists and demagogues, and the ruling party, during the Nehru days, harbouring too many admirers, worshipers and Trojan Horses of world communism. In political practice it does not look unusual for communism having an army of ideological guerillas in India and this Chinese fifth column, operating in the country has been doing splendid service to the enemy through propaganda, mis-representation and political sabotage. Democracy's rulers as ordinary mortals think more about their present interests than about the future and this aspect very dangerously manifesting in democracy's election returns. Today also the real and immediate threat to China can be her past-enemy—Japan who in no time can build a powerful military machine shadowing the dragon. The Japanese crimes against China, before and during the Second World War were so horrendous and shocking that no Chinese patriot can absolve Japan of it even after the many capital punishments awarded to Japanese war criminals by the Military Tribunal For The Far East. Then why China does not take Japan as the main enemy and not taking revenge on her? The reasons are obvious. Whatever the military pretensions of China once Japan decides to rearm, and re-equip herself there will be no present power in Asia to match her technology and gallantry. That such rearmament will cause an abrupt shift in Asia's balance of power also is never in doubt. Contrary to her policy in the world war days, post-war Japan has replaced China as the Asian ally of the United States, and as a result, the American nuclear umbrella is hanging over the Far East to guarantee the security of the Sun God worshippers. Japan continues the dangerous target and the impossible target also for China to challenge, and cleverly the former turns her face away from the latter's abominable war crimes. Who can absolve Japan of the Rape of Nanking in which nearly two lakh Chinese perished in 1936? This Chinese policy is, in spite of Japan remaining in the anti-communist Western camp as the committed strategic ally of Western democracies, especially of the United States. The Japanese policy in peace has been the product of the confrontationist Cold War days.

227) Every country in Asia harbours a domestic pro-China political lobby as the apologist of Chinese imperialism. These anti-state ambassadors act as the open-world spearheads of red-imperialism anywhere. In Japan also, there is a not too powerful pro-China communist party, but the Japanese will not tolerate a domestic spearhead as China's fifth column. If China wants to avenge the massive crimes committed on her by Japan during the first half of the 20th century, that revenge should have come ruthlessly. On Japanese war crimes, what is the policy China is pursuing? She knows that any saber-rattling against Japan is beset with dangerous consequences, and so the Chinese calm against the latter's crimes. The dragon is scary that once Japan rearms and breaks out of the shell of constitutional monasticism, there will be no stopping her. China is able to win the wars against Tibet, India and Indo-China only because the Asian Tiger-Japan has been sleeping under a self-applied anesthesia. In that context, it is to be asked why in Korea and Vietnam, China jumped against that biggest military power of the United States. China made that jump only after Mao and Chau En Lai could read the American mind very correctly that post-war America has reached the retreat mode and is climbing down to make cowardly, ungallant, demagogic surrenders. The first post-war test of the American will was made by Stalin in the Berlin-Blockade of 1948, where America defensibly avoided a head-on US-Russia collision. The world remembers that in 1948 America alone had the atom bomb. Unlike their experience in Korea, the communists won the Vietnam war hands down. From the Vietnam triumph, China could judge more thoroughly that post-war America is a fatigued-nation, hesitant to employ her unmatched fire-power to win. It was this American dithering and dilemma to defend Chiang Kai Shek, and finally deserting Chiang at the turning point (Civil War) that inspired and emboldened China to enter the Korean and Vietnam conflicts. China reaped half-victory in Korea, but in Vietnam it was wholesale triumph for the Viet Cong. But in spite of these victories, the most legitimate right of China to recapture and incorporate Taiwan with the mainland still remains an unrealized dream, as the American determination to defend the island continues firm. In the above background, the plea that India is the only obstacle to Chinese paramountcy in the east, and so China is always looking at India as her arch-rival, appears unreal.

228) Nehru acted apologetic towards China, as the former was suffering from a fear-induced comraderie with the Chinese enemy—a conduct utterly baffling the politicians, patriots and statesmen. This Nehruvian modesty demoted India into a credulous accomplice of Chinese imperialism in Korea and Tibet. But after 1962, Nehru himself will admit that what China gave back in thanksgiving was betrayal and backstab. This Chinese policy of pouncing upon the weak and bowing before the strong, is nothing but she playing the art of the possible. Nehru was refusing to read this dangerous message in spite of the many warnings given by friends and patrons and more by the warnings of history. When he opened his eyes to see the ghastliness of China's deceit, it was too late, and he was crest-fallen.

229) After China's aggression and annexation of Indian territory, pitiable to see the continuing vassal-like stand of India before the enemy. To justify enemy aggression, the Indian left was ready to go to the point of talking treason, and that conduct becoming boldly expressive during the war itself. Confined to Kerala and West Bengal, the communists may appear a lesser security risk geopolitically, but in the event of a Chinese victory over India, these two Indian states and their leaders shall be the legitimate inheritors of communist power, as it happened in post-war Eastern Europe. As the Hungarian Revolution of 1956 split World Communism into two, the Chinese attack on India (1962) sowed the seeds to split in the Indian Communist Party. Just after the Chinese attack, the central committee of the CPI, with a large majority passed a resolutions condemning China and supporting India. But this resolution was not published, though the media did know it. Against this patriotic resolution leaders like A.K. Gopalan and EMS Namboodirippad were furious and they later walked out to form the pro-China Indian Communist Part (Marxist) who, of the two factions, became more popular and powerful. Had this resolution been duly published at once, perhaps the Marxist Party would have gone into eclipse—but CPI (the other faction) did not bother to give it wide publicity. Strange that even after 1962, India hesitates to make a clear and open demand to China to vacate occupied territory in Aksai Chin. The agitating Tibetans are furious that India consistently fails to argue for Tibetan autonomy again guaranteed in the Sino-Indian agreement of 1954. Fighting shy of a defiant Chinese response, India has banned Dalai Lama (now residing in India at Dharmasala in Himachal Pradesh) from engaging in political activities of any kind within India's borders. It is an unpardonable breach of promise that India is refusing to reiterate the Tibetan cause in negotiations and

policy declarations made in international meets. In fact Indian diplomacy has forgotten the case of Tibetans long ago. Fear-complex and defeatism continuing to rule the ruler's mind in New Delhi, this weak stand once again proves so imprudent as pacifying the enemy. If India finds it dangerous to go to war with China (as both are nuclear powers) why does she fail to make a plain speak on occupied territory? Why India failed to launch diplomatic offensives to arraign the powerful free world against China's crimes against humanity? As said above, the first thing India will tell China is that in the event of the latter refusing to vacate Indian territory, the former will be compelled to withdraw recognition to Chinese suzerainty over Tibet, and also that India will be placing the case before the United Nations and other world fora for immediate review and action for Tibetan rights and independence. The Chinese reaction to this move also, as usual, will be angry and violent, and she may even rouse her belligerent feathers by restarting new arms-shows along the border. India, not being cowed down by these orchestrated remonstrances and threats, can launch a propaganda war, projecting and spearheading the cause of Dalai Lama, and these endeavours will be carried forward by exposing the sins of the dragon. It was India's ungallant submission to China's rape of Tibet that dissuaded and discouraged the powerful world democracies from championing more aggressively the cause of Tibet and Dalai Lama. India's unending silence in this respect is now pushing a desperate Dalai Lama to declare that he wants only autonomy for Tibet, but willing to accept Chinese suzerainty over his homeland. In 1952, the Tibetan delegation visiting Peking for negotiations was forced to sign the China—drafted-17-Point Treaty on dotted lines. The first thing a fleeing Dalai Lama did after crossing into India (Tezpur) in 1959 was to repudiate this Treaty of coercion and fraud. The Tibetan supremo, after an exhausting wait, now appears dismayed and frustrated, and in a climb down he limits his demand into autonomy. After Deng Ziao Ping came to power, several rounds of talks were held, but all negotiations reaching deadlock only because Beijing is determined not to concede anything like autonomy. Recently, Dalai Lama shed his temporal powers and allowed a prime minister in exile to be elected by the Tibetan diaspora. On the other side, China hopes that with the death of Dalai Lama, the Tibetan war of independence will recede into history and memory. But the émigré Tibetans are furious that it is because of Dalai Lama's injunctions that the revolt has been held in check, and the Tibetans, both inside and outside are determined to carry violent fight even after the exit of Dalai Lama from the scene. This Tibetan resolve, India is duty bound to encourage and bolster up, if necessary by withdrawing recognition to Chinese suzerainty. As usual, for any Indian attempt to de-recognize, the Chinese reaction will be as bad as battle cry or mobilization which are the usual communist tactics in bad situations. Without making a dangerous challenge to her imperialism in Tibet, China will not heed the Indian calls for a reasonable, negotiated settlement of the border dispute, which significantly was a non-issue during the Kuomintang days. At the height of the Second World War, Winston Churchill exhorted his countrymen to live dangerously, but free Indians are yet to experience what is dangerous living, though often unknowingly they run into serious dangers.

The Left Intellectuals

230) The political left and the dithery intellectuals in India warn their motherland that China is a mighty country economically, militarily and geographically, and any militant stand by India will lead to a second Sino-Indian war—a war which also India cannot win on any account. For avoiding war, they argue although impliedly, that India shall surrender her territory to the Chinese warlord, who stand assured that the Indian Left are there as their Trojan Horse, and any debate in India to go to war with the latter will be politically and ideologically resisted by these proxies deployed in India. The left-intellectuals also plead for China emphatically. Political resistance from within the country itself will ensure half-victory for China in the run up to a new war. Before casting the die in favour of Tibet, India will make calls to Asian governments, more particularly Japan, South Korea, Indonesia, Philippines, Australia, Thailand, Singapore and Malaysia about the imperial

shadow the dragon has already cast over the region, and the need of these countries too, as part of their self-defence, to support the cause of Tibet more determinedly. If India pleading for Tibetan autonomy will lead to war, how can China assume that her occupation and colonization of Tibet will not lead to war? So long as the moves are peaceful China will only ignore it, these countries having no programme to enforce these claims through use of force. To perpetuate her overlordship over Tibet, China is now building elaborate infrastructure in the plateau, both military and civil. The recently built rail road from China to Tibet is the latest imperial monument, intended to perpetuate Chinese hegemony. Who can deny the story that it was the introduction of railways in India in 1853 that changed the course of colonial history? Railways helped Lord Dalhousie and the British to consolidate and fortify their Indian empire, and successfully they put down the 1857-revolt involving many kings, princes and queens and hundreds of thousands of revolters. To begin with, China carried out a massacre in Tibet, and against this impost of red imperialism through terror, India failed to raise even a murmur of protest. Beijing is fast converting Tibet into a military camp, while India is lying low and silent. If India launches the offensive for withdrawal of recognition to Tibet, China is bound to realize the complex problems coming in its wake. Pitiable that even after 1962, India's China-policy continues the defeatism and fear complex of the Nehru days, more or less copying the stereotype endeavours of the past to buy peace at any cost. It is the continuing weakness of Indian democracy that the post-1962 India also failed to produce a leader to standup up to Mao and Chau En Lai. Where she finds the challenge real and powerful, China relents on the negotiating table; where the response is mute, diplomatic and negotiatory, she postpones and postpones until the enemy, getting tired of the process, silently capitulates. When the border deadlock prolongs, the continuing status quo is wholly advantageous to the aggressor. The Chinese are stalling and stonewalling a negotiated solution, because they hope a long status quo will only legitimize aggression. Patriotic India mourns that a person like Sardar Patel would have met the

Chinese threat ably patriotically and courageously. When Atal Behari Vajpayee came to power in 1998, the political world hoped that he would jettison Non-Alignment, and follow an activist China policy, seeking a just deal on Tibet and the border. Indians hoped that he would pointedly tell China to keep her word on Tibetan autonomy. But Vajpayee not only followed the policy of appeasement, but reiterated China's suzerainty over Tibet. For making this vaulting concession, what did India get in return? India developing trade with China on fast track can be seen a positive development in economic relations, but it is to the existential interests of India that the rulers shall give priority and primacy. Now Sino-Indian trade is booming, as both countries are on high-speed economic reconstruction. At the same time, the Chinese belligerence on Arunachal Pradesh and her callous intrusions into India's domestic politics in Kashmir, are the new tests to measure India's will to meet the enemy point blank. Because of the low key reaction of India, China is building roads not only in Tibet but in Pak Occupied Kashmir (POK) also and this Chinese encroachment into Kashmir is a blunt-intrusion into the internal affairs of India. The enemy entering Kashmir territory means committing new aggression and Pakistan is happy to play the suicidal game. The next Chinese step will be she herself building her own roads in POK, and raise new claims. Another border-salvo fired by China recently is about the length of the India-China border. The real length of the Sino-Indian border is more than 4,500 kms., but China now claims that the length is only 2,000 kms. and the remaining 2,500 kms. is the border between Kashmir and China. Disputed border means China can redraw the map of Jammu and Kashmir in a way to exclude Aksai Chin and make it part of Tibet, and thus part of China. A new Chinese attempt is to block and harness the headwaters of Brahmaputra river in Tibet, divert it northwards and desertify and destroy the greenery, flora and fauna in India's North East and Bengal including the Sunderbans. China denies this story only to hide it for sometime, as she played with her wrong maps before 1962. Against this new outrage, India has only protest notes to deliver. When fickle political leadership reigns in Delhi, China assumes she can play any nefarious, insulting game. As during 1959-62, is not China planning to slap another war on India? Wars descends when least expected by the victim. By making a resolute stand, India has to demonstrate her power to resist China, but having no powerful leader as political visionary, India, again and again stands down to be ridden rough. China occupied more than 38000 square kilometers in Aksai Chin, and in order to perpetuate the conquest she is making another false claim on Arunachal Pradesh. Political commentators assume that the claim on Arunachal is kept alive as a bargaining chip against Aksai Chin. If India agrees to cede Aksai Chin, China, may be willing to drop her claim on Arunachal Pradesh. Why not China make a wholesale claim for Uttar Pradesh, Bihar, Assam and Bengal, and then bargain that if West Bengal and Assam are surrendered, she will drop her claim on Uttar Pradesh and Bihar? There will be no end to China's territorial high-handedness, so long as India continues the underdog, pleading her case at China's door.

231) Under the new commercial policy, India's trade volumes with China are increasing fast to hit the $100 billion mark, and this is fantastic economic business regarding India. But trading profits are no substitute for national territory. In another context I relate the story of the trade interests of Japan and Germany before the outbreak of the two World Wars. For Germany, it was her trade with her prospective enemies that was helping her to keep her economy dynamic and powerful, and the expanding war machine well oiled. Only by sacrificing those huge economic profits she had to go to war. Before Pearl Harbour, Japan's main trading-partner and supplier of energy and industrial raw material was the United States, but the former chose war, suicidally sacrificing these vital interests. But regarding India, her share of trade with China in 1962 was negligible. Even if it was large and critical, India had to forgo it during war. When the enemy, after unleashing open aggression, attempts to justify the crime through the untenable excuses of a haughty aggressor, can the victim submit to the invader's insulting excuses? Aggressors justify conquests through their arguments of conceit very much pre-fabricated and kept ready in their diplomatic armoury before the aggression has even been contemplated. Such arguments in fact become worse affronts. War, in the nuclear age, is not only terrible but suicidal for combatants, and if war is dangerous, it is dangerous for both sides. If one party is blunt enough to declare that she can outlive even a nuclear catastrophe, that is as much bluff as a capital lie. Mao once declared that China is a huge country, and in the event of a nuclear catastrophe, a large part of China's population will still survive to carry forward the revolution. Perhaps he was referring to Noah's Arc during the great deluge. Such bluffs sometimes work, but in the strategic world, it did not have takers except his partisans and ideologues, and this truth Mao himself was well-aware. At the same time the political biography of Mao is the story of a hard core pragmatist, realist and strategist, and above all a committed patriot and imperialist. If he was sincere to his theory, why did he not go for a nuclear war with the United States on the Taiwan issue, or with Russia on the Ussuri or Amur borders—the flash point for long? During the Indo-Pak War of 1965, when Lal Bahadur Shastri gave a curt reply to the threatening Mao, the latter quietly beat the retreat. When there came an opponent to call his bluff, Mao showed the statesmanly wisdom to make it safe for China. In the Chinese Civil War, it was his strategic retreats, withdrawals and guerilla tactics at turning points that enabled him to win ultimately. He challenged America in Korea and Vietnam, because he was certain that post-war America has decayed into a fickle, irresolute society, fearing war and death. Also he could correctly assess the poor mettle of the spineless leaders parading Washington under the camaflouge of demagogic platitudes. For any country, war is the last option, but when the enemy decides to strike, the opponent cannot prevent it by running away. An unresolved border is an inflammable border, which can go aflame any moment. If there is another war on India's northern borders, for that tragedy, the blame will again fall on China, but she emphatically will reject the charge. In the present state of affairs, China is waiting to force India into another armed conflict, which the former knows she cannot win as easily as in 1962. The fate of a new Sino-Indian war also will ultimately depend on who will then be sitting in the White House. China fears a Reagon or George W. Bush, but not a Ford or Carter or Obama.

232) In human affairs, war had never been the safe option, but the inevitable option for the defender. When the enemy is at the gate, the opponent is left with no other choice but to engage. Still the rulers repeat the refrain that wars are dangerous, and therefore shall be averted at any cost. At the same time the negligent and the ungallant assumes that the occasion to exercise the dangerous option is far, far away. The question facing India is whether she has done all things in her power, short of war, to warn China to unmake her aggression on Indian soil? When Manmohan Singh—the Indian Prime Minister visited Arunachal Pradesh recently, China protested that a foreigner is crossing into China without Chinese passport. This conduct again shows the contemptuous way China is treating India and her political leadership. The Indian reaction to this brazen insult ought to have been decisive and defiant, but Manmohan is no Hu Jintao, or Jiang Zemin. The South Block, afflicted by the surrender slogans of the Nehru days, this time also the Indian reaction was mute and frail. When an Indian diplomat hailing from Arunachal wanted to visit China, China reacted that the diplomat needs no visa, as he is already a Chinese national, in spite of he being a member of the Indian diplomatic corps. Of late, China started issuing a special sheet-visa to the citizens of POK, declaring that she does not recognize Indian authority over Kashmir—a stand running counter to the original stand of both the PRC and Nationalist China. In 1948, it was Nationalist China who vetoed the resolution in the UN Security Council, accusing India of aggression in Kashmir. But in October 2009, the same China (but PRC) is objecting to the visit of Manmohan Singh to Arunachal Pradesh, in connection with assembly elections. What do these Chinese about-turns and volte faces indicate? While China is insulting India every now and then India stands aside as the silent, fearful guy. Is it impossible for India change into a dynamic border policy? Challenging China's suzerainty claim over Tibet is India's strategic trump card, and China is deeply apprehensive of this move. And never it is too late for India to demand the enemy vacate Indian territory, occupied by aggression. There is no doubt that such demand can lead to a diplomatic impasse sometimes forcing both sides to call off the trade-talks now vigorously on acceleration. Violent responses are Red-China's established policy. Any Indian demand to vacate aggression is certainly to fall on the deaf ears of the dragon, and then what will be India's next step? India will tell China in black and white that Tibet is autonomous territory. Such autonomy, so clearly guaranteed to the Lamas in the 1954 Agreement also is illegally and treacherously violated and steamrolled by China, and therefore the Tibetan war of independence, both within and without, deserves to get the moral support of India and the world. For embarking on this thunderous policy change, India has to launch diplomatic offensives to enlist the support of the world's leading democracies like the United States, Canada, Britain, France, Germany, Japan, Malaysia, Singapore, Philippines, Indonesia, Australia, South Korea, etc. for the humane cause. A powerful push by India was certain to receive the support of the Bush administration, but now the Obama administration, retreative and hesitant, will be reluctant to join this campaign for fear of displeasing aggressive China. During the course of his first term, Obama gave the message that he has no active or clear policy to check Chinese imperialism, and he was for compromise everywhere. India also is bound to fear that this Obama policy will act the dampener on any dynamic Indian move, challenging China. India going silent on the massive human rights crimes China commits in Tibet and Xinjiang, is the very grave issue facing the international community. These rights-violations India has to bring before the activist world in clear focus, but she is shirking in the duty. The recent revolt in Xinjiang gives new impetus to the Tibetan revolters. During the Second World War, when Chiang Kai Shek made an attempt to subjugate Xinjiang under the cover of the war, the Allies asked him to turn back. The rulers of Red China too are at their age-old ambition to conquer, and incorporate this region as a full-fledged province of China. By forcibly settling more and more Han immigrants in the province, the majority—Muslim Uyghurs fear that they are being reduced into a minority, and the fear of demographic aggression resulted in the Uyghur revolt of July 2009. This revolt caused the death of more than 200 Uyghur protesters, but unofficial estimates put the figure at a more than a thousand, both dead and injured. The rulers in Beijing give no other reason than the communist refrain that the protesters are merely foreign agents and state enemies, supporting the bourgeois secessionists. With a heavy hand China suppressed the revolt. Again such revolts erupt continuously, but Beijing asserts that there will be no review of her Sinjiang policy, and the crackdowns will continue as the usual course of action. Certain that these developments in Sinjiang come a shot in the arm for the Tibetan revolters, but with no foreign armed help forthcoming, the protesters are there only to be gunned down by the mercenaries of Beijing.

Asia Groping in the Dark

233) To meet the common threat from China, Free Asia, unallied and aimless, is groping in the dark, the Asian policy against Chinese imperialism suffering from a total absence of initiatives and strategy. They fail to highlight the human rights violations in places like Tibet, Sinjiang and Inner Mongolia. Against the large-scale political executions taking place inside China, the Asian response has been fear and silence. Human rights activists in China are banned, and many are either driven underground or driven abroad. The popular revolts breaking out across the Middle Kingdom are mostly unreported and unacknowledged, and thus blacked out from the world view. The Tiananmen genocide of 1989 ought to have been taken up for a more aggressive debate by the democratic world and human rights bodies, but done only as an 'as usual' incident. The world media, and particularly the leftist media, are very conveniently ignoring it, as part of they trivialising the rights-violations taking place in communist states. Perhaps the media will raise the alibi that it is an unworthy cause to be fought for, as the result of these onslaughts would be as barren as a cry in the wilderness. Regarding the anti-human rights regime in China, this media policy will take the major share of the blame. The Asian media

has a duty to come forward to wage a vigorous and purposive battle in this respect. The intelligence machinery in India needs to be re-organized and reequipped to collect the latest information, especially about the Tibetan and Uyghur revolts. In democratic Asia, China enjoys a big advantage in covering up these sins, as her Asian neighbours play this subject as safe as pleasing the Chinese ears. In this case India and other Asian democracies have to learn from the challenging responses coming from the west, particularly against the Chinese crackdown of Olympic Torch protesters, and the subdued Chinese response against Western charges.

234) Post-war Japan, who should to have played the critical role in the containment of China, has been forced to stand aside. The United States and the world human rights bodies, of late, maintain a diplomatic moderation and silence over the totalitarian crimes against human rights and the servitude China imposes upon her people-making up a fifth of the humanity inhabiting the earth. This speaks of the unpardonable neglect by world democracies of rights violations taking place inside China. India taking a tough stand against China on these violations will certainly persuade other Asian democrats also to challenge China on these sins. The resulting diplomatic and military postures of China are assumed to be violent enough to threaten the Asian peace, but India is duty bound to stand her ground, and meet China's muscle-flexing resolutely. Can China be allowed to steamroll on her neighbours again on the reason that the democratic states in Asia are defeasibly restrained? A dangerous China, at the same time, is a powerful China also, with her fast-growing economic and military muscle. According to recent developments and border incidents the immediate victim of her muscle flexing will again be India and not another Asian country. But the real fear of China is a rearmed Japan across the straits, but the latter after the 1946 Peace Constitution is living more monastic than the monastic Tibet. The strategic reality that India single-handedly cannot confront an armed China in power balance, continues, while India is far less adept at the art of balance of terror. Why do China take India as her prime-target? Because free India, right from the dawn of independence,

is non-violent and soft, faithfully following the Nehru legacy of goodwill through capitulation. The Indian climbdown supplies China with the space for her subverting exercises far and wide. Languishing as the soft target, the enemy taking India again and again for a rough ride is no surprise. Then the question very relevant is why China fails to go belligerent against Taiwan or South Korea or Japan? The reason is obvious. Presently these are impossible tasks for her militarily, as any such attempt will place her face to face with the mailed fist of the United States. In 1895, in a military contest, China was forced to cede Korea and Formosa to Japan. In spite of being thrashed and humiliated in the 1962-war, why India fails to evolve a strategy to bolster up her security through military alliance with a big power, and why she stands continuously exposed to Chinese threats is permanent mystery. New Delhi will know that till India equips herself with powerful arms and powerful friends, China will not consider the Indian demands with concern. The stalemate in the border hardens even after India going nuclear. To ensure national security, it has become inevitable that India enter into military pacts with the powerful democracies of Asia and the west, and declare she is no more the victim of the discredited NAM construct parading as appendage to the world left-movement. At the same time, strategically it is too important for India to awaken Japan for rearmament, as that step itself alone will neutralise the dragon to a great extent. If China grows powerful, there are so many powerful countries in the world, and there are rising powers in Asia too to counter balance it. If China and India are growing markets for each other, any decline in commerce will affect both countries equally badly, as trade is a two way process. It is wrong to contend that Communist China targets India as the only potential Asian challenge to Chinese hegemony. Through a radically overhauled military strategy, India can send the message that she is not the India of the Nehru days any more, and that 21st century India means different business. A change of policy, though a hard choice for India has become inevitable.

235) After seizing Tibet by naked conquest, the dragon, repeats through the treaty of 1954, that Tibet is autonomous.

When the religion and tenets of the monks vapours off under the 'new regime' of totalitarian terror the democratic world look only frustrated about the fate of the hapless Tibetans. In the recent past, a leading English daily in India published a report that China considers the 2008 American suggestion to speak to Dalai Lama, as bad as suggesting to the United States to talk to the terror supremo Osama Bin Laden. This pro-China report, written by a reporter of the newspaper, to the shock of all democrats, suggests that there is no use in the international community pressurising China, when Beijing is defiant enough to dismiss the suggestion at the threshold itself. That China-friendly reporter again asks what is the use of America making reform suggestions which China looks at with contempt? In fact that Indian newspaper is playing the role of spokesman and apologist of Chinese terror and genocide in Tibet. The report pours scorn on the unarmed Tibetan protesters and martyrs fighting with their blood alone to recapture the liberty they lost in 1950. The leftist Indian media, predominantly pro-China and anti-national, is toeing the Chinese version shunted out from Beijing, and now they are daring enough to compare Dalai Lama with the 9/11 terrorist-baron Osama Bin Ladan. Can Indian media's servitude to Beijing be more abysmal!

236) If political China is not liberalised urgently by the rulers themselves, she too will be heading for the fate met by Soviet Union in 1989. Again a reference to history appears relevant. During the Czarist rule spanning many centuries, the Russian territory expanded eastward and southward manifold. In Russian political experience, the difference between Czarism and Communism was the difference between civilization and banditry. Under the Czars, the people enjoyed all rights except the political right to challenge the power of the monarch. They possessed the rights of worship and religion, economic freedom and to a large extent the right of expression and the freedoms of art and culture. On cultural, educational and artistic freedoms, there was absolute non-interference by the state. Even trade union and press freedoms were allowed, and during the 19th century there grew up powerful trade unions all over Russia, who later would back up the many anti-Tsarist revolts, including

the February Revolution of 1917. Compare these monarchic restrictions with the totalitarian control imposed even on man's, biological and physical wants and totally banning his thinking rights, by Lenin and Stalin. The moment Lenin got power, he unleashed a reign of terror through murder and genocide, which move really appalled and paralysed the Russian mind's power to react. Communist revolutionaries had promised eldorado to the people, and if the people can reach heavens through the wave of a totalitarian magic wand who will not want it! By playing beastly political fraud on the people, through false promises and betrayals, the whole nation was dragged unawares into the dungeon of terror, and the cheated people fated to contend with the tragedy of that promised land of milk honey turning into the hellish quagmire of physical wants, state terror abject misery and enslavement. Simply because philosopher Karl Marx, and a power-hungry Lenin advocated total subjection and enslavement of man's mind, body and property to monstrous state terror, should his promoters and followers force mankind to live in hell only to prove Karl Marx correct? Historians and political critics argue that unlike Kant, Hegel and Niestzche who served as Marx's philosopher models, Marx fails to prove his arguments through practical application, empiricism, common sense and logic. He was in great hurry to mount a revolution in Germany (his native land) under the Social Democratic Party, but even after the 1848 Revolution rocking many European capitals including Berlin, he failed to move a powerful body of rebels, and failed to march to his native land at the head of a revolutionary brigade. When Marx failed to explain his theory in real practice, his unknown disciples in Russia-Lenin and Trotsky, whom the former had no occasion to see and groom, filled all gaps in his theory by the decrees of state terror. At the same time, Lenin very conveniently and deceitfully blacked out the story of the radical conversion underwent by Marx himself after his disastrous experience in the Paris Commune of 1871, in which political stampede, more than 24000 of his partisans were killed and hundreds of thousands orphaned. Stunned by this reverse Marx in his 1872 Amsterdam speech, radically alters his original theory, discounting the relevance of many of its clauses in the art of mounting a revolution. Lenin wanted total power for himself, and made Marxism the main instrument for power capture, but blacking out what Marx redefined and redeclared in 1872. In his rash collectivization drive, Lenin brought the Russian economy wholly to a grinding halt, precipitating huge manmade shortages, famines and mass deaths. The Russia watchers estimate that more than thirty-five million people perished under the Stalin purge and collectivization, and this tragedy was perpetrated through his inhuman economic experimentations in Leninist social re-engineering. This abominable mass slaughter was committed to prove Karl Marx correct, and to cement the Lenin-Stalin dictatorship. To say that the Soviet citizen was demoted into a slave, is a comparison defaming slavery itself, because slaves also retain so many rights which the Soviet subjects were robbed of. Under communist rule, the human rights condition of the Soviet citizen has gone down many times worse than Czarist serfs. That such a horrendous, beastly society lasted more than 70 years, itself is surprising, but once again pointing to the docile 'rights response' of the Russian society, never wanting in revolutionary adventurism during the 19th and 20th centuries. The pre-Revolution Russian society was uniquely adventures including the Decembrists. Even among the moderates among political activists there were too many assassins, and during the 19th century, the minimum Russian rebel target was political murder, the rebel not knowing any middle road.

237) The popular majority in Russia never supported a Bolshevik Revolution (October) and Bolshevik power, but through a surprise insurrection, Lenin seized power. This Lenin triumph was tricky and terrific and he executed this feat taking advantage of the liberal policies of Luvov and Kerensky governments. A lot of liberalists fell before the magic promise of Lenin to end the ongoing world war, and thus to end the seemingly endless war-agonies of the Russian people, through the masterstroke of a surrendering withdrawal. This unpatriotic, ungallant promise Lenin fulfilled in letter and spirit. But once reaching power, in a surprise move he was swallowing all past promises. He threw away the political mask, and embarked on

the path of bloody state-terror. He suppressed all opposition parties in the country through shocking cruelty. He introduced the demoniac art of elimination of political opponents through mass-shootings, and the first shock was applied by gunning down around 700 political dissidents point blank in St. Petersburg and around, immediately after October 25. This genocidal art of Lenin underwent multiple changes and perfections under his estranged disciple—Joseph Stalin. In his last days, Lenin suspected Stalin as a Caucasian bandit, amassing too much power as the Secretary of the Central Committee office, originally not a powerful one. But Lenin after the assassination attempt on him, was gradually suffering paralysis and in this confusion Stalin's power increased very fast. Lenin was alarmed and he secretly enlisted the help of Trotsky to remove Stalin. But Stalin's wife...who was working in Lenin office knew this conspiracy and promptly informed Stalin. An enraged Stalin took up the phone and called Lenin's wife Krupskaya and abused her. This abuse steeled the Lenin resolve to remove Stalin from the post of secretary, but fate was on Stalin side. Lenin's paralysis worsened and gradually he lost the power of speech. Before he lost the power of speech, Lenin dictated his last will and testament to his secretary and that document remained in the possession of Lenin's wife Krupskaya. Lenin died shortly but without removing Stalin from the secretaryship of the Central Committee. As Lenin lay in paralysis the post or the Secretary of the CC increased enormously and about this build of power Lenin became suspicious and apprehensive and wanted to make Trotsky, the latecomer in the Bolshevik party, his successor. But Trotsky was arrogant and tactless and he displeased many members in the Politbureau and Central Committee because of his adamant stand for total revolution. Trotsky, who had escaped to New York from Tsarist imprisonment knew about the February Revolution and he was not enthused by his own Socialist Party colleagues who were too liberal. On reaching Russia he quarrelled with the Mensheviks. Even from earlier days Lenin was very much impressed with the organizing skill and adventurism of Trotsky, and had tried his best to bring him under the Bolshevik fold. But it was only in July 1917 that Trotsky joined the Bolshevik Party and took active part in the coup of 25th October 1917, which brought Bolsheviks to power. It was Trotsky's organizing skill and military strategy that brought final victory to the Bolshevists in the civil war that continued for more than five years. It is believed by historians that but for Trotsky, the Bolshevik Revolution would have fizzled out as the February Revolution foundered after eight months. It is often commented that if Trotsky so decided, he could have captured the top post from Lenin himself, but Trotsky's loyalty to Lenin was complete.

238) As said earlier Trotsky's ability excelled all others and most of the members of the Politbureau did not like Trotsky and they were envious. Prominent party members like Kamanev and Zinoviev would oppose his elevation to leadership after the death of Lenin. As Lenin lay bedridden for years, the Stalin scheme succeeded. As party secretary he could remove old members and enroll new members to committees and very soon the party machine was manipulated to contain more Stalin loyalists. On many occasions Trotsky opposed the views of Lenin in policies when Stalin offered full support to Lenin. Stalin and other Politbreau members were resentful that Trotsky—the latecomer was seizing the leadership of the party pushing aside the long-time loyalists like Kamaniev, Zinoviev, Stalin, etc. Anyhow these members never suspected their future betrayer in Stalin, whereas Lenin suspected that the arbitrary power enjoyed and exercised by Stalin was dangerous to party ideology. Had Lenin survived the stroke and came back to active politics, the fate of Stalin would have been sealed forever. Lenin fell into a coma and his new comradeship with Trotsky could not fully materialise. Lenin died in 1924 and the power struggle between the nationalists and the internationalists will continue till 1929. Most of the members in the Central Committee and the Politbureau feared that if Trotsky succeeds as leader, their position in the party will be in jeopardy, Stalin incited this fear and he for the time being was appearing most accommodative. Members of the Politbureau like Bukharin, Kamaniev, Zinoviev, etc. failed to see their future assassin hiding in Stalin and they voted against Trotsky and in favour of

Stalin. Immediately after the death of Lenin, Krupskaya (Lenin widow) introduced a resolution in the Central Committee to endorse and publish the testament of Lenin, but the committee decided that it need not be published. If published, the party was bound to oust Stalin not only from the secretaryship, but from the party itself. Stalin, by this time could influence all prominent members to his side and this freezing and secreting the testament of Lenin came to the rescue of Stalin. The top members of the Central Committee and the Politbureau never knew that by voting in favour of Stalin they were embracing their own future assassin. By 1928, Trotsky was expelled from Soviet Russia.

239) Lenin's resolve to remove Stalin could not be enforced, as he never recovered from the stroke and died and the rest is the story of the Great Terror. Stalinist terror, deceit and brain-washing propaganda made it impossible to dislodge his corps of hyenas holding the reigns of state terror in Kremlin, and this ruthless terror continued till his death in 1953. The chief of Stalin's Secret-Police Avanti Beria and his team will run amuck to kill, to keep the Russian political society eternally tremulous.

240) The Hitlerite plan to destroy Bolshevism in 1941 failed because he made the wrong strategy of attacking Russia without coordinating his strategy with Japan. Just before Hitler launched the Barbarossa against Russia, Stalin has concluded a No War Pact with Japan. The fatal flaw of the Axis campaign was the total lack of military coordination between Germany and Japan. Japan, Germany and Italy had already become part of the Tripartite Alliance formed in Berlin in 1941, and then how could the No War Pact be signed between Russia and Japan? Critics doubt that the Barbarossa was not clearly intimated to Japan, and Hitler acted on his own as he received no warnings from Japan about the Pearl Harbour strike. In September 1939, Germany and Russia joined in the conquest of Poland starting the Second World War. When the Russo-Japanese No War Pact was signed only days before the Barbarossa, it may not have sounded so much discordant among the Axis as Stalin by then had not somersaulted into the Allied Comp. Was it possible for Hitler to have intervened effectively against the Russo-Japanese

No War Pact of 1941 as he alone then knew that the Barbarossa was imminent.

241) It was and it is the world democracy's political default to plan the defeat of communism through honest means. The democratic programme being decent and transparent, it was bound to fail against the communist stock of betrayals, lies and ruthless crackdowns. And as if in an abominable political self-contradiction, there emerged, during the Second World War, the democratic-Bolshevik alliance, supplying the long wanted, long-awaited moral halo to the communist movement till then estranged, despised and looked down upon by the democrats. When the Bolshevists took over Russia and sank the country under state-terror, the outside world decided to shun Soviet Russia from the mainstream of international inter course. The trade embargo imposed by Europe and the free world pushed Russia into famine and misery. Soviet authorities made earnest attempts to repair and refurbish her image, but all these moves taking her to the final collapse in 1989. This Soviet-model terror and genocide has been borrowed by Mao only to copy it verbatim and unload it on China from 1949 to 1976. Only after Mao's death in 1976, the reformist Deng Ziao Ping, long in political wilderness, came forward to seize the party leadership, and execute an about-turn to derevolutionise and decollectivise the structure and character of the totalitarian misadventures of Mao. Till the death of Mao, China's economic condition was horror story, into which grinder of repression not thousands but tens of millions were thrown in. Critics once guestimated the number of martyrs as less bloody than Stalin's communes and show trials, but latest research would put it around 65 million. The Great Leap Forward of 1959-60 ended in total disaster. The ensuing Cultural Revolution starting in 1966, and lasting up to the death of Mao in 1976, was taking the country to the brink of economic and cultural collapse. In 1976, both Mao Tse Tung and Chau En Lai died, and the age of mindless terror was set to recede. In the party, Chau En Lai represented the rightist and moderate faction, but only on condition of unconditionally accepting Mao's leadership. Mao and Chau, well aware of their own different motives and policies, endeavoured to coexist, both showing pragmatism to acknowledge the role of each other in Chinese politics. This cooperation which started during the Long March of 1934-35 continued till their death. In the beginning of the Long March, the official position of Chau En Lai in the party was higher to Mao Tse Tung. During the march, or rather in the power struggle taking place during the Long March itself, Mao was set to take over the party leadership, and Chau voluntarily stood down to accept a position below Mao, and this cooperation continued till the death of Chau in February 1976. Mao died in October the same year. In the long March, Chu The, Liu Shao Chi, Chen Yei, and Deng Ziao Ping also were the participants. When Chau founded the Paris unit of the CCP in 1921, Deng was recruited as Chau's imeograph operator. Within ten months after the death of Mao in 1976, a bitter struggle in the party exploded into the open. On the one side was the moderates represented by the future Prime Minister Hua Guofeng. They were opposed by the conservative radicals, led by Mao's widow Jiang Quing and this radical group nick named the "Gang of Four". The moderates led by Hua Guo Feng won the power struggle and Hua became the prime minister. Hereafter the long sidelined and demoted Deng Ziao Ping will rise into prominence as the man of China's new destiny. It is history that Hua was responsible to bring Deng Xiao Ping into the politbureau and that decision alone was responsible for Hua's downfall later. Deng would use his new position to oust Hua himself from power. Deng was a moderate, spearheading the liberalization of the economy and he wanted to pull China away from communes and collectivism. Communism in power carries the impossible task of proving Karl Marx unfalsiable and infallible, but in real practice the infallibility concept became possible to be held aloft only through the secrecy of the Iron Curtain. Within the Curtain also Marx will stand up through wholesale terror. The claim of infallibility was a complete lie in real life and the question is how long can an anti-people regime declaring war on the people survive? The communists, unlike the other revolutionaries promise that they will open a new era, steamrolling the logics of man and history. At the same time the world was warning the communists that disaster is in the offing, as human life cannot be permanently shackled by the inhuman perversions of any man-hating philosopher. The fall of the Soviet Union, was predicted by worldly commonsense that a state attempting to destroy creativity cannot endure. Among the communists, the reformist leaders of China will learn the lessons of history not only from the economic bankruptcy of the Soviets, but more from their own political debacles and tragedies like the Great Leap Forward and the Cultural Revolution. Much before 1989, the Chinese reformists moved for change in 1978, and since 1983 they moved resolutely for the big change. This change over was later justified by the fall of the Soviet state and her European satellites in 1989. When China repudiated Karl Marx and took the country to the capitalist road of Adam Smith, Ricardo and Keynes through economic counter-revolution, the world communist movement will stand dumb-faced, failing to offer any explanation for the sudden fall of Marxist-Leninist infallibility. Communist silence was due to political shock. This was thunderous confession that Marx and Lenin are wrong. China changed course and escaped the counter-revolutionary storm gathering over her skies. She fore-warned herself that the Soviet locomotive was passing through the precipitous edge of an ideological abyss, and so the former shall go for emergency measures to change course and reform.